GW01606907

CORNISH MINE DISASTERS

CORNISH MINE DISASTERS

By Cyril Noall

Edited, with an Introduction

By Philip Payton
BSc, PhD, FRHistS.

DYLLANSOW
TRURAN

First published 1989 by Dyllansow Truran, 'Trewolsta', Trewirgie, Redruth,Kernow

ISBN 1 85022 032 8

Typeset by St. George Typesetting, Commercial Centre, Wilson Way,
Pool Industrial Estate, Redruth, Cornwall

Sources

In general, the best accounts of Cornish mining accidents are to be found in the files of the Cornish and regional Press. Those principally consulted were the *Sherborne Mercury*, *Royal Cornwall Gazette*, *West Briton*, *Penzance Gazette*, *Cornish Telegraph*, *Cornishman*, and *Western Morning News*. The *Mining Journal* has also proved a valuable source of information, whilst other specialist publications, such as the *Mining Magazine* and the all-too-short-lived *Mining and Smelting Magazine* were also examined. Occasional use was also made of various standard works on Cornish mining, acknowledgements to which are made in the text.

Acknowledgements

I would like to thank all those who helped in various ways during the writing of this book. In particular, I must express my grateful acknowledgements to John H. Trounson, of Redruth, Chairman of the Cornish Mines Development Association, for his kindness in reading the manuscript and for the loan of photographs from his marvellous collection on Cornish mining. Justin Brooke of Marazion, was, as always, happy to supply valuable information from his extensive files. Mention must also be made of the following: W. J. North, of Calartha, Pendeen; Douglas Vosper, Saltash; H. L. Douch, Curator, and R. D. Penhallurick of the County Museum, Truro; P. L. Hull, Archivist, County Record Office, Truro; Terry Knight, of the Local History Section, Redruth Library; D. B. Barton, South Africa; C. J. Davies, Truro; staff of the British Library Newspaper Library, Colindale, London; staff of the Penzance (Morrab Gardens) Library, Penzance; and the Trustees of the St. Ives Museum.

Editor's note: Cyril Noall wrote these acknowledgements some time before his death and, as many readers with a knowledge of Cornish affairs will readily appreciate, several number are by now ''dated''. In particular, we must record the passing of Douglas Vosper, the noted local historian, and of John H. Trounson, the doyen of the Cornish mining industry.

P. J. P.

CONTENTS

Introduction

The untimely death of Cyril Noall in April 1985 at the relatively youthful age of 65 deprived Cornwall of one of her ablest and most committed scholars, leaving even those who knew him only through his many books and articles with a sense of loss and the recognition that the field of Cornish Studies was by Cyril's death diminished. Cyril Noall was a St. Ives man born and bred and, although his interest extended across the whole of Cornwall, it was his home town and its surrounding district of Penwith that was for him the over-riding, consuming passion. As Curator of the St. Ives Museum he acquired a local knowledge and expertise second to none, earning an early reputation as archivist, journalist and historian. He was active in the Old Cornwall movement, was a great supporter of the Royal Institution of Cornwall, and for his services to Cornwall was initiated as a Bard of the Cornish Gorseth at Callington in 1959, taking the Bardic name Scryfer Por'ya (Writer of St. Ives).

Although Cyril Noall suffered from impaired eyesight, which had prevented him from taking-up an academic career, he triumphed over his disability to produce a stream of publications, many of which were models of their type and have stood the test of time as Cornish classics. As one of the more prolific authors of the D. Bradford Barton/Tor Mark Press publishing house he helped pioneer the early growth of what is now a thriving and genuinely indigenous Cornish publishing industry. He is remembered especially, perhaps, as a mining historian. His "trilogy" — *Botallack*, *Levant*, *Geevor* — drew an extraordinary and vivid picture of the history of tin and copper mining on the Atlantic-battered cliffs at the very edge of Penwith and the end of Cornwall, and his *The St. Ives Mining District, Volume 1* lent an intimate and detailed account of several well-known but many more obscure and hitherto unresearched workings. Likewise, *The St. Just Mining District* revealed the hidden histories of mines such as Great Trevegean and Wheal Bostraze.

However, Cyril Noall's interest in Cornish history was by no means confined to mining. He was equally at home with maritime themes, his *Cornish Seines and Seiners* (a delightful play on words, for those who know) emerging as the standard account of the pilchard fishing industry. Significant too were *Smuggling in Cornwall* and *Cornish Lights and Shipwrecks*, while his collaboration with Graham Farr produced the important three-volumed *Wreck and Rescue Round the Cornish Coast*, a history of Cornwall's lifeboats. In other areas of research he turned his hand successfully, for example, to *A History of Cornish Mail and Stage Coaches*, with his native St. Ives featuring inevitably as a major focus for his attentions. Along with his *The Story of St. Ives* and *Yesterday's*

Town, St. Ives was his sumptuous and widely acclaimed *The Book of St. Ives.*

But despite his reputation and accomplished record, Cyril remained a modest and in several respects retiring man, avoiding the limelight and eschewing the accolades and attentions sometimes showered upon successful writers. In an affectionate obituary the *Western Morning News* concluded that,

> A bachelor, with no close relatives, he lived alone. Mr. Noall appeared to be content with his own company, as he daily trudged the roads and country lanes of his beloved St. Ives and its surroundings, deep in thought, recognising no one unless spoken to. But he was a courteous and friendly man, and St. Ives was very proud of him.[1]

Reflecting, indeed complementing, his character and personality was his style of writing. He composed his work with an almost Edwardian precision, with a concern for detail and an always careful choice of words and phrases. Often rather formal, his style was nonetheless easy on the reader, accurate to a fault and yet always picturesque and engaging. He belonged unashamedly to the old school of narrative historians, with a concern for history as literature and a desire to excite and inspire his readership. As one coming to serious Cornish scholarship at a time when Cyril Noall's literary career was at its height, I was one of those excited and inspired by his example. In a memorable Introduction to his *Botallack* were words and images which, for me, were as evocotive and arousing as Du Maurier's "Last night I dreamt I went to Manderlay again":

> Situated only a few miles from the Land's End, its engine houses cling precariously to the sides of rugged cliffs against which the Atlantic surges in rough weather with tremendous violence, making the solid rock quiver with its fury. At two places — Wheal Cock and the Crowns — the workings extend for some distance under the sea, so that, at Wheal Cock especially, the workmen were sometimes obliged to retreat in terror at the crashing of waves and boulders just a few feet above their heads.[2]

"... stand atop those majestic cliffs at the Crowns ...",[3] commanded Noall, "For here, all around, lie the evidences of an enterprise conceived and executed with skill and daring, by a unique breed of men".[4] These were words designed to stir and indeed they have, stirring readers to an appreciation of the singular environment of Cornish mining, and encouraging others to learn more, sometimes prompting new research in new areas of Cornish history.

Cyril Noall's ability to inspire through his use of language was matched by his gift of description, his talent for capturing the quintessential character and mood of place. Here, for example, is his pen-picture of the hinterland that lies beyond St. Ives:

> Some of the most varied and beautiful scenery in Cornwall is to be found here ... The district is bounded on the east by that part of St. Ives Bay extending from the ancient fishing port of St. Ives along an indented shore of dark headlands and contrasting golden beaches towards Lelant Towans and the western side of Hayle Estuary. The pleasant woodlands at Lelant, rising above the river, flourish in the shelter of Trencrom Hill, whilst in similar fashion Carbis Bay and St. Ives nestle below the heights of Worvas, Penbeagle and Rosewall. Beyond, the bleak moors and "high countries" of the western parishes sweep away under a wide sky towards the limits of Bolerium. To the north and west these moors command magnificent views of the Atlantic Ocean; but between them and the rugged shore lies a narrow fertile plain patterned with the complicated tracery of an ancient Celtic field system.[5]

Cyril had a number of projects in hand at the time of his death in 1985, and amongst a collection of literary effects left in the care of Dyllansow Truran, the Cornish publishing house, was the draft manuscript for a book on *Cornish Mine Disasters*, along with an incomplete set of accompanying photographs. That draft, of course, forms the basis of this present volume, and I considered it a great honour when Leonard Truran approched me with the suggestion that I help steer Cyril's book towards publication by assisting in the editorial process, expanding the illustration collection, and writing an introduction to set both Mr. Noall and Cornish mining disasters within their historical contexts. As one who had, now almost twenty years ago, come across and been affected by the works of Cyril Noall in my almost desperate ransacking of libraries for Cornish books of quality (and continuous badgering of Cornish publishers for their latest lists of titles), I felt that I would be repaying some kind of personal debt in helping his book to see the light of day. Others were similarly eager to be of assistance, those deserving particular mention including Roger Penhallurick of the Royal Institution of Cornwall, Justin Brooke of Marazion, and Dr. James Whetter, editor of the *Cornish Banner*. Thanks, too, must go to the *Mining Journal*, Rigby Ltd., and HMSO for their ready assistance with illustrations.

The appearance of this book is, of course, much more than the mere repayment of debt, more even than a posthumous tribute to the scholarship and devotion to Cornwall of Cyril Noall. Most importantly, it fills a hitherto glaring gap in Cornish mining history and is an original contribution of considerable strength to the body of knowledge that comprises Cornish Studies. Mining disasters, in Cornwall and elsewhere, have always exited curiosity; poignant and melancholy events, somehow very human and telling in the fascination that they arouse. Tales of hardship and sorrow in days gone by do have a peculiar attraction, the pathos appealing in some strange way to our own fears and vulnerabilities (a sublime fear that fascinates), and it is odd that there has not, until now, been a full treatment of Cornish mining disasters.

Although there were sensational and spectacular disasters, like those of Levant or East Wheal Rose, which excited widespread and continuing interest (and have lingered in Cornish folk-memory), accidents were — as Cyril Noall intimates — an everyday and almost commonplace facet of the Cornish mining scene. Mines are by their very nature dangerous places, a danger excacerbated in nineteenth-century Cornwall by the application of technological contraptions whose functions might trap the unwary or unlucky, and a danger ever-present by virtue of the close proximity of workplace and home in the Cornish mining districts. In areas such as St. Just, Wendron and Gwennap (and in a fashion soon emulated overseas in places like Moonta and Wallaroo Mines) the mining landscape was a bewildering and ad hoc collection of engine-houses, stamping mills, and open shafts interspersed with miners' cottages and even small-holdings, the whole inter-linked with a complicated pattern of criss-crossing and interconnecting lanes and paths. In such an environment it was not uncommon for the traveller late at night to fall down an unguarded shaft by the roadside, or for a child to wander from its home and come to grief in the machinery of a nearby mine. A. K. Hamilton Jenkin recorded an old Cornish rhyme which warned the unwary against the dangers of mining paraphenalia:

Balance-bob work up and down,
Pumping the water from underground,
Over a while the inion (engine) do lash,
Scat the old man (or woman) back in the shaft.[6]

This ever-present danger was a reflection of the general level of conditions in working-class Cornwall in the last century. Mining accidents were but one threat to life and limb (all too often one reads in contemporary newspaper reports of commonplace domestic accidents, like the frequent death by internal scalding suffered by small children who had in unsupervised moments sipped from the pots heating on stoves) and, despite the ameliorating and improving influences of Methodism, human existence was often harsh. Cornwall was "West Barbary" — the land of food riots, smuggling and "wrecking" — the lot of the ordinary Cornish man or woman captured in the verses of John Harris, the nineteenth-century miner-poet:

The grey-headed man, clad in rags as he goes,
And the water-cress girl, with frost in her toes,
I saw them to-day creeping down the dark lane,
And they trembled with cold, and were weeping with pain.[7]

Our fascination with the details, often lurid, of these disasters of long ago must always be tempered by the knowledge that those who suffered were real people, flesh and blood like ourselves. Cyril Noall was acutely aware of this, and his narrative is full of the details that bring to life again the many characters whose deaths it charts — Christian names and surnames (so many of them typically Cornish such as Spargo and Trevorrow, but with the occasional interloper like Moffat), date of birth or age at death, place of home or work, names and circumstances of kinfolk — including the inevitable widows and fatherless children with hungry mouths to feed. Quite apart from the tragedy of the accidents themselves, there could be far-reaching ramifications. In 1858, for example, one William Tonkin from St. Cleer, near Liskeard, was killed in an accident in Craddock Moor Mine, an old working whose crumbling engine-house, engine pool, and burrows, together with a second stack a little to the west, are on the moorland ridge which overlooks Tremar Coombe and St. Cleer Churchtown. Amongst the several children left to mourn his loss was his namesake, William, who was taken under the kindly wing of James Richards, a mine captain of Tremar, who eventually adopted him.[8]

The crumbling engine-house of Craddock Moor Mine, on Bodmin Moor

In 1866 James Richards became involved in the strikes that swept the Caradon mines, a turbulence which, had the Cornish mining industry survived as a major element of the Cornish economy, might have proved the precursor of a fully-fledged Labour movement in the Cornish mines. But 1866 also marked the crash of Cornish copper, heralding the demise of the mining industry and precipitating the widespread emigration of the potential trade unionists who took their new ideas on the organisation of Labour to mining fields abroad such as Moonta in South Australia and Butte in Montana. Richards had taken the side of the men during the strikes, and in the unpleasantness and economic downturn of the aftermath he too decided that he must seek alternative employment overseas. His destination was rather nearer home, however, for he was appointed to the Glen Roy mine on the Isle of Man. Young William Tonkin went with his adopted father to Glen Roy. The irony of the tale is that, while William left mining to take over the "New Inn" in the Manx settlement of Laxey, James Richards remained intimately concerned with Manx mining, only to die as a result of injuries *he* sustained in an accident while dismantling machinery at the Rushden mines. A further irony is that Richards' natural son, William Henry, was himself partially incapacitated as a result of his participation in the rescue effort at a Snaefell mining disaster.

William Tonkin's gravestone, St. Cleer Church

Cornish mining history is littered with these cruel twists and quirks of fate. In 1902, for example, Thomas Ninnes from Cross Roads, near Moonta on South Australia's Yorke Peninsula, was killed in an accident in the South Mine on the Broken Hill silverlead fields of New South Wales. For his mother it was an especially tragic occurance, for she had lost her husband in so very similar circumstances many years before in an accident in the St. Ives Consols mine in Cornwall. The ever-present threat of sudden death or bereavement must have weighed heavy upon Cornish hearts, and it is hardly surprising that Methodism emerged as a religious, moral and social force of some considerable importance. Offering practical help and "improvement" in this world and anticipating the glories of that to come, Methodism encouraged an atmosphere of trust (or fatalism, depending on one's point of view) which enabled the individual to face the dangers of life:

Far down in the earth's dark bosom
  The miner mines the ore:
Death lurks in the dark behind him
  And hides in the rock before.
Yet never alone is the Christian
  Who lives by faith and prayer;
For God is a friend unfailing,
  And God is everywhere.[9]

Many Cornish miners experienced this faith very deeply, as in the case of Charles Trenberth who, "Working with his father in a stope near Taylor's Shaft ... went into a level, where he could be alone, and there, fully surrendering himself to Christ, a great joy and peace filled his soul".[10] For men like Trenberth, faith offered protection from the ever-present dangers of the mine, and yet if he was "taken" in an accident it would be an expression of God's Will, an almost welcome release from the ills of this world and a special calling for admittance into the next. It created an attitude of mind which, for the modern reader, perhaps, seems excessively morbid. There is, indeed, a certain morbidity in the old Cornish "burying tune", a hymn of widespread currency in the last century, noted by historians as diverse as Hamilton Jenkin and Geoffrey Blainey:

'Sing from the chamber to the grave',
I hear the dying miner say;
'A sound of melody I crave
Upon my burial day'.

'Sing sweetly whilst you travel on
And keep the funeral slow;
The angels sing where I am gone
And you should sing below.

'Then bear me gently to my grave,
And as you pass along,
Remember, 'twas my wish to have
A pleasant funeral song'.[11]

Likewise, the hymn "Thee We Adore" — with its line "What e'er we do, where'er we be, we are travelling to the grave" — was popular amongst Cornish communities at home and abroad. "Lead, kindly Light" was similarly popular in Methodist Cornwall, almost rivalling "Trelawny" in its claim to be a Cornish National Anthem, its words curiously appropriate for a mining people so given to emigration: "Lead, kindly Light, amid the encircling gloom, ... Keep thou my feet; I do not ask to see/The distant scene — one step enough for me.".[12]

But fatalism, morbidity even, was tempered by its humour, for even the most sober of Cornish Methodists could see the funny side of death as well as life. The emigration experience no doubt prompted the joke, "There do be some people that do say when we die we do go to Bolivian",[13] and overseas the Cornish emigrant communities retained their dry, quick-witted humour that had marked them at home. The oft-repeated story recorded by Blainey in his *The Rise of Broken Hill* is an exemplar. In this, a man went to break the sad news to the wife of a miner who had just been killed in a mining accident. When, in answer to the man's insistent knocking, the wife opened her door, she was more than surprised to find herself addressed with the melancholy greeting: "Good afternoon Widow Tregonning". She protested vigorously that she was no widow and that her husband was at that very moment at work in the mine, to which the news-breaker replied by asking her if she would "... like to take a bet on it"![14]

This earthy, sometimes self-mocking, yet fatalistic humour was best expressed in the cartoons of Oswald Pryor, whose caricatures reflected exactly the ambience of Cornish folk and the idiom of Cornish speech.[15] A number of his cartoons revealed a pre-occupation with death and funerals: "Ow did'ee enjoy your trip 'ome to Cornwall, Maister Treeloar? — Splendid, John; I sing'd to fower funerals" or "Ole man Trebuzza's been and dropped dead on 'is ninety-fourth birthday — Baint surprised. 'E was always delicate". Rather more, however, dwelt upon the dangers of mining or the consequences of accidents. In one cartoon a grandmother and small child pass an open shaft as the man-skip prepares to descend. In wonder they declare, "Lor, I wouldn't like to go down with a little rope like that!" to which the response flashes from the skip, "Be worse without un, Missus". In another an indignant miner complains about the state of an adit: "This place edden fit for a man to go into, Cap'n. Come in and have a look at un". A number deal with the effects of explosions, typically with a worldly-wise Cornish miner

"Lor', I wouldn't like to go down with a little rope like that!"
"Be worse without un, Missus."

Oswald Pryor's commentary on mine safety (Courtesy Rigby Ltd.)

responding to the inquisitive captain: "Had any experience with explosives? — Exper'unce, Cap'n! I've been blawed to bits three times" or "Accidents! I've had three legs broke, now". Perhaps the most delightful and authentic cartoon is that which represents the conversation between captain and stoker in the boiler-house. "What steps would you take if steam pressure went up to two hundred pounds?'', asks the frock-coated captain in tones of authority. ''Longest ones I could, Cap'n'', comes the cheeky but honest reply from the perspiring Cousin Jack.

Such fatalistic humour might represent a certain good-natured resignation to one's lot in life, but there were several improvements

"This place edden fit for a man to go into, Cap'n. Come in and have a look at un."

A further example of Pryor's ''fatalistic humour'' (Courtesy Rigby Ltd.)

which did do something to ease the condition of the labouring miner in the last century. The opening of the West Cornwall Miners' Hospital at Barncoose, near Redruth, in 1863 came none too soon but many of the larger mines had already been operating for some years a "club and doctor" fund to which miners could contribute when in employment and on which they could draw when incapacitated through illness or accident. Some technological advances, most notably the introduction of Bickford's Safety Fuse circa 1830, helped improve conditions in Cornish mines, and some technologists — most notably Sir Humphry Davy — were genuinely concerned for the welfare of the men and balmaidens employed at Cornish mines. Ironically, Davy's best-known invention, the miners' safety lamp (with which he is dipicted in the statue at the head of Market Jew Street in Penzance), was designed to benefit colliers in districts outside of Cornwall! But legislation relating to the coal-fields also benefitted metalliferrous mining areas such as Cornwall, the achievement of certain standards in the collieries prompting the investigation of standards in mines other than those of coal. A Royal Commission for this purpose was set-up in 1860 and in 1872 the resultant Metalliferous Mines Regulation Act came into force. Boys under twelve years of age could no longer work underground and those under sixteen could work no more than ten hours per day. More stringent safety rules in the construction of shaft ladder-ways were introduced, shaft openings and adits were to be more properly guarded, and changing rooms ("dries") were to be provided at the larger mines. All manner of other provisions similarly allowed for the safer operation of Cornish mines and the improved welfare of their employees.

However, by 1872 the great days of Cornish mining had already passed. Copper was already into its terminal decline and, although tin was seemingly on the point of boom in 1872, the tin industry was by 1874 also in desperate trouble in Cornwall (mainly due to overseas competition, principally from Australia). The 1872 Act came too late, therefore, to have any overwhelming or revolutionary impact upon Cornish life, for the position and importance of mining was already in decline. It is interesting, however, that in the brief and unsuccessful attempts at combination by Cornish miners in 1866 and again in 1874 there is some evidence of the influence of the debate which attended the Commission's enquiries and consequent Act. Had mining survived as a major Cornish industry and a vigorous Labour movement arisen as a result, we may speculate that conditions and welfare would have been amongst the trade unionists' principal concerns, perhaps counter-balancing that fatalism and resignation noted above.[16] Indeed, it is important to note that in the Australian colony of Victoria — where many Cornish miners had gone to find work in the goldfields, and had become involved in the creation of the Bendigo Miners' Association in

1872 and the Australia-wide union, the Amalgamated Miners' Association, in 1874 — miners' combinations profoundly influenced the Regulation of Mines Act of 1874.

Of course, in emigrating overseas many Cornish individuals and families were seeking an improved quality of life, and, for some, emigration would have been an escape from conditions at home and in the mines. However, the conditions encountered abroad could on occasions be as bad — or even worse — than those experienced in Cornwall. Many overseas mines were notoriously "unhealthy", those of Cuba and South America acquiring especially unsavoury reputations. In Cornwall it was not uncommon for folk to contract "miners' complaint" — an all-encompassing term covering all sorts of lung disorders from consumption to phthisis, silicosis, and presumably radon-induced lung cancer — but the impact of employment in overseas mines could bring even worse results. At Broken Hill there was the threat of plumbism or "getting leaded" and in the Transvaal was the "African phthsisis" caused by the "... malignant quartz that hid the gold and filled the lungs of the Cornish pioneers".[17] The experience of Henry Crougey, born near Carn Marth in a little cottage almost on the edge of Gwennap Pit in March 1825, would have been typical of many. As a youth he sung in the Wesleyan choir at Carharrack, and at the age of 21 married Ann Bray of Twelveheads. Some fifteen months later the couple emigrated to Chile, where Henry toiled in the copper mines for over twelve years. From Chile they moved briefly to California, and from there in 1865 to Burra in South Australia where Henry again worked as a copper miner. In 1877 they moved to Ballarat and Clunes in Victoria before returning to South Australia, where Henry found employment in the Moonta Mines. Unfortunately, Henry's Australian cycle had been increasingly dogged by the effects of "miners' complaint", which he had contracted all those years ago in Chile, and — although he did remarkably well to survive until the very respectable age of 85 — the disease incapacitated him in later life and finally killed him, at his daughter's home in Broken Hill in 1910.[18]

If disease could maim and kill abroad as ruthlessly as it did in Cornwall, then so too could mining accidents themselves. In emigrating to the Moonta and Wallaroo copper mines in South Australia, for example, the Cornish miners found conditions at surface and underground which in many respects bore close comparison with those that obtained in Cornwall. Amongst these were the steady catalogue of mining accidents, all too familiar in cause and effect to those that had been witnessed at home. As well as collapses of ground, there were the usual scaldings, boiler explosions, machinery crushings, "falling away" from ladders, and so on. As in Cornwall, sometimes children were involved — as in 1874 when William Northey (a son of Captain Northey) fell down a shaft at the Devon Consols mine near Wallaroo, or in 1886 when seven year-old Joseph Williams was killed by riding a plunger pole at Hughes' Shaft, Moonta Mines. Underground explosions accounted for some loss of life at Moonta, as in 1878 when William Bennett, James Crabbe, and Edward Quintrell were killed; an enquiry attributing the explosion to the negligence of one John Roberts. Rock falls, such as that which killed Henry Angwin in the Kurilla mine in 1879, occurred from time to time. Accidents involving man-skips could also result in deaths — as in 1893, for instance, when William Hobb from Cross Roads put his head out of the skip in which he was travelling and had it dashed against the shaft wall.[19]

Anxious relatives congregate at Taylor's Shaft, Wallaroo Mines, 13 January 1904. (Courtesy South Australian Archives)

One extraordinary disaster — in which, miraculously, there was no direct loss of life — was the great fire at Wallaroo Mines in 1904. This fire, which started and raged underground and resulted in the total ruination of Taylor's Shaft, was first noticed at three o'clock on the afternoon of 13th January. Very quickly groups of anxious relatives congregated at the pit-head, waiting for news of those trapped underground, a scene which anticipated in a most striking way the similar gatherings of wives and friends at the Levant disaster in Cornwall in 1919. As the flames were brought under control, parties of volunteers went below to rescue those overcome by fumes and smoke. One miner recalled later the scene as the choking men were brought to surface:

> ... there must have been ... from 150 to 220 men and they were all gassed. It was a pitiful sight to see those men brought up gassed, some of them being helpless, while others were dead to the world. As one after the other were brought to the surface, it was like bringing wounded from a battlefield. And the strongest and largest men seemed to be the most affected. Some of them were brought up preaching and praying, others came up laughing, and some crying, and some very quiet.[20]

Despite the obvious trauma of the event, and the widespread destruction caused by the fire, there were no immediate deaths, although many of those who had suffered were never restored to their full health, a number dying prematurely as a result of the lingering effects of that day.

Emigration, then, was no panacea — at least as far as mining conditions and accidents were concerned — and the Cousin Jack abroad was as equally at the mercy of the dangers of the mine as was his counterpart in Cornwall. Even in North America or Australia, where the activities of organised Labour combined with enlightened legislation to produce at least some advance in industrial standards, the improvements were piecemeal and probably did not represent any significant superiority over the advances that were made in Cornwall over the same period. In the final analysis, the Cornish miner took his chances amidst the sometimes destructive forces of the industrial revolution in his bid to seek remuneration for the skills he had to offer, a course of action that in the nineteenth-century atmosphere of "laissez-faire" seemed entirely reasonable, proper, and indeed natural. If the miner took his chances but came to grief amidst those destructive forces — open shafts, unguarded machinery, temperamental boilers, and the like — then that was the way of the industrial world, in the normal course of affairs prompting no other judgement than "accidental death":

> Coroner's Inquest: On Tuesday the 28th ult., at the Cornish Arms Inn, in the parish of Constantine, on the body of George James, a boy about 12 years of age, who worked as a Stamps boy in Wheal Vyvyan mine, in that parish. It appeared from the evidence, that on Monday afternoon, between one and two O'clock, deceased was accidentally jammed by a crank attached to the axis of the stamp wheel, and killed on the spot. Verdict, accidental death.[21]

Or,

> At West Caradon Mine, James Clemo, aged 15, was rolling some stuff underground, and on arriving at the plot for depositing it, he was about to take the candle from the fore part of the barrow which he had emptied, and put one foot on it to do so, when it overturned, and precipitated him down the shaft, a depth of 104 fathoms. His mutilated body presented a sad spectacle; the remains were collected, and conveyed to his home. An

inquest was held before Mr. Hamley, coroner, and a verdict returned of "accidental death".[22]

The Grim Reminder

George Seymour's "grim reminder" of the ever-present threat of death in the Cornish mines. First published in the *Mining Journal* in the 1870s, this sketch reappeared in the booklet *The Man-Machine* in 1977 and is reproduced here courtesy of the *Mining Journal*

We are today, perhaps, removed from the worst of such "Victorian values". But Cyril Noall's book, giving chapter and verse as it does to the disabilities and misfortunes (and heroism) of the nineteenth-century

Cornish mineworker, is a chastening reminder of the days that have gone before and a fitting tribute to the courage and tenacity of Cornish men and women.

Philip Payton,
St. Cleer, Cornwall.
November 1988.

References

1. *Western Morning News*, 19 April 1985.
2. Cyril Noall, *Botallack*, D. B. Barton, Truro, 1972, p 7.
3. Ibid.
4. Ibid.
5. Cyril Noall, *The St. Ives Mining District, Volume I*, Dyllansow Truran, Redruth, 1982, p xi.
6. A. K. Hamilton Jenkin, *The Cornish Miner*, 1927, republished, David & Charles, Newton Abbot, 1972, p 256.
7. D. M. Thomas, (ed), *The Granite Kingdom: Poems of Cornwall*, D. B. Barton, Truro, 1970, p 59.
8. S. Stuart and A. Williamson, *Cornish Miners in The Isle of Man*, n.d., pp 15-16.
9. Philip Payton, *The Cornish Miner in Australia: Cousin Jack Down Under*, Dyllansow Truran, Redruth, 1984, p 166.
10. *Australian Christian Commonwealth*, 5 April 1907.
11. Hamilton Jenkin, Op. Cit., p 283; Geoffrey Blainey, *The Rush That Never Ended: A History of Australian Mining*, Melbourne University Press, Melbourne, 1963, republished, 1974, p 120.
12. Philip Payton, *Cornish Carols From Australia*, Dyllansow Truran, Redruth, 1984, pp vii-x.
13. South Australian Archives, PRG 96, *Oswald Pryor Papers.*
14. Geoffrey Blainey, *The Rise of Broken Hill*, Macmillan, London, 1968, p 94.
15. Oswald Pryor, *Cornish Pasty: A Selection of Cartoons*, Rigby, Adelaide, 1976, pp 8, 9, 17, 32, 67, 70, 81, 83, 97.
16. Bernard Deacon, "Attempts at Unionism by Cornish Metal Miners in 1866," *Cornish Studies*, 10, 1982, and "Heroic Individualists? The Cornish Miners and the Five-Week Month 1872-74", *Cornish Studies*, 14, 1986.
17. Hamilton Jenkin, Op.Cit., p 330.
18. *Australian Christian Commonwealth*, 17 June 1910.
19. South Australian Archives, D6010 (Misc), Max A. Slee, *Mining Accidents, 1866-1900*, 1977.
20. South Australian Archives, D5342 (T), Peter Thomas, *Scrapbook Relating to Kapunda, Burra, Wallaroo and Moonta Mines.*
21. *West Briton*, 3 March 1837.
22. *West Briton*, 26 April 1850.

Foreword

From earliest times, mining has been considered one of the dangerous occupations. The metals and fuel on which civilisation depends have been won only at a very high price in human life and suffering, for Nature guards her buried treasures well, and exacts a grim toll from those who would wrest them from her. In recent years, it is true, the many remarkable advances in mining technology which have taken place, together with rigidly enforced safety measures, have done much to render underground work less hazardous than it once was, besides placing at the miner's disposal aids to efficiency undreamed of by his predecessors. No longer does he grope his way through levels by the dim light of a guttering candle, nor beat his boryer into the solid rock by sheer muscle power. Compressed air now drives his tools and flushes the fumes of explosives from advancing ends. The diamond drill probes the way ahead, revealing not only the nature of the ground and its mineral content, but giving ample warning of old flooded workings and other dangers. Yet, despite these improvements, accidents have not been eliminated. Rocks still fall from overhead, killing or maiming those working below; men still miss their footing and drop hundreds of feet down shafts to their deaths. Tribute is still demanded, and must be paid, until that day — still, seemingly, far distant, — when remotely controlled robots can replace human skill in the deep underground.

The worst mining disasters have been confined to the collieries, where explosions of gas and coal dust have sometimes caused the deaths of hundreds of miners in a single catastrophe. In Cornwall, the mines are entirely metalliferous in character, and so have been exempt from this particular hazard. It is, indeed, a rather curious fact that the safety lamp invented by that noted Cornishman, Sir Humphry Davy, proved of little service in his native Cornwall, though it saved many lives elsewhere. However, Cornwall has experienced nearly every other known type of mining disaster, including at least one which appears to be quite unique in industrial history — the collapse of the man-engine at Levant in 1919.

A survey of these accidents, such as is attempted in the following pages, inevitably involves the recounting of many harrowing stories of men killed and injured in a wide variety of ways, by blasting, flooding, fire, entombment and a host of others. The painful details of these cannot but make melancholy reading; but fortunately there is a brighter side to the picture which must also be shown. For though so many died, others had miraculous escapes, whilst the dedication shown by those engaged in rescue operations lies beyond praise, their courage at least partly off-setting the terrible sacrifice of human life in so many of these tragedies.

Were any further justification required for investigating these grim records of the past, it is to be found in the fascinating details of the mining technology of an earlier age which they disclose. The methods used by former generations of miners were extremely primitive, yet often displayed an astonishing degree of ingenuity and improvisation, which enabled the most difficult tasks to be successfully accomplished with a minimum of effort. The 'old men' were, indeed, highly adept in modifying their limited equipment to serve entirely new and complex purposes. "If you can't schemey you must louster," ran an old local saying; and the Cornish miner constantly demonstrated how well he knew to use his cunning to spare himself unnecessary labour.

Such matters are, however, it must be acknowledged, merely incidental to the main purpose of this book, which is to record the high price paid in suffering and death by the men and women who devoted their skill to the development of Cornwall's oldest industry. May it serve as a memorial, however inadequate, to the Cornish miners of earlier and more recent times who lost their lives when pursuing their ancient calling.

Cyril Noall

The Shaft

There can be few people in Cornwall who have not, at some time or other, stood nervously at the top of an old mine shaft and tossed a stone into its yawning maw, then bent their heads to catch the seconds-long reverberations of its descent into the mysterious depths, hundreds of feet below. This is always an eerie, rather frightening experience as the noisy clattering gradually fades into silence or terminates in the sibilance of a distant splash. To even the most unimaginative it brings a vivid awareness of those deep, dark caverns where long-dead generations of miners toiled by the light of flickering candles to win Cornwall's buried wealth of tin and copper, often at the price of their lives. Of the inescapable dangers by which mining has always been beset, the falling stone speaks with convincing clarity. Suppose that missile to be not idly thrown into a disused shaft, but accidentally detached from the side of one still working, with an unsuspecting miner standing in its path many fathoms below; or visualise a man rather than a stone, losing his grip upon the ladder, and falling, falling, tossed like a shuttlecock from one granite wall to another until he reaches bottom — man no longer, but a shattered, broken lump of flesh and bone. So thinking, the stone-thrower shrinks back from the sinister black opening with an involuntary shudder, and accounts himself fortunate that his daily occupation does not require him to forsake the friendly sunshine and face such perils as these.

The shaft is the highway leading into the mine; but, because the metal-bearing lodes often lie far underground it usually takes the form of a vertical rather than a horizontal road. In some cases — as when mines are opened in cliffs or the sides of hills — horizontal shafts, or *adits*, may be driven to reach the ore-body; whilst diagonal or sloping shafts are sometimes sunk to follow the underlie of a dipping lode. But, in the main, they are perpendicular, as this type affords greater facility in working and leads to a more logical layout of the mine.

In the earliest 'hole-in-the-ground' type of working there was only one shaft, which had to serve a variety of purposes — providing a footway for the men, passage for the removed tinstuff and 'deads,' drainage for the water, and ventilation. As the mines grew deeper, and were enlarged, anciliary shafts would be sunk from surface to reach the lode at different points, which were then connected by horizontal *levels* underground. As shafts increased in number, they became more specialised in use, thus avoiding the time-wasting confusion found in the all-purpose variety. In this way, winding shafts, pumping shafts and air shafts came into being, the larger mines possessing several of each of these distinctive types.

Most shafts were equipped with ladders for climbing. These were constructed with wooden sides, the earlier ones also having wooden staves, but in the later examples iron staves were used. There was always a set of ladders in the pumping shaft placed near the pump rods, and quite unprotected, their purpose being to assist in the maintenance of the machinery. This footway was generally the most direct to the bottom of the mine, but also a dangerous one, owing to its proximity to the moving rods; its convenience nevertheless caused it to be widely used by the miners in getting to their work, accidents sometimes resulting thereby. Ladders were also frequently met with in the winding shafts through which the mineral was sent to surface; here they were sometimes, but not invariably, protected by a casing of wood. Where ore was raised by chain and kibbles swinging loosely in the shaft, even with a partition between there was considerble danger, for should the chain break — a not uncommon occurrence — the falling kibble could wreak havoc throughout the shaft; hence the rule that men must stand in a level until the kibble had passed them. Where there was no complete casing, the men were also exposed to the risk of pieces of stone falling on them and the other dangers of an open shaft. When winding was accomplished by skips, running in guides, the danger arising from a breaking chain was considerably lessened, the skip then being confined to its course in falling to the bottom. In a few mines, special shafts, originally used for pumping or winding, were appropriated exclusively for footways. In these, the shaft was generally divided into lengths of about three to five fathoms by wooden platforms, called *sollars*, which filled the whole area of the shaft except for a small opening just large enough for a man to pass through, called the *man-hole*. The ladders rested upon the sollars. These footways were both comfortable and safe. The ladders were of easy lengths, and inclined at a convenient angle for climbing, whilst the frequent sollars greatly lessened the risk of serious injury if a man fell away.

The most usual mode of descent, however, was by the ladders in the engine shaft to reach adit level (the lowest point from which water could be discharged from the mine by gravity) and from thence to the bottom by ladders placed in *winzes* — short underground shafts used for interconnecting the different levels. This was a very safe way, as the winzes were on average only twenty fathoms deep, this distance itself often being divided into two or three stages. But always, the crucial point so far as the safety and comfort of the miners went, was the angle at which the ladders were placed. In very old mines, they were often quite perpendicular, making ascent difficult and dangerous. Occasionally, it was necessary to set ladders at too 'flat' an angle, however, and this could be just as fatiguing for the men.

But, however well erected and maintained, accidents in footways were always liable to occur. When using them, the miner was often burdened with tools and other impediments; and what with these, and the darkness, and the wet and slimy staves, it is not to be wondered at that mishaps did occur. On July 17 1821 as Richard Bonds was ascending the engine shaft at Wheal Buller his foot unfortunately slipped just when he reached surface, and he fell to the bottom. When taken up, his body was found to be most dreadfully injured, and he died almost immediately after being conveyed home. When Richard Rule was leaving work at

A ladder-way in Dolcoath, circa 1890 (Courtesy Royal Institution of Cornwall)

Dolcoath mine on February 26 1823, and had also nearly ascended to 'grass,' one of the staves of the ladder gave way, so that he was thrown backwards down the shaft and killed. Again, a young man called Mark Smith, employed at North Fowey Consols, was climbing the shaft after his day's labour on November 10 1847, when he missed his footing and fell to the bottom with fatal results. Death in a different and more terrible form awaited James Prideaux when he fell in the engine shaft at Polgine mine, Camborne, in February 1838, for he struck some machinery and by it was fatally mangled. So often it happened that these men, tired out after their 'core' underground, lost hold when nearly at the top of the long ladderway, so near to 'grass' and safety. There were, of course, others who fell in from surface, perhaps from misjudging the edge, or by slipping. In one week's issue of the *Royal Cornwall Gazette* (August 4 1810) it was reported that one man had been killed by falling in Wheal Crenver, in Crowan, and a boy of fourteen, called Arthur Orwall, working near the edge of a shaft in Wheal Gorland, Gwennap, by the ground giving way.

The collapse of a ladder when laden with men could produce very serious consequences. Fortunately, this type of accident seems to have been comparatively rare. One example of it occurred in Dolcoath during February 1884. A pair of men, last core by night, were on their way down to the 376 fathom level in New Sump shaft. They had reached the 326 fathom level between Wheal Harriet shaft and Old Sump shaft and were descending still further when a ladder holding seven of the party gave way between the 326 and the 338, carrying the men with it. One, hearing his comrade shout, "The ladder is going!" jumped off. John Richards, 60, of St. Ives, had his left leg broken in two places and his foot bruised. William Pope, of Camborne, had both thighs broken and sustained serious head injuries. John Spargo, of Illogan Highway, suffered a serious leg injury. Edward Angove, of Camborne, fell nearly the whole of the 72 feet between the levels, but escaped with only a few scratches to his right hand. More remarkable still, Frederick Chinn fell all the way, and had not a scratch, but felt rather sore from the shaking. Three other men on the ladder also completely escaped injury. It must be accounted miraculous that none of them was killed.

Maintenance of pitwork and machinery has been a frequent source of death in the mines. This work, carried out against a background of total darkness, and with a yawning gulf waiting below to swallow the careless or over-confident miner, always contains a large element of risk. A grim example of its dangers occurred at Tolvaddon, in 1863. This was a copper mine in the Marazion district, and it was the practice here to carry out repairs to the pitwork on Saturday afternoons. The shaft involved in this accident was a combined engine and winding shaft. The winding section was most securely cased off both from the engine shaft and from the level which passed behind it. The engine part was six feet long by five feet wide, and inclined at an angle of 22 degrees from the vertical. The ladders ran in long lengths down the shaft, but the men could step out at every ten fathoms upon a floor fitting closely all through the shaft. "In this respect" (wrote the Government inspector who visited the mine after the accident) "I never saw a better landing place." When new pitwork was required, it was sent down through the engine shaft by a series of trap doors fitted to the sollars; and on Saturday afternoons, these doors, normally closed, were opened for the passage of such material. On other occasions, the men entering the shaft from the level stepped out on to the trapdoor and took the ladders, but when this door was raised they stepped on a plank about a foot wide, on which the door rested. On this particular Saturday a lad named Charles Vincent and his father were working at the 50 fathom level when the lad went to go to the 40 to collect a pick which had been left there, but on entering the shaft, and not thinking of the open trapdoor, he stepped in in the usual manner, fell through to the 80 fathom level, and was killed.

More fortunate was a young miner named Craze, employed at South Crofty. In May 1873, whilst attempting to move a piece of timber with an iron bar he fell headlong down a shaft 80 fathoms deep. The bar fell to the bottom, but ten fathoms down his body was caught by a narrow plank placed across the shaft, and there he lay insensible for about an hour and a half. On returning to consciousness, he walked with great difficultly to that part of the mine in which his comrades were working. When he told them what had happened they thought he was joking, but when he again lapsed into unconsciousness through loss of blood, they realised that he had had a truly marvellous escape from death. An experience such as this must indeed be accounted quite exceptional. Far more typical was an accident which occurred at St. Ives Consols in September 1910. Bryant J. Trevithick, a shaft carpenter, assisted by another man was fixing a pump-runner about 180 feet from surface when, hearing shouts of warning, they both stepped back to a place of safety. In doing so, however, their candles went out, and in the dark Trevithick missed his footing and fell forty feet, receiving injuries from which he soon after died.

Another grim accident of this kind occurred at Wheal Fortune, part of Great Consols mine, Gwennap, in June 1853. Benjamin Kellow, aged 36, and Richard Tregoning were walking to their place of work along the 120 fm. level E. when Kellow's candle, which he had placed on his barrow, was extinguished by falling water. He called to his comrade, who was a short distance ahead, to give him a light, but as Tregoning was re-lighting the candle from his own a drop of water fell from the back of the level and put it out also. Both men were now in total darkness; and Kellow left Tregoning to go up to the 90 to fetch a light. Tregoning waited for nearly

St. Ives Consols, early 20th Century (Courtesy Royal Institution of Cornwall)

two hours, but finding his comrade did not return he recollected that the previous week they had left a bag of powder down at the 140. In pitch darkness he groped his way down to that level and brought some of it up to the 120 where he had left his dag. Having some dry hemp in the bottom of his hat he contrived, by striking a piece of mundic stone with the dag, to ignite the powder and the hemp. Having thus obtained a light he went in search of Kellow, and found him lying quite dead and fearfully mutilated on the sollar at the 140. In going up the 90 Kellow had to cross a whim shaft over a roadway divided from it by a casing, but it appeared that in endeavouring to find his way in the dark, he went in front of the casing instead of behind it, and so fell down the shaft.

Unfamiliarity with the layout of a mine could be just as dangerous as the want of a light, especially if the miner concerned was an inexperienced youngster. On July 11 1866 Josephus Trevithick, aged 15, whilst working in the 160 fm. level of Tincroft, Illogan, was asked by his comrades to fetch two spanners weighing ten pounds from the bottom of the level, and bring them up to a sollar, but mistaking his whereabouts took them further up the shaft than was necessary. Seeing him come up, William Carpenter, his brother-in-law, exclaimed, "Josephus, why do you bring up the spanners here for; they are wanted down on the sollar." Without answering, Trevithick turned to go down, slipped his left hand and his right foot and fell a distance of seven fathoms. He was still alive, but unconscious, when found, and died shortly afterwards.

Some of these old mining accidents are invested with what can only be described an eerie quality, and none more so than that which took place at South Condurrow on January 16 1867, when a signal bell was used to inform those at surface whether an injured miner lived or died. Thomas Muffitt, of Copper Bottom Gate, Crowan, and his comrade Henry Berryman, being unable to work at their accustomed place in Flat Rod shaft because of water, were engaged in timbering in the 25 fm. level of Sump shaft. Berryman was standing on the ladder sollar with Muffitt four feet above him. Muffitt had fixed two boards in upon the main pieces and asked his comrade to hand up a third piece. Berryman, whose back was to the shaft, slipped and overbalanced and fell down the shaft. Muffitt descended the ladder as fast as possible and found Berryman alive but unconscious. He carried the injured man into the level, and having fetched another miner to remain with him, went to grass to tell the captain of the accident. Before leaving, he left instructions that if Berryman should die in the meantime the signal bell should be rung four times, but if he lived ten rings were to be given. Whilst he was speaking to the captain the bell rang ten times, but before they could send down the skip the bell gave four rings, signifying that Berryman was dead.

The fortitude often displayed by badly injured miners was never better exemplified than by William Daniel at Wheal Owles in April 1867.

Accompanied by Captain Hollow, he had to cross a winze by means of a plank. Captain Hollow went over first, but when Daniel stepped on the timber it slipped and he fell 40 feet, alighting on the lower part of his back. He appeared little hurt externally but had sustained fatal internal injuries:

> "Against the cheering words of his companions who opposed his conviction that he was dying, but said he was quite prepared and happy and would readily attempt to reach the surface. He was helped up the ladders, and all the way spoke cheerfully and resignedly of his fast approaching death. Near the surface the end came. He asked to stand aside from the ladder in a level and there calmly breathed his last — his companions, to the close, more anxious for his recovery than he seemed himself. He leaves a widow, seven children and the character of an excellent miner and a true Christian." *(Cornish Telegraph)*

There were occasions, however, when the dreadful experiences they suffered caused miners to become temporarily deranged. Such an incident occurred at Pednandrea mine, Redruth, on August 9 1828. John Stephens, aged 25, usually known as 'Cousin Jack Cobbler,' and two brothers called Thomas were stripping the shaft and drawing materials from the mine which had closed about a year previously. They had to remove a quarter piece, which was a stay for poppet heads, from above the shaft's mouth, but as soon as one end of it had been cut away with a dag Stephens and one of the Thomas brothers fell into the shaft. Thomas, after dropping about twelve feet, contrived to stop his further descent by clinging with hands and feet to the sides of one of the angles of the shaft, and here held on till a rope was sent down, by means of which he was saved. John Stephens fell further down and was buried by rubbish, all the collar of the shaft having run in. Though every effort was made for more than two months to recover his body, it could not be found, and the shaft was then closed over.

When Thomas was hauled to the surface after his remarkable escape from what looked like certain death, he was so affected by the terrifying experience he had undergone that his conduct for a while was that of a madman. He ran wildly away, no one knew where, but at length was found in a pigs' house, when proper measures were taken to restore him to sanity. Twenty six years later, in April 1854, Pednandrea mine was reopened. During the following September, when clearing up the 32 fathom level under adit, the body of John Stephens was discovered lying on its left side at the bottom of the level. It had on a blue coat with metal buttons, a coarse woollen shirt, and stockings and shoes, and was identified by William Thomas, brother of the rescued miner, by means of the coat and buttons. At the long delayed inquest on the dead man one of the witnesses was Mrs Anthony Michell, of Redruth, who had seen

Stephens rescued from the shaft in 1828 and had gone in search of him after he ran off in a distracted state. The jury returned a verdict of 'accidental death.'

Falls into shafts by men operating the winding gear at surface also sometimes occurred, and often proved fatal. William Andrewartha, a 'lander' at Wheal Mirth, Lelant, was standing near the landing stage at about ten o'clock on the night of January 30 1904 when the kibble arrived from underground. He signalled to the engine-driver to stop, which was done. Andrewartha, however, forgot to move a lever which would have closed the landing doors over the shaft, and so when he pushed the wagon forward to receive the contents of the kibble, both man and wagon went into the shaft, falling a depth of 72 feet. Death must have been instantaneous, as the head was battered and the brain protruded.

Wheal Mirth (or Merth). (Noall collection)

Mention has already been made of stones falling down shafts and striking miners working at a lower depth. The *Sherborne Mercury* of February 3 1806 reported that on Monday evening (January 27, probably) "one Samuel Osborn, a sober and worthy young man, was killed in Penberthy Mine, near Marazion. He was descending to the bottom in the ladders, when a lad, who was working at a higher level, carelessly, but not intentionally, let a stone fall into the shaft, which hit him on the head and dashed out his brains."

This was not the only way in which such mishaps could happen. On May 7 1860, William Stevens Quick, a tutworker at Wheal Kitty, in Lelant, crossed Bolitho's shaft from the 30 fathom level, where he had been working, to a plat to eat his 'crowst,' but in returning across the shaft was struck on the head by a stone of seven or eight pounds weight which had fallen from the kibble at the 20. Other miners saw him stagger towards his pitch, and then his light went out. He died from the effects of the blow the following day. During the inquest held at Balnoon — a now vanished mining village near Halsetown — Captain Rosewarne, an underground agent who was descending the shaft at the time, described how the stone fell from the kibble through a jerking of the chain at the moment it was taken 'in draught' by the whim. Kibbles themselves could become lethal missiles if the chains or ropes holding them happened to break. William Dunstone was killed by this means in Tincroft mine, Illogan, on February 7 1843, the kibble accidentally falling from the 72 to the 81 fathom level where he and his comrades were raising tin stuff. In a similar fashion, a man named Sanders who was helping to clear an old shaft at Hardhead, near Bodmin, sixteen fathoms from surface, on April 12 1873, died when struck by a kibble which had become detached from its chain after being emptied.

A more unusual accident of this kind took place at Coldreath Iron Mine in Roche parish on March 4 1854. William Hancock, 31, was lowering himself by the whim rope when his cousin, John Hancock, also took hold of the rope to descend in the same way. Their combined weight overbalanced the kibble and caused the whim to run, forcing the kibble up to the poppet heads with such violence that the rope broke, and the kibble fell back into the shaft, killing William Hancock and injuring his cousin. There was a very good footway provided by which they should have gone down, and the men had been frequently cautioned about making use of the rope for descending.

An inquest was held at the 'Bird in Hand' inn, Sancreed, on May 19 1866 on Richard Pengelly, who had been killed in a skip accident at Balleswidden, again by following a dangerous and unauthorised practice during the course of his work. Having completed his 'core' in one of the deep levels and partially filled the skip with his tin stuff, he seated himself on top of the skip to ascend to surface instead of using the ladderway. On reaching a height of 20 fathoms above the level, the wire-rope parted at its junction with the chain which connected it to the skip, and he fell with it to the bottom of the shaft into about two fathoms of water, where he was drowned. He left a widow and four children. The customary verdict of 'accidental death' was returned.

An incident of peculiar horror took place at Binner Downs mine, just to the east of Leedstown in June, 1828. A miner named Speer, aged seventy-two — men were often obliged to continue working into extreme old age before State pensions were established — was killed by the breaking of a chain on a steam whim. As the kibble, then on its way up, approached the top of the shaft, the chain parted, sending the bucket to the bottom; but the section of chain still attached to the whim recoiled, and, coming in contact with Speer's arm, made several turns around it. His arm and shoulder were nearly wrenched off, completely exposing the heart and lungs; and he died instantly. The unfortunate man left an aged and bed-ridden widow in great poverty and distress; his three sons had all been killed in mining accidents within the space of a few years. Such was the reverse side of the coin of romantic Cornish mining so often presented by superficial writers on the subject.

A sensible means of preventing shaft accidents caused by falling objects was to erect a *penthouse* above the heads of miners working there. The neglect, through misapplied economy measures, to provide such a shield, led to a most unfortunate accident at Combellack mine on June 14 1877. Combellack is situated about three miles from Helston near the side of the Falmouth road. Three men called Date, Old and Rowling were working 42 fathoms underground sinking the engine shaft, when they suddenly heard a hissing sound. Date looked up, saw something falling down the shaft, and gave a warning shout. He himself made a bound and managed to reach the side, but before either of the others had time to move, the kibble and a large portion of the shaft's side came down on them. The kibble stuck Old on the head and killed him instantly, his brains being dashed all about. Rowling was also struck on the head and died within a few minutes. The mishap was caused by the kibble rope taking fire — probably through friction, though it was also conjectured that a spark from a small engine placed near the whim might have been the cause. At the inquest, held at Helston, the jury returned a verdict of manslaughter against the manager, because of his failure to erect a penthouse for the protection of the men. He was subsequently tried for his offence at the Assizes, but acquitted. Rowling had been injured in the same shaft six months previously by stones falling down, yet nothing had been done to make the place safer. During the enquiry, a witness stated that when similar sinking operations were carried out at nearby New Trumpet and Lovell, the men had a penthouse at every ten fathoms.

The ropes used for hauling kibbles up and down shafts wore out very quickly, and their frequent renewal was a heavy item of expense for the mine adventurers. Eventually, chains were substituted for them, being much more durable and less liable to break. However, the links did sometimes snap; and an occurence of this kind at Dolcoath on the morning of March 4 1863 led to an unusual fatal accident. Three miners were working in the section called Wheal Harriet, Thomas Kessel filling the kibbles and sending the stuff to grass, whilst Nicholas Bate trammed the ore to him. When one of the filled kibbles was being drawn to surface, the chain broke and it fell down through the north part of the shaft. Kessel, Bate and a third man called Samuel Jewell at once set to work to repair the damage; but whilst they were so employed a scale of ground fell from the side of the shaft. To avoid the falling rock, Kessel stepped back, and fell away in the North Gunnis to a depth of about thirteen fathoms. Bate went down after him and found his comrade in the bottom of the level four fathoms under the 220, lying face downwards on his right side. He was still alive but unconscious, and died about five mintues after being taken up. Bate believed that when they pulled the chain in order to clear it, they brought away the ground as well. He had not previously noticed the ground to be loose, whilst the whim chain was apparently a good one and of the proper size. It came out at the inquest, that when a chain broke, the men were required to fetch it at once, this being a rule in all mines.

Going Down in a Kibble

George Seymour's depiction of the dangerous practice of descending in a Kibble. (Courtesy *Mining Journal*)

A most unusual accident resulting from a falling kibble occurred at Wheal Clowance, situated about two miles south-east of Gwinear, on April 17 1820. Captain Edward Jennings was descending the shaft in one kibble as another, empty, was ascending. The rope of the latter broke, and it fell upon that in which the captain was riding; he was thrown out, precipitated to the bottom of the shaft, and instantly killed. Generally speaking, riding to surface in kibbles was a practice frowned on in most mines, and in many definitely forbidden by the rules. This is not to be wondered at, considering the danger; for the bucket, not running in guides, could be upset by any chance obstruction, whilst there was also a risk of its being over-wound at the top, with equally disastrous consequences to any 'passenger.' Occasionally, however, circumstances made the use of the kibble for this purpose almost unavoidable. Such a necessity arose at St. Ives Consols during March 1887, and it resulted in a fatal accident. Whilst working in the old adit level, seventeen fathoms down, some workmen who were blasting away stuff from the old Bank shaft, allowed some loose material to run in from surface, which blocked the regular way leading to that part of the workings. Captain Mitchell advised the miners not to attempt to resume work by lowering themselves in a bucket by the horse-whim — the only other means of access — but being tributers, and eager to get on with the job, they ignored his advice. The miners — there were four in this pare — made the kibble more secure, as they thought, by adding a strong hemp rope to the wire rope, whereby it was suspended, the former acting as a 'stay' to which they clung when riding. After they had been working below for a while, Edwin Trevorrow asked to be 'wound up;' but when he had nearly reached surface the wire rope parted. Joseph Tonkin, who was standing below, heard a shriek, and then saw the kibble coming down, striking fire from the sides in its fall. He jumped back to avoid it, and the kibble passed on its way to the bottom of the perpendicular shaft. There they found Trevorrow dead with head injuries, and another kibble lying on top of him. At the inquest, it came out that the wire rope was of very doubtful vintage and condition. One of the witnesses conceded that it was "a little over three years old," having been "a little used at West Providence before it was used at St. Ives Consols;" but had to amend his statement when the Government Inspector pointed out that West Providence had been stopped "three years last October." He then admitted that he did not know how long the rope had been used in the latter mine. The jury strongly censured Captain Mitchell for "not severely forbidding the men descending in the kibble," but mercifully refrained from bringing in a verdict of manslaughter against him.

The caving in of ground has always been a common — perhaps the commonest — source of accidents in Cornish mines. A later section of this book has been devoted to them; but whilst on the present subject a

The gravestone of Edwin Trevorrow, who was killed in St. Ives Consols on 15 March 1887, in Balnoon Cemetery, St. Ives (Noall collection)

few examples of shaft accidents caused by this means may be given. On March 14 1811 a pare of men went down into some old workings at Wheal Kitty, in Lelant, to clear away the deads, "but," says the *Sherborne Mercury*, "for want of taking with them the timber allotted for the support of the old workings a large quantity of one of the shafts gave way and buried three poor fellows under the rubbish, and their bodies were not taken out till the following day." One of the miners belonged to Col. Halse's Corps of St. Ives Volunteers, and he was buried two days later with full military honours, an 'immense concourse' of people attending the service. A similar fate befell Captain Phillips, his son, and a labourer in Holmbush mine near Callington on February 16 1843. About four hundred kibbles of stuff fell away in the shaft, which carried the captain with it and buried the other two.

What was described as an 'almost miraculous' escape occurred at Ding Dong in March 1853. Captain Truran had been engaged in dialling and was talking with some miners near a shaft when a mass of rubbish which included one large stone of about a ton in weight, fell away, carrying two men with it to a depth of five fathoms. One, called Carbis, was completely buried in the mass from which he was only extricated with great difficulty, suffering from bruises to the back and shoulders. One of his shoes was cut to pieces by the heavy rock, and he had a truly wonderful escape from death. Another miner, named Cock, of Madron, fell on the rock and fractured both bones of his leg.

As mines grew deeper, the amount of ladder climbing required to reach the lower pitches each day began adversely to affect both the miners' health and output. Depths of a thousand and even fifteen hundred feet were attained; which meant that the men had to perform the equivalent of a stiff mountaineering climb in addition to their arduous underground 'core.' As a result, heart disease and other ailments became common among them, their earnings dropped, and the mines suffered a loss of profitability. In an attempt to solve this problem, Mr. C. Fox and the Royal Cornwall Polytechnic Society in 1834 offered a prize for the design of a machine to convey miners up and down shafts in mines. The premium was in due course awarded to Michael Loam and the adventurers of Tresavean mine, near Lanner, where his *man-engine* was installed in 1842.

This device had the great practical merit of being based on the traditional Cornish beam pumping engine, found on almost every mine in Cornwall, and could thus be easily introduced and maintained without very expensive alterations or changes in working methods. In its original form, two parallel wooden rods were set side by side in the shaft, each being fitted with a series of steps or little platforms set twelve feet apart, which was also the length of stroke of the engine. The rods moved in contrary directions, the steps on the rods coming opposite to each other at the top and bottom of every stroke. Thus, a miner, stepping from one side to the other at these times would be carried either up or down the shaft in twelve feet stages, according to whether he stepped in at the

Cornish miners riding a man-engine (at Dolcoath, circa 1892)
(Courtesy Royal Institution of Cornwall)

commencement of a rising or a descending movement of the rod. A simplier version was also devised, making use of only one moving rod, the corresponding platforms being fixed to the side of the shaft on either side of the rod, to separate the ascending and descending streams of men.

The man-engine proved a convenient and popular means of conveyance with the men; but, doubtless owing to a policy of short-sighted economy, and difficulties in adapting crooked, narrow shafts for its use, the machine was not introduced as widely into the mines as its widespread fame would imply. Indeed, only a relatively small proportion of Cornish miners ever benefitted from Loam's invention. This was a regrettable matter; but to illustrate the difficulties involved in installing it in an old mine, it may be mentioned that it took Captain Hollow and the adventurers of Wheal Providence, at Carbis Bay, fully four years to convert Dunstan's shaft to receive a man-engine, the work being successfully completed in November 1869. For the first 90 fathoms of its depth, the shaft was sunk in decomposed granite; so at that depth the old timber had to be removed, and the sides built elliptically upwards with massive blocks of granite which rested on the solid 'country' below, and, at intervals, on turned arches. At 100 fathoms, a huge excavation had to be made for a balance-bob, which assisted the up-stroke of the rod, but this part of the work paid for itself, owing to the tin which was found there.

In general, the man-engine had a good safety record, but it was too much to expect the machine to be completely foolproof. Grim evidence of this was provided at Tresavean soon after Michael Loam's engine had been put to work. A little boy of eleven, riding with his father on the same platform, through the latter's inattention, fell off and was killed. A similar accident occurred to James Goldsworthy in the engine shaft at the United Mines in January 1865. Whilst descending by the man-engine to commence work with the afternoon 'core,' he missed his hold and fell about twenty fathoms, being dead when found. Most accidents of this kind were caused by carelessness or forgetfulness — a case of 'familiarity breeding contempt' for what was, potentially, a lethal machine. On March 27 1873 Edward Thomas, of Tuckingmill, and his son-in-law, John Quentrall, were riding the man-engine at Cook's Kitchen when, just four fathoms from surface, Thomas, with one foot on the sollar and the other on the stage of the man-engine, tried to take a light from Quentrall's candle. This made him a little too late for the down stroke of the machine, and he fell a depth of eight fathoms. In ten minutes he was got to grass, where examination disclosed a spinal injury. The poor man lingered in excruciating agony for eleven days before death brought a merciful release. Another form of danger attending the man-engine arose from neglect of the rules which prevented ascending and descending miners from meeting on the rod. An example of this occurred at Dolcoath on June 24 1877. About seven in the morning Walter Williams, aged 55, was coming up on the man-engine when he met a boy going down. Somehow or other Williams missed his footing, came in contact with the engine-rod, and sustained a severe compound fracture of the right leg.

However, such accidents as these, few and far between as they were, did nothing to shake the general confidence that was reposed in the machine. For the man-engine itself seemed perfectly safe; only failure on the part of its human passengers to observe commonsense precautions could result in injury or death. Or so it was everywhere believed. There was, however, one man-engine which was destined to shatter this illusion, and in so doing to produce one of the most terrible disasters in Cornish mining history. This was the man-engine at Levant — that fabulous submarine mine situated on the cliffs at St. Just, whose workings extend for over a mile out under the bed of the Atlantic Ocean.

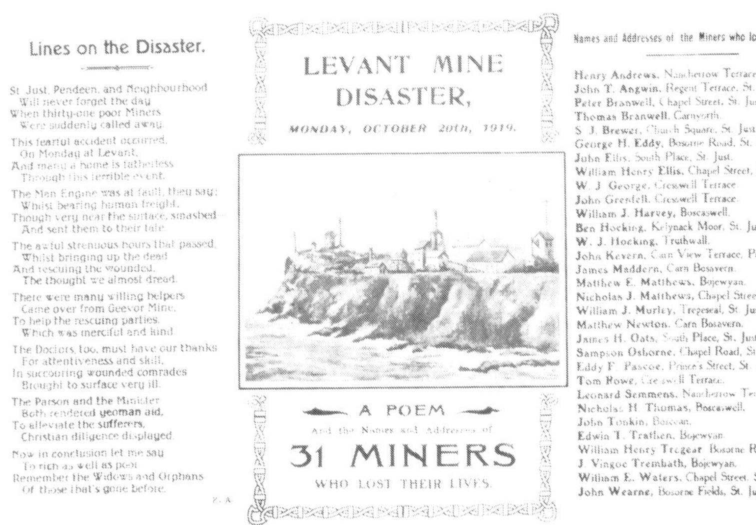

Lines on the Disaster.

St Just, Pendeen, and Neighbourhood
Will never forget the day
When thirty-one poor Miners
Were suddenly called away.

This fearful accident occurred,
On Monday at Levant,
And many a home is fatherless
Through this terrible event.

The Man Engine was at fault, they say:
Whilst bearing human freight,
Though very near the surface, smashed
And sent them to their fate.

The awful strenuous hours that passed,
Whilst bringing up the dead
And rescuing the wounded,
The thought we almost dread.

There were many willing helpers
Came over from Geevor Mine,
To help the rescuing parties,
Which was merciful and kind.

The Doctors, too, must have our thanks
For attentiveness and skill,
In succouring wounded comrades
Brought to surface very ill.

The Parson and the Minister
Both rendered yeoman aid,
To alleviate the sufferers,
Christian diligence displayed.

Now in conclusion let me say
To rich as well as poor
Remember the Widows and Orphans
Of those that's gone before.

Z. A.

LEVANT MINE DISASTER,

MONDAY, OCTOBER 20th, 1919.

A POEM

And the Names and Addresses of

31 MINERS

WHO LOST THEIR LIVES.

Names and Addresses of the Miners who lost their lives.

Henry Andrews, Nancherrow Terrace, St. Just.
John T. Angwin, Regent Terrace, St. Just.
Peter Branwell, Chapel Street, St. Just.
Thomas Branwell, Carnyorth.
S. J. Brewer, Church Square, St. Just.
George H. Eddy, Bosorne Road, St. Just.
John Ellis, South Place, St. Just.
William Henry Ellis, Chapel Street, St. Just.
W. J. George, Cresswell Terrace.
John Grenfell, Cresswell Terrace.
William J. Harvey, Boscaswell.
Ben Hocking, Kelynack Moor, St. Just.
W. J. Hocking, Truthwall.
John Kevern, Carn View Terrace, Pendeen.
James Maddern, Carn Bosavern.
Matthew E. Matthews, Bojewyan.
Nicholas J. Matthews, Chapel Street, St. Just.
William J. Murley, Trepeseal, St. Just.
Matthew Newton, Carn Bosavern.
James H. Oats, South Place, St. Just
Sampson Osborne, Chapel Road, St. Just.
Eddy F. Pascoe, Prince's Street, St. Just.
Tom Rowe, Cresswell Terrace.
Leonard Semmens, Nancherrow Terrace, St. Just.
Nicholas H. Thomas, Boscaswell.
John Tonkin, Boscean.
Edwin T. Trathen, Bojewyan.
William Henry Tregear, Bosorne Road, St. Just.
J. Vingoe Trembath, Bojewyan.
William E. Waters, Chapel Street, St. Just.
John Wearne, Bosorne Fields, St. Just

A contemporary verse, written to commemorate the 31 Cornish miners who lost their lives at Levant on Monday 20 October 1919 (Noall collection)

This engine and its history have already been described in the author's *Levant* (1970). It will suffice to state here that it was installed to a depth of 170 fathoms from surface in 1857, and extended in two stages to its ultimate depth of 266 fathoms by 1898. Several relatively minor accidents occurred with the machine from time to time; but the mishap which should really have alerted the management to its dangerous potentialities took place on February 19 1908. Between fifty and a hundred miners of the forenoon shift were ascending to surface when the rod or pole — a massive timber baulk measuring a foot square — snapped, throwing several men down the shaft, while the sudden drop inflicted a severe shaking on the others. Those who were caught and crushed by the fallen rod cried out to be released, and alarm was increased by the falling of stones and other debris in the shaft. With considerable difficultly the more severely injured were brought to surface, where the wildest rumours had been circulating regarding the extent of the accident.

It was clear from what had happened that the safety devices with which the man-engine was fitted were inadequate to prevent serious consequences in the event of a breakage; but the warning went unheeded. The outcome was the terrible disaster of October 20 1919.

On this occassion, a breakage occurred in one of the two 'caps' by which the rod was attached to the quadrant beam of the engine above the shaft. The engine was almost fully loaded with men ascending from the mine, the rod, with its heavy load, falling a distance of 10′ 6″ on to the safety catches. Some of these failed; and the rod also broke sixty fathoms below the cap. The upper portion, carrying thirty men, fell 46 fathoms to the 70 fathom level, destroying the platforms as it fell. In the shaft, all was chaos and confusion. Some men had marvellous escapes; but no less than thirty-one died amid the welter of crushing timber and stones. The scenes at surface, as relatives of the miners flocked to await news of their loved ones were more reminiscent of large-scale colliery disasters than of Cornish mining tragedies. The event left a grim impression on the local community, and its poignant memories still have not completely faded.

Ingenious invention as the man-engine undoubtedly was, it yet had its limitations. Apart from the fact that it could not be used at all in many mines because of the unsuitability of their shafts, it was also somewhat slow in operation, and a miner could spend up to half-an-hour of his working day stepping off and on its platforms, to say nothing of additional time lost in walking through levels and descending winzes to get to his underground pitch. Something more adaptable and speedier than this cumbersome machine was required; and the answer was supplied by the *gig* or *cage*. This was a logical development of the horse-whim and kibble arrangement, which from comparatively early times had been employed to raise ore and water from underground. The horse, however, was replaced by a fast-working powerful engine; the primitive kibble or bucket by a rectangular iron box (the gig) divided into two sections or cubicles placed vertically one over the other; and the ponderous rope or chain by a slender but strong steel cable. The gig was

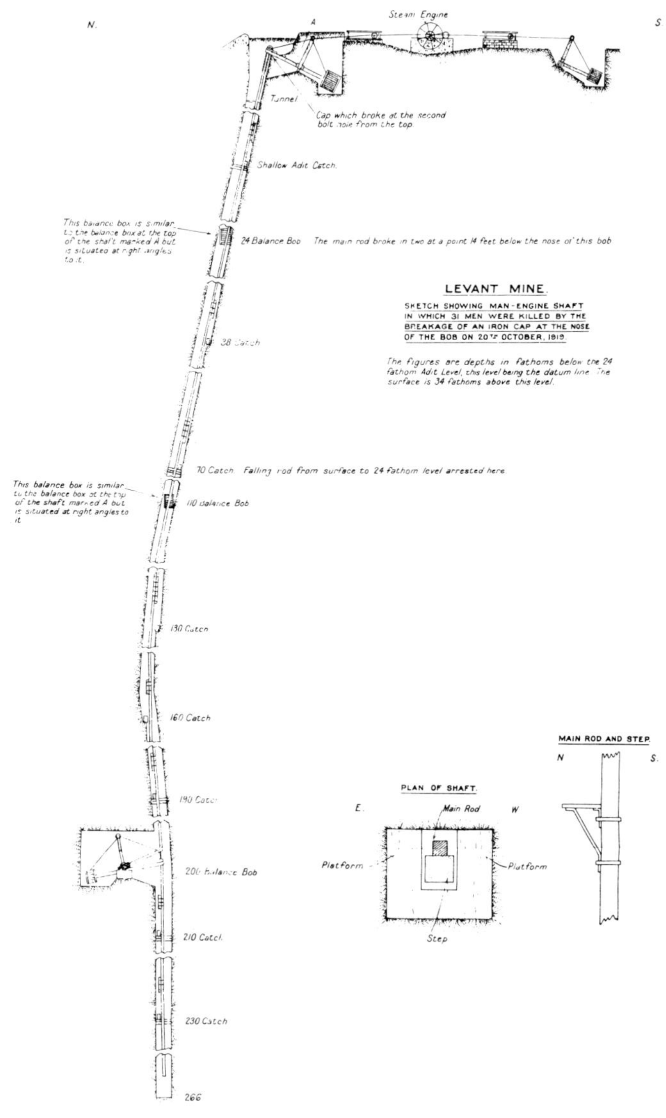

(a) and (b) Diagrams from HM Inspector of Mines' report on the Levant Mine disaster of 1919 (Courtesy Justin Brooke and HMSO)

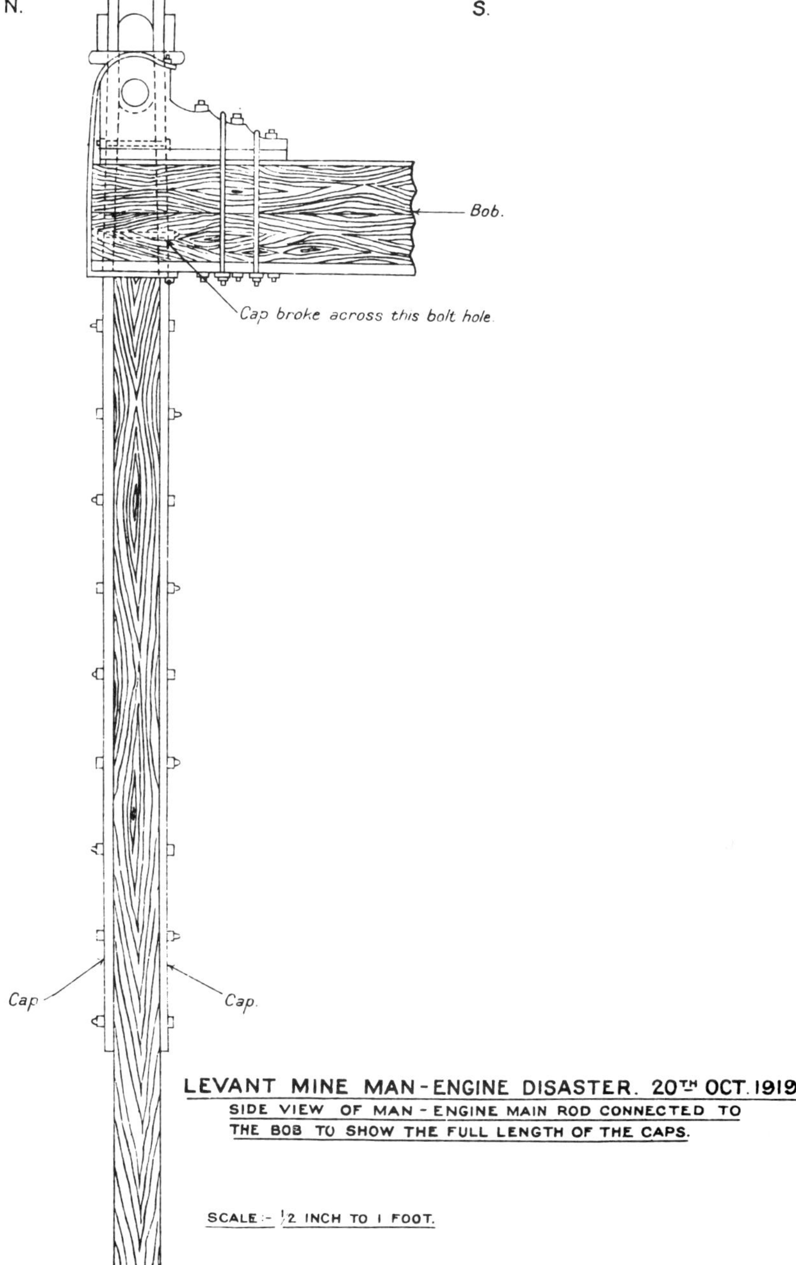

LEVANT MINE MAN-ENGINE DISASTER. 20TH OCT. 1919.

SIDE VIEW OF MAN-ENGINE MAIN ROD CONNECTED TO THE BOB TO SHOW THE FULL LENGTH OF THE CAPS.

SCALE:- 1/2 INCH TO 1 FOOT.

The main shaft at Levant on 20 October 1919, photographed shortly after the accident (Courtesy Royal Institution of Cornwall)

Anxious relatives at Levant, 21 October 1919. (Courtesy Royal Institution of Cornwall)

fitted with wheels, which enabled it to run smoothly over a specially prepared wooden trackway in the shaft, and safety catches were also introduced to hold the gig in the event of the cable snapping. It could be easily fitted into shafts which would have been impossible for the man-engine to work in, whilst its speed was so great that the time required to ascend even a deep shaft could be measured in seconds rather than minutes. Its introduction represented a further notable improvement in the miner's working conditions, and also assisted him materially in improving his output (and hence his earnings) by reducing the time required to get to his workplace.

The gig nevertheless had its dangers, and some serious accidents resulted, either from failure of the human or mechanical element involved. One of the most appalling of these took place at Wheal Agar, which adjoins the village of Pool and the former Carn Brea railway station, mid-way between Camborne and Redruth, in the early morning of August 15 1883. The cage involved in this disaster appears to have been of the usual type, being made of iron, and divided into two compartments; it was worked by a steam capstan, or whim, and was situated in the engine shaft on the left of the road which divides East Pool from Wheal Agar. It must have been a very uncomfortable vehicle to ride in, for the men in the lower chamber could not stand properly; there was an opening on two sides with a bar in the centre, to which the miners clung. At the time of the accident the cage was being operated by John Long, the 'lander,' who controlled its ascents and descents in accordance with signals received from below. He brought up one set of men who had been working 'last core at night,' and then sent down the cage for a second set. Ten miners crammed themselves into the vehicle's two compartments, and three more scrambled up on its top. Another young man was prevented from climbing on to the gig at the 190 plat. As it ascended the shaft the men were singing, as they usually did on such occasions, and the journey continued in a normal fashion until it had reached the entrance of the shaft and its top was actually two and a half feet above the landing step. The 'lip' — a piece of iron usually thrown back to rest the skip upon when it reached the surface full of mineral — had not been put down, as it was not used for the gig. The lander had made a signal to the whim-driver to inform him of the near approach of the cage, and had the bell-rope in his hand about to ring 'stop.' The cage was but slowly ascending when Long heard something breaking. He had just a moment before he caught sight of the heads of the miners in the upper compartment, and glanced up to see what was the matter. At the same instant one of the men — Long did not know his identity — exclaimed "What is that going up overhead?" Long saw that the rope was parting, and felt so frightened that 'his blood almost turned to water.' Henry Carbines (or Carbis), one of the three men standing on top of the cage, sprang off and landed safely in the usual way, but his companions did not have time to follow him. Two other men, named Lenten and Symons, were waiting their turn to descend as soon as the cage made its return journey down the shaft, and being anxious to secure good places, were about to place their feet on it when, like Long, they saw the rope going and withdrew — just in the nick of time. As Carbines alighted, his back, for an instant, was to the shaft, but on turning round he was bewildered and appalled at seeing the rope had parted, and that the cage, with his comrades still aboard, was hurtling into the abyss with fearful rapidity.

Down below, some miners — including the young man who had not been allowed on during the ascent — then impatiently awaiting the gig's return at the 190 plat, suddenly heard a terrible noise in the shaft. Thinking that the cage had broken away or that there had been a fall of 'stuff,' they withdrew hastily into the level, and then went by ladder up to the 130 level, where they found the gig with two bodies inside, both badly mutilated. The shaft, as it happened, was downright (perpendicular) as far as this level, but then ran on the underlie to the 170, after which it became downright again; the cage, consequently, had been arrested in its frightful fall by the angle at the start of the underlie at the 130. Examination revealed that the cage had left the skip-road at the 70 fathom level, from where to the 110 the eastern side of the road was ripped up. At the 110 a body was found; and at this place the cage again got into the road, remaining there until it ran into the plot at the 130 where it stopped and partly overturned. Two bodies were found at this point, but the velocity and lateration in position of the cage had the effect of precipitating the remaining men further down the shaft. Two others were discovered at the 175, two at the 205, and three at the 225, or bottom of the mine. All had been appallingly mutilated in their headlong fall. Their brains were scattered all the way down the shaft, their heads being reduced almost to a jelly, and in one or two cases decapitated. Their bodies, also, were smashed in an indescribable manner, limbs having been torn off and fearful wounds inflicted. These pitiful remains were carefully collected and wrapped in coarse flannel, or 'bla' shag,' preperatory to being brought to surface. The 80 fathom level had to be specially cleared for the purpose, and after drawing them up the ladderway by ropes, they were conveyed to the new shaft and there sent up in pairs in the kibbles. They were then taken to the carpenter's shop and placed in coffins, to await interment. One very strange story related of this disaster is that the shriek given by the men in the cage as they felt themselves suddenly falling into the depths was distinctly heard by some workmen on the turnpike road sixty yards from the top of the shaft, who immediately knew that some terrible calamity had occurred.

The names of those who perished in the accident were:

Charles Osborne, single, Gulval.
George Clemence, single, Redruth.
Charles Trevena, married, Redruth.
Paul Pope, single, Illogan Highway.
James Caddy, single, Illogan.
Joseph Roberts, married, Illogan.
William Cavill, single, Redruth.
Edward Dave, single, Redruth.
Thomas Cock, —, Redruth.
Thomas Richards, single, Redruth.
Henry Thomas, single, Redruth.
Francis Henry Woolcock, single, St. Agnes.

Three causative factors appear to have been involved in this terrible affair — the worst of its kind in the annals of Cornish mining. In the first place, the cage itself was greatly overloaded. Its maximum permitted capacity was eight men; but ten squeezed themselves into its narrow compartments and three more had perched themselves on top, hanging on by the chain — a practice absolutely forbidden by the rules. The great danger of riding in this position had been proved on earlier occasions; at East Pool a miner so placed when the skip ran to the top of the 'shears' was literally bent and broken in two; whilst on another occasion a miner had his head cut off by the skip in Pendarves United. Then, the rope by which the cage was suspended appears to have been unsuitable, and not normally employed for such work. This rope snapped some twelve feet above the gig, and was a capstan-rope, put on in place of the whim-rope which had itself parted shortly before the accident. But what made the accident inevitable, once these failures had occurred, was the lack of any safety devices on the cage itself. Safety-catches had already been invented, and were in use in many of the Californian and Australian mines; they were self-acting and so constructed that if the rope, through breakage, became detached from the upper part of the gig, then these catches, placed on either side of the gig, would open and incise themselves into the runners fixed to the shaft, and so arrest its descent.

It might seem that when a cage fell away in this fashion, all those riding in it would be doomed to an inescapable death. Sometimes, however, quite remarkable escapes were recorded. Perhaps the most astonishing of these occurred at Dolcoath mine, Camborne, on May 31, 1892. For several hours during the afternoon parties of men had been raised and lowered by cage in the eastern shaft without incident. Then, two shaftsmen and two miners got into the cage at the 375 level to ride up, but when it reached the 254 level, the shaft of the fly-wheel of the winding engine suddenly broke in two, and down the deep shaft went the cage and its four startled inmates like a stone. The breaking wheel hurled pieces of iron for long distances at surface, and strong timber was crushed into matchwood. A shieve wheel, eleven feet high, and with wrought iron spokes was 'doubled up like a big bundle of cabbage plant,' and hurled to the threshold of the engine-house door by the force of the flying wire rope. There were two enginemen on the whim who, with commendable promptitude, at once applied the brake to the drum with every ounce of strength their muscles would yield. Fire and smoke produced by friction arose from the drum as they strained on the lever; but owing to the spur-wheel coming in contact with the lever, their efforts were not as effectual as they otherwise would have been. So down the shaft still flew the cage and the apparently doomed men. Their feelings were almost indescribable. It seemed as if every drop of blood rushed to their heads, then ebbed to their hearts, leaving a clear conviction that they would in another moment be killed. But both sensations were so lightning-like — there was so brief a time for experiencing or for uttering a prayer, that had they been dashed to pieces they scarcely believed they would have felt it. The cage continued to hurtle down to the 376, where there was a sharp turn in the shaft from the downright to the underlie. This sudden change in direction, coupled with the desperate efforts of the enginemen to slow its fall with the brake, here brought it to a violent halt. But for this, all the men would most probably have been killed; certainly the two in the lower chamber would have been drowned in the water at the bottom of the skip shaft, near the 400 fathom level. As it was, they were unhurt, save for general soreness, fright, and one black eye. One of the timbermen, called Jewell, must have been born under a lucky star, for he had previously escaped when buried by rock in an earlier, fatal accident at the mine; and had also marvellously eluded being killed when entangled with the capstan-rope at West Frances. The event was a seven-day wonder at Camborne; and the men's survival had certainly been miraculous. The big, heavy box in which they were riding had fallen like a thunderbolt for 756 feet down a well. Some idea of its velocity may be gathered from the fact that after the wire rope had left the huge ten-ton horizontal drum, it whirled around with the brake down on it like the wheels of a train travelling at 40 m.p.h. Much praise was bestowed on the plucky enginemen who stuck to their seemingly hopeless task amidst the awful crash of falling iron and timber. When it was over, they appeared white as sheets, and wet with sweat — the result of the agony and toil to save their fellow workmen in the falling cage.

Another remarkable escape of this kind happened at Wheal Agar on September 11 1882. A miner was in the cage in the shaft when the fastening broke, and it plummeted down a distance of twenty fathoms, finally upsetting in about seventy fathoms of water. The man was flung out, and he swam and supported himself on the surface until assistance arrived. On being taken to the Miners' Hospital, at Redruth, he was found to have sustained serious shoulder, head and arm injuries; but the fact that he had been rescued alive after such a terrifying experience was accounted almost unbelievable.

One miner was actually drowned in a skip, while others narrowly escaped sharing his fate in a singular accident a few years later at Wheal Basset, lying to the south-west of Redruth. During the Christmas holiday a breakdown occurred in the lower part of the lift which drained the mine, and this allowed twenty fathoms of water to collect in the bottom of the shaft. The shaftsmen, whose duty it was to go down and examine the pitwork neglected to do so 'because it was Christmas time.' If this usual preliminary survey had been carried out the accumulation of water would have been discovered, and no one would have been sent down in the gig until it had been drained. But, ignorant of the deadly pool waiting below, the miners of the first core got into the vehicle at six in the morning and were lowered to the 180 fathom level. As it plunged into the water, three succeeded in climbing to the top of the gig, and seizing the knocker line, signalled to be drawn to surface. The other three were not so fortunate, for they were washed out of the skip. One managed to grasp a wire rope, and by it climbed ten fathoms in darkness to the 170. Another, by a tremendous effort, managed to get into a winze and climbed up through this to the level above. The last, however, a young man of Stithians, called Edwin Dunstan, aged about eighteen, was drowned. The miner who ascended the winze lost his boots, hat and jacket in the water, whilst the one who climbed by the rope received a bad blow on the head. As soon as the gig arrived at surface, the three men on it were rescued from their perilous situation, and three more who had been awaiting their turn to descend to the 190, were at once lowered to the 170, where they searched around and brought up the other two survivers, who were almost exhausted by the superhuman efforts they had made to save themselves. Search was also made for Dunstan, but his body could not then be found. One curious feature about this accident is that the skip had been lowered empty, according to regulations, before the first manned descent was made, without anything amiss being discovered. One can only assume it was not sent down far enough to reach the water. There was a general feeling that the negligent shaftsmen ought to have been prosecuted, but at the inquest on Dunstan, the jury, also apparently infected by the Christmas spirit, contented themselves with the mild rider that rules for the shaftsmen's guidance should be posted in the mine!

In this instance, the accident had been the result of carelessness and neglect of duty, but the great majority of these mishaps occurred through the breakage of the winding rope. Two men died through this cause at

North Basset when the cage was being drawn to surface on one occasion. One of the dead miners had a pick driven through his side in the fall, but the one who escaped was so little hurt that he was soon able to resume work.

A much more serious disaster of this nature took place at Botallack on April 18 1863; but here the winding arrangements were of a quite different nature. Botallack, like Levant, is a submarine mine, its shafts and engine houses being most spectacularly situated on the bold, high cliffs about two miles from St. Just. Access to the undersea section, which extended for about a third of a mile out under the Atlantic, was gained by the celebrated Boscawen diagonal shaft running at an angle of 32½ degrees from the horizontal. A narrow gauge railway track was laid through the greater length of the shaft, on which a small carriage for the men and a separate skip for mineral was hauled up and down by the winding engine on the cliff. On April 18 1863 as the carriage, containing eight men and a boy, was being raised from the 100 fathom level, the winding chain broke, and the vehicle began to run back down the shaft with terrifying velocity. It had been fitted with safety devices; but these, partly through the inattention of the brakesman riding on it, and partly through the counteracting effect of the weight of trailing chain, failed to operate. The carriage hurtled down the track, throwing out several men on the way, until it was stopped by colliding with timbers at the 190 level. All the occupants were killed, their bodies being shockingly mutilated. However, despite this accident, when the Prince and Princess of Wales visited Botallack two years later, they made a journey to the bottom of the mine in the very carriage in which the men had taken their last fatal ride, the vehicle having suffered no material injury in the disaster.

Mention has already been made of accidents resulting to miners through their improper use of kibbles — intended only for drawing mineral — as a means of travelling up the shafts. When kibbles gave way to skips — large rectangular containers — the men continued, in some mines, to employ them for this purpose, despite the threat of fines and dismissal if they were caught. This happened even where man-engines or cages had been provided, the miners apparently preferring the risks of skip-riding to the trouble of a little extra underground walking or ladder-work to reach the shafts containing these appliances. Needless to say, this foolish practice produced an inevitable crop of accidents. One such occurred at West Seton mine, near Camborne, during the early morning of November 26 1887. Five miners who had been working in the 264 fathom level decided to come up in the skip, although it was against the rules. They made a signal for the skip to be drawn up, and reached surface safely, but were then carried on to the poppet heads without stopping. As a result, three of the men were injured, one of them, James Curnow, being badly crushed. The whim-driver, seeing what had happened, threw the skip about eighteen inches, and Curnow was released, but died of his injuries a few weeks later. The engineman gave evidence at the inquest that the indicator, showing the exact position of the skip in the shaft, was out of order, and although it gave a variation in reading equal to no more than half a stroke of the engine, this had been sufficient to bring the skip to the poppet heads, causing the accident. He could not see the shaft from the engine-house, but depended on the lander. Unfortunately, there was no lander on duty at that time of morning, so he had nothing but the faulty indicator to depend on. However, the over-winding of the skip would not have mattered in the least had there been no men in it. Conflicting evidence was given as to connivance by the engineman in the miners' misuse of the vehicle; but it seems clear from other cases of the same nature that this did sometimes occur. The jury's verdict was: "Accidentally killed through being wound up to the poppet heads; and we unanimously recommend a cage being provided for the men by the mine authorities." Considering the great depth from which the men had to climb after a hard night's labour underground, could anyone seriously blame them for rising up in the convenient but treacherous skip? The responsibility for such an accident as this clearly lay more with the management than the men.

The same excuse could not be offered in respect of an accident which occurred at Dolcoath on October 9 1882. Dolcoath was the deepest mine in Cornwall, and three miners who had been tramming and filling at the 352 fathom level on the first core by night finished their work a little late (eleven o'clock), and feeling tired, resolved to ride up in the skip. They were joined by a shaftsman, William Mitchell, of Beacon, and a boy who had been working with him in the new sump shaft. Mitchell actually jumped on top of the skip, and rode up with his feet resting on one edge and his back on the other. When they arrived at a point about twenty feet from surface, the driver suddenly stopped the skip — a custom adopted more by night than day, for fear the lander might be away from the brace. While the skip was thus poised motionless in the shaft, Mitchell, in order to escape detection by the agents, and so avoid a fine, jumped out of the skip into the ladder-way, intending to climb the remaining distance. However, he either missed his footing, or else was jerked off by the skip, which at that moment began to move again, and fell away into the shaft. He had not told his comrades of his attention to get off, and though they heard a strange sound, they did not take much notice of it. When surface was reached, he was found to be missing, and a search was at once instituted for him in the shaft. Descending the ladders, Captain James Rhodda and two shaftsmen found Mitchell five fathoms below the 40 fathom level, lying on a piece of dividing timber with his feet hanging in the shaft. Both legs and one arm were broken and the other torn off; needless to say, he was quite dead. It was remarked afterwards how fear of detection had caused him to sit on top of the skip, as there had been plenty of room inside. No blame could be attached to those operating the skip at surface, as they were completely unaware that men were riding up. But what made the accident so unnecessary and tragic was that the men knew perfectly well that the man-engine was working at the time, and yet preferred to hazard their lives in the skip.

Shafts can be dangerous when working; they can be equally dangerous when closed, as witnessed the large number of mishaps occasioned by people falling into disused workings; and they can also be dangerous for those who try to make them safe for the public. On January 17 1874 two brothers named John and William Berriman, together with the latter's son, a boy aged about thirteen, were engaged in 'sollaring over' an old shaft in a field near Wheal Trenwith engine house, at St. Ives. Granite stones had been laid across the shaft with a hold in the firm soil about three fathoms from surface; the interstices were carefully filled in, and the hole covered with rubbish, preparatory to levelling in from above, when William Berriman, who was on the cover, felt something giving way, and at the same moment, John, who was above, saw him and his own son going down into the shaft, amidst a heap of stones and rubbish. He heard the lad calling to him, and having procured help, the father went down and extricated him from the heap of stones in which he was partially buried. He brought the injured boy to grass in his arms, holding on by the windlass-rope. No trace could be found of his brother, or of the covering stones. Twenty volunteers came forward and offered to search for the missing man, and necessary equipment was provided by the neighbouring mines. The rescue work proved exceedingly dangerous owing to the condition of the shaft, and it was late on the following day before the miner's body was recovered. They found it near the collapsed covering stones, head and feet together, and jammed down into a crevice. The accident had been caused either by the granite slabs not being long enough to obtain a firm hold in the ground, or by being flawed.

At about the same time, a similar accident occurred in the Great Western mines, between Penzance and Helston. Two men, a father and son named Foss, were removing part of the collar of the disused Annie shaft when the ground gave way, and they fell to a depth of eighty fathoms. The *Mining Journal* asserted that the shaft was sufficiently protected against casual intrusion, "but not against such interference as caused the death of these unhappy men" — which leaves one wondering just what their purpose had been.

The mining districts of Cornwall are riddled with old shafts, some left completely open and unfenced, others sealed with timbers now completely rotten, and others so well hidden by vegetation that their very existence is today unknown. Every now and again one hears an amusing

Wheal Trenwith, circa 1850 (Noall collection)

story of a shaft opening under someone's kitchen floor, or of a tractor suddenly sinking when ploughing a field. But though such incidents may arouse a smile, the menace presented by these unfenced or unrecorded shafts should never be minimised. They represent a danger to the whole community; and the efforts now being made to render them secure deserve every possible support.

The Level

During the earliest period of underground mining, rocks were broken by the ancient method known as 'fire-setting.' Faggots of wood were piled against the rock face and set on fire, water then being thrown over the heated surface, causing it to fracture. An alternative technique was to drill an oblique hole in the rock with a hand drill into which two semi-cylindrical rods of iron, called 'feather,' were inserted, a steel wedge then being driven between them, so splitting off a section. The labour involved in hewing out shafts and levels by such primitive means must have been tremendous, especially where the 'country' was hard; so, to keep the toil required to a minimum, all openings were made as narrow as possible, particularly the levels. Barrows were usually employed for bringing the excavated material to shaft, and the levels were driven just high and wide enough to allow for their passage. In some instances levels were cut even narrower, the miners then having to drag the stuff behind them on sleds.

The introduction of blasting into Cornwall during the late 17th century changed all this, enabling excavations to be made more rapidly on a more generous scale, providing much less cramped working conditions. Another tremendous improvement came in the 1870s with the pneumatic drill, superseding the old boryer and hammer, which speeded up still further the process of tunnelling through rock. The levels in a modern mine can be driven as wide and as high as circumstances require, and in a mere fraction of the time needed when men broke out the ground by the sheer force of their own muscles and sinews.

It might be imagined that the level, from its very nature, was a much safer place to work in than the shaft. Such an impression is certainly fostered by those neat little plans published in mining books and elsewhere in which levels are depicted as ruler-straight horizontal lines. The reality, however, was often vastly different, levels in old mines not infrequently being crooked as serpents, and as dangerous. The floor usually contained depressions filled with water, some being large excavations which had to be crossed on treacherous slippery planks, where a false step could easily result in a fatality.

Miners often had to ascend from the level into a *rise* to reach their pitches. Where ladders were provided, these places were usually safe enough; but sometimes men had to climb up by chains, holding on with both hands, digging their toes into any roughness in the rock on one side and pressing their backs firmly against the other. By this means, they often managed to raise themselves to considerable heights, but the risks were not inconsiderable. For descending winzes and sumps, chain ladders, or a rope and windlass were often used. With the later method, one foot or leg was placed in a loop, the rope grasped in the hands, and the free leg used as a 'fender' to prevent rubbing or striking against the rock. It was a less hazardous method than this description might imply, but accidents nevertheless occurred by the miner losing hold and falling to the bottom. A much greater source of danger was presented by the shafts passing through the levels, these being, in the old days, quite open and unprotected, as they should have been, by a light gate or a chain drawn across them.

However, all these causes combined were far less productive of mishaps than unexpected falls of rock or ground. Where levels were driven through granite or other hard rock the risk of a roof collapse was relatively slight, though the possibility of a large piece flawed by blasting or natural causes suddenly giving way could never entirely be discounted. In soft ground, a 'run' might occur at any time, and could only be guarded against by shoring up the excavations with strong timbers. The danger was greatest not in the comparatively narrow levels, but in those places where the lode had been stoped away for a considerable height and depth, producing large caverns whose sides and roofs had to be shored with extreme thoroughness to ensure safety. In the majority of Cornish mines the lodes were not excessively wide; but large 'bunches' of metalliferous ground were always likely to be met with, these sometimes being of enormous size, like the fabulous 'carbonas' at St. Ives Consols, Rosewall Hill, and a few other mines. Absolute forests of timbering were used in such huge caves as these to prevent the hollowed ground from coming together and entombing all the men working in them.

Sometimes, when a collapse of ground occurred, the miners received no warning; but at others, clear indications of an impending 'run' were given, perhaps by a bending or cracking beam, or the falling away of a little stone or trickle of earth - forerunner of the avalanche to follow. Those who ignored such warnings often paid for their indifference with their lives. On May 5 1869, three tutworkers began their days 'core' at eight in the morning by cutting 'hitches' — places for the ends of timber supports — in the 120 fathom level at Wheal Seton, lying to the north of Camborne. They continued at this work for two hours, at which time James Boase was holding the borer and Tobias Rodda striking, whilst Thomas Davey stood about four feet behind them. Suddenly a small stone, about the size of a hen's egg, fell down and struck Boase on the right knee. Boase stopped work to rub his knee, and Rodda enquired from where the stone had come. "I reckon from the stull overhead," replied the injured miner. However, none of them took any further notice of the incident, and commenced to work again. A moment later, however, there was a tremendous crash. Davey, terrified, ran back into the level for five or six fathoms, but then returned, seeing Rodda's light still burning. The latter was safe, but Boase lay on his face, dead, having been buried by a 'scale' of ground which had come away from overhead. A large stone rested on the back of his neck and a rock of at least a ton on his legs, one of which was severed above the ankle. The ground from which the rock fell had not been wrought, but was known to be 'drummy' or loose, yet the miners had not considered the place dangerous to work in. The warning stone that fell should have disillusioned them; but they paid no heed, and it was fortunate that the rock, when crashing down, did not kill them all.

Tributers, who were paid according to the value of the stuff they sent up, were, perhaps, more liable to run risks by working in unsafe ground than the tutmen, whose terms of contract made them, in effect, mere hired labourers. An interesting illustration of this occurred at the phenomenally rich St. Ives Consols on March 12 1873. Roberts, an old miner of 72, had taken up an abandoned pitch in the 87 fathom level, despite warnings from the agents of the danger he was running. Some men had left the pitch the month before for this reason, but Bennetts was not to be deterred, the inducement which led him to incur such risk being the ease with which a quantity of tin stuff was to be won there without hard work. What made the danger even greater for him was his deafness, so that he could not hear any warning sounds. About midday, another miner observed that a quantity of stuff had broken away on the Standard lode and blocked the pitch where Bennetts was working. He searched, and found Bennetts' jacket, then went through another level to the opposite side, hoping to find his comrade safe, but failing to see him came up for help. Several hours elapsed before the missing man was discovered — dead — and brought out. The body was in a most singular position, suspended by the heels in a hollow, sufficient rubbish having fallen down around the shoulders just to bury his head. The only apparent injury was to the ankles, caused probably in freeing the body. Hundreds of tons of stuff had fallen away, carrying him with it, but he had been caught by the feet, and his head only buried in this extraordinary manner, death being caused by suffocation.

Some further examples, briefly described, will help to establish the general pattern of this class of accident. On September 22 1845 Richard Pike was working with a bar in Poldory mine, Gwennap, bringing down some stuff, when a large 'run' occurred and buried him, breaking his arms and neck. He was found to be dead when extricated with a rope. Pike had almost certainly wrought his own destruction by the incautious use of the bar; but the same cannot be said of Henry Trevorrow, killed at Wheal Providence, near St. Ives, in September 1866, when the ground suddenly gave way above the place where he was working in the 150 fathom level, a huge rock weighing six hundredweight falling directly on his head. The circumstances (though not recorded) were probably similar in the case of an unnamed Lelant miner killed at North Binner mine on

March 11 1806 "by an immense rock and a large body of earth falling on him and crushing him to death" (*Sherborne Mercury*.)

On December 22 1849, William Keast and John Jane were working together in Restormel Iron Mines when a large rock of about four tons weight broke away unexpectedly from the upper part of the adit, killing Keast instantly and injuring Jane so badly that he died after being taken home. John Stephens and Thomas Richards were stoping at Wheal Josiah, Devon Great Consols, at about eight in the morning of December 14 1864 when some of the earthwork gave way. Stephens' skull was

St. Ives Consols, circa 1870 (Courtesy Royal Institution of Cornwall)

fractured, causing instant death, whilst Richards escaped with a fractured thigh and lesser injuries. Death in an unusual form came to Charles Tonkin in Perran Iron Mine, Perranzabuloe, on October 27 1858. Falling ground hurled him forward with great force against a board on which the barrows were wheeled, killing him instantaneously. A pare of miners were stoping away a piece of ground in the back of the 60 fathom level in West Frances on November 17 1874 when the ground gave way from above, crashed through a sollar, and buried James Negus under seven feet of stuff. One of his comrades rushed to help, and found him still alive and able to speak. It took two hours to get him free, but he died later. The sollar was a good one, but quite unable to stand the weight of material — five to eight tons — which came crashing down on it from a height of five feet. Death by choking proved to be the grim fate of Gabriel Thomas, at Botallack on February 16 1872, when some stuff fell away in the place where he was working. He was found lying against the opposite wall, where the 'run' had thrown him, with a large piece of ground pressing on his neck, which prevented him from breathing.

Equally sad was the fate of Charles Bottrell Toll, of Perran Downs, killed in a curious and very unfortunate way at East Wheal Grylls in February 1865. Toll left home to go to work on the last core by day, being engaged alone on driving the 17 fathom level at £1 5s. a fathom and 6s. 8d. in the £ for tin. From the 17 fathom level to the 30 fathom level (the adit) a lode had been worked out and a stull built at the top of it a year before. Timber was introduced into the matrix of the lode, with a bearing of 9 inches on each side, about six feet below the 17 fathom level and the place filled up with stuff, over which the roadway of that level was continued. Ever since, men had worked over and under the stull, and it was considered quite safe.

Toll did not return home at his proper time, and his wife becoming alarmed, James Pope, Henry Pearce and Jeremiah Andrew went underground at midnight to search for him. They found the footway and stull had gone down, and Toll lay with his barrow and ten or fifteen tons of rubbish sixty feet below. There was a large, deep cut in his forehead, which if not sufficient to cause death must have rendered him insensible and made his end comparatively painless. At the inquest, held at the Falmouth Packet inn, St. Hilary, the miner who had put in the stull and worked under it for twelve months, stated he had examined it a month before the accident and found the timber substantial and good. The sole reason for the failure, in his opinion, was that, as a result of recent heavy rains, surface water had poured down an old shaft and on the stull; percolating through, this had carried away the ground on which the lower timbers rested; and so when Toll wheeled his barrow across, the structure collapsed and precipitated him to the bottom. The jury returned a verdict of 'accidental death.'

So one could go on, compiling an enormous catalogue of these accidents, which have been all too depressingly frequent and fatal. It is, therefore, with some relief that we turn to those cases in which miners buried or entombed by falls of rock managed to survive their fearful ordeal, being released after hours or days of imprisonment through the heroic efforts of rescue teams. A typical case occurred at West Tolgus on December 30 1876, when Nicholas Seccombe was almost buried alive by the sudden collapse of a scale of ground estimated at fully ten tons. His comrades extricated him as speedily as possible, but some hours elapsed before he could be brought to surface. Miraculously, no bones had been broken, but he sustained severe bruising and was badly shocked. Two men similarly buried under earth which fell on them in Levant mine during March 1834 were also extricated by the prompt exertions of their comrades, both being relatively uninjured.

The remarkable story of a miner trapped by a fall of earth in an adit in the Ludgvan area appeared in the *Cornish Telegraph* of February 21 1872. This adit was about a mile long, and very low and narrow, so that a man could only crawl through it. The passage became choked by an obstruction, which threatened to flood the mine. Accordingly, the captain ordered Will Thomas to clear it — a dangerous and unpleasant task which, because of the restricted space in the adit, he had to carry out alone. Thomas entered it through its portal, intending to make his way to surface up the ladders in the shaft after clearing the blockage. However, when his comrades finished their 'core' there was no sign of him. At first, they were not unduly alarmed, even after learning he had failed to turn up at his home, as they believed he must have come up safely but had then stopped to gossip with an old friend at Ludgvan. However, hours passed, and he still did not return; so, late that night, one of his companions, moved by the pitiful entreaties of Thomas' young wife, rounded up the fellow members of his 'core' and set out in search of him.

The narrowness of the adit made it necessary for the leader to go in alone; and though he was used to such work, big drops of sweat stood out on his face as he crawled along, expecting any moment to come upon the dead body of his friend. Once, indeed, though no coward, he almost turned back, but overcame his fears, and pressed forwards, calling out every now and then to the missing man. But his shouts evoked no answer, except the purling of the little stream that ran along the bottom of the adit and the hollow echo of his own voice. He had crawled about a third of a mile when far away he heard a muffled shriek. A cold shiver ran through the rescuer as that dismal sound pealed along the adit, but he shouted back lustily that help was near, and crawled on faster than before. Eventually he heard a deep groan, then the low mutter of someone praying, and knew he was nearing the place where Thomas must be trapped. At last, squeezing through the narrowest part of the passage, he came upon the unfortunate man who had been wedged in by a slip of earth. Pinned down on his face — obliged to throw back his head, which was the only part of his body he could move, to keep the stream from entering his mouth and drowning him — Will Thomas' predicament was indeed a desperate one. Seeing the agony he was in from keeping his head in that position, the rescuer took off his own coat and, rolling it up, placed it under Will's chin. Then, pouring some brandy down his throat, he bade him cheer up whilst he went back to the shaft for more help. Thomas gave a gasp, and pitifully begged not to be left alone. During the long hours of pain and darkness in which he had cried out so often for someone to save him, his hopes sometimes being raised by an imagined footfall, then falling prey to despair when no one came, had made a child of him. However, his rescuer made him see that there was no help for it — that he must be left on his own again if he were to be saved. So, assistance was brought; and slowly the burden of earth that held Thomas fast was removed — no easy task in that confined space, yet one that had to be performed as quickly as possible if he were not to die of exhaustion. It was late the next day before they brought Will Thomas out of the shaft, and those who stood about it said he was dead. But they were wrong. Many hours passed before he returned to consciousness and recognised his wife who was watching over him; and a long time more before he took his spell of work with his comrades again. But he did well, and seemed none the worse for the time when he lay some twenty hours or more fast in an adit.

Another fine rescue was performed at Balleswidden mine, St. Just, on May 14 1858. Following a 'run' in the soft, decomposed granite in which this mine was sunk, it was feared that a man and boy had either been killed or entombed when their above-ground clothes remained unclaimed long after their shift was over. It was some time before a search could be instituted, owing to the great change which had taken place in the appearance of the workings, but at length a man named Martin Wallish succeeded in making himself heard by the missing miners. By spilling through the shaft a distance of about six feet, an entrance was effected into the dark dungeon where they had been trapped. The man, Joseph Edward, and the boy, Henry Edwards, stated that they bored a hole about ten o'clock the previous day, when the ground gave way, and shut them in. They called for help, but at length became too exhausted to continue, and they gave up everything as lost. Their incarceration lasted twenty-seven hours. Great praise was bestowed on the agents and timbermen for their efforts in rescuing the trapped men.

Such cases of entombment did not always, unfortunately, have a happy ending. In one of his broadsheets, Henry Quick, the eccentric Zennor poet, relates the pathetic story of an accident at Towednack in which a miner was imprisoned in a narrow conduit by a fall of rock on his legs:-

> His comrades had gone before him,
> And he just the belt had passed,
> When poor Martins to them called,
> "My two legs, they are stuck fast."

His friends almost pulled him asunder in efforts to draw him clear, and brought him food and warm drinks, but without avail. Deep down in this damp narrow hole he lingered for some days until the chill reached his heart. Hundreds of people would gather round the shaft's mouth to learn how the rescue operations were proceeding below; but when eventually they succeeded in making an opening sufficiently large to extricate him, the poor man was already dead.

In February 1889 while a party of four miners were stoping in the 44 fathom level of the old workings in Drakewalls mine, Gunnislake, several hundred tons of sand and refuse fell about them. John Rule and William Bant, two young men from Calstock, were entombed, but the others were unhurt. It was said that the stope where they were working was some distance above the level, and that the men were letting rubble fall to fill a space or make a rise, but much more came away than was intended. Another theory was that they had undermined an old gunnis which had previously been filled with sand, and that this ran in on them, when the timbers of a very old disused shaft gave way. A rescue party of sixteen miners worked in relays in the hope of freeing the trapped men. The work went on without cease for four and a half days before they were reached. The rescue party never lost heart, as they heard knockings at intervals during the progress of their labours. Both men were got out alive and appeared active and cheerful, though they had had no food all the time they were entombed.

Dolcoath, richest and deepest of all the Cornish mines, was the scene of at least two serious accidents resulting from the collapse of stulls. The first of these, the story of which appears to be but little known, occurred on November 18 1872. Thomas Henry Borlase, a miner of Troon, went underground at eight o'clock that morning to work between the 200 and 212 fathom levels near Wheal Harriet shaft, accompanied by two young comrades — Simon Davies Bastion (14) and William Henry Moffat (16). About four o'clock that afternoon, at the end of their shift, the two lads left work and walked to the shaft, where they stood on the tramroad at the southern side of the lode waiting to ascend. It appears that three others were waiting near them in the level, but Borlase still remained at his work. Suddenly, and without warning, a large piece of ground above the boys broke away and came crashing down on them. It carried away the timber and swept on down into the shaft, taking with it the lads and many tons of displaced rubbish. The amount of stuff involved was said to be 'prodigious' — at least four hundred tons — and the rush of this mass down a perpendicular shaft 1,400 feet deep made an appalling sight and sound. Their bodies were carried into the 'bottoms' between the 212 and 224 fathom levels, and deeply covered with rubbish.

A man named Thomas Oxnam working in the 224 fathom level rushed to the shaft to ascertain the cause of the terrible crashing noise made by the falling earth and timber, but was struck down and buried with the boys. Thomas Henry Oxnam, his son, who was working with him, saw there was danger, and catching up his younger brother in this arms, ran back to an arch in the level. The candles were blown out, but on striking a light he saw that his father was missing. He thought the older man had been caught by some of the stull timber as it hurtled past.

The other miners immediately set to work to dig out their buried comrades, and further assistance was despatched from surface. After four hours' toiling they uncovered Moffat's body which was so frightfully mangled as to be almost unrecognisable. Bastion's mutilated remains were recovered a little later; but Oxnam had been more deeply buried, and it was not till the afternoon of the third day that he was found among the heap of displaced ground, rock and broken timber under the 224 level, just below the place where he had been standing when the slip occurred. He was lying on his face, with his skull crushed. The piece of ground which fell and caused the accident was an overhang, but the men considered it firm and sound, as no stoping had taken place beneath it for fully three years. General confidence was also felt in the firmness of the stull then being erected a little below the 212 level; it had great strength and would have borne any weight that might reasonably have been put upon it. One of the shaftsmen stated that the stull was loaded, but it required a great many additional tons to carry it away.

The second of these stull collapses at Dolcoath resulted in one of the most spectacular mining disasters ever recorded in Cornwall. The setting of this appalling catastrophe was appropriately dramatic; for it took place nearly half-a-mile underground in the great forty feet wide level. A party of workmen were engaged in strengthening the enormous stull or penthouse of timbers supporting the roof; this stull suddenly gave way — it was popularly said that 'the bottom of Dolcoath ran together' — and eight of them were engulfed by thousands of tons of rock, only one miner being subsequently extricated alive. To understand fully what occurred, it is necessary to know something of the layout of that part of the mine where the mishap occurred. As mentioned previously, the lodes in Cornish mines are generally rather narrow, but that at Dolcoath proved exceptionally large, and increased in size with depth, so that at the lowest workings to the East of Engine shaft it attained a width of 20-30 feet. At the time of the disaster (September 20 1898) the deepest level was the 425 under adit, or 453 fathoms from surface. The collapse occurred a little above this in the 412. The lode on which the shaft had been sunk did not follow a consistently perpendicular line from surface. This shaft ran vertically to the 125 fathom level, then sloped diagonally, following the dip to the lode, and the angle gradually increased until at the bottom level it reached 48 degrees, running southward, or a little over four feet in a fathom. On both sides of the lode the country rock was granite. In stoping away the lode, the miners sometimes left arches standing to support the overhang; but elsewhere large timbers were placed across the workings approximately at right angles to the underlie of the lode. The timber used was principally pitchpine, 18-20 inches in diameter, and propped, where necessary, by pitchpine or large pieces of Norway timber 12-14 inches in diameter. Near the bottom, the shaft did not dip as sharply as the lode; and levels were driven from the shaft toward it. Two winzes (or small shafts) were also sunk for the 412 level on the lode itself, at a distance of 15 fathoms, and the stull which collapsed was actually a penthouse to protect the pare working in No. 2 winze and the stopes above it. The lode had been taken away at the 412 about eight fathoms in height, and the stull props rested on sills, about three feet of ground having been taken out to lay the timbers on the level. The scene presented in this great cavern, with the sides and roof supported by the largest balk timbers procurable and the miners working away at the gigantic lode was truly a wonderful one. Only a few months before the disaster Mr. J. C. Burrow took a flashlight photograph of the stull, which gives a vivid impression of this awe-inspiring place.

J. C. Burrow's photograph of the 412 fathom level in Dolcoath, taken shortly before the appalling accident on 20 September 1893 (Courtesy Royal Institution of Cornwall)

This immense stull lay underneath a smaller one, the space between then being nearly filled with broken rock or 'attle', which extended nearly up to the 400 fathom level. This great cavity had been stoped or worked away to a length of 35-40 yards, 10 yards in width and up to 11 or 12 fathoms in height, with only 2-3 yards of solid ground between its apex and the floor of the 400. Above the massive timbers of the 412 stull were sheeting planks or slabs on which about three fathoms of 'deads' were piled. Some of the stull pieces were strengthened with 'studdies' and 'legs.' The 400 fathom level was a very narrow one, driven through thousands of tons of rubbish which had some time previously run together in the higher part of the mine. Hence, above the 412 fathom stull a mass of loose stuff extended over a hundred fathoms in height, separated only by the narrow portion of unwrought ground immediately below the 400 fathom level from the 412 stull timbers.

From these details a truly frightening picture emerges. One visualises the great lode, altogether bigger and richer than anything known elsewhere in the county, thrusting steeply downwards through the solid granite thousands of feet below grass, its upper part riddled with levels, gunnies and winzes, which in turn had been largely re-filled with deads and fallen ground; then keeping up this mass of loose and broken rock, a frail structure of timbers — massive timbers, it is true, yet mere matchwood compared with the titanic burden that had been called upon to bear; and finally, underneath it all, the minute and insignificant figures of the miners themselves, still nibbling away at the soft ore-stuff like mites in a great cheese, ever widening and weakening its base, until at last, unable to bear the fantastic strain any longer, the whole mass comes crashing down, burying the authors of all this ruin in its fall. It is not too far-fetched to say that the disaster was caused by Dolcoath being too rich. The ore-ground was so valuable that nearly all of it was taken away, too little being left to support the roof. As a result the deeper she went, the more hollow she became, and the more dangerous to those working in the bottom.

Cornish miners have always been a superstitious race, and it is said that some of the Dolcoath men entertained a strange foreboding of this great catastrophe. It was noted that Henry Saunders had fallen six fathoms in Tincroft the previous Saturday and sustained no injury; and that since accidents were believed to come not singly, but in threes, there would cetainly be someone killed between Redruth and Camborne in the following seven days! The agents, however, had a more rational cause for apprehending danger. Only the day prior to the collapse Captain Josiah Thomas, the celebrated manager of Dolcoath, visited the 412 with Captain James Johns, the chief underground agent, who was responsible for the timbering of the mine. Captain Johns stated afterwards that the roof appeared firm, and that he would not have been afraid to sleep there twelve hours; "I knew, however, that sometime the ground would have to be strengthened, and considered it would go weak, and it would be wiser to do so before it was needed than when it was too late." Captain Johns clearly had his doubts about the stull; and these doubts were so strong that he immediately instructed some timbermen to put in a large piece of 20-inch timber, which had already been sent down, and another one, which would follow, to strengthen it.

The working party, which went below at seven o'clock the following morning, included a boy and four students from the Camborne School of Mines. The great stull, on which they set to work an hour later, was in the back of the 412 fathom level, fifty fathoms east of New East shaft. It consisted of about 22 pieces of 18-inch square pitchpine timbers, the average length being about 33 or 34 feet, fixed at an incline from head to foot of 40-45 degrees, and set from 2 feet to 2 feet 3 ins. apart. The second, smaller, stull was fixed eighteen feet above the first, and crossbeams were set in level from the heads of the pieces to the footwall and then filled in with debris for 18 or 20 feet above, where preparations had already been made to fix a third stull before taking away the ground above. During his visit, Captain Johns had noticed that one of the western pieces under the deads was bending, and he told John Pollard, chief timberman, to put in a new piece beneath it. He did not consider the bending to be the result of pressure from behind, but of natural decay of the wood — a somewhat surprising conclusion seeing that the stull was quite new, having been put in only six months before. It seems much more likely that the ground was already settling, preparatory to a fall.

Repair work on the stull proceeded throughout the morning without incident. The accident took place at one o'clock, at which time six of the party — Arnall, Williams, Davies, Roberts, Hicks, Jones and Gregory — chanced to be at the western end of the structure, close to the level opening into this 30-40 foot wide gunny. Their 'boss' — Charles White — with six others and a boy, were further in, right under the stull itself, and so nearer to the point of danger. They were making ready to put in one of the new 24 foot long timber balks from the hanging side to the footwall of the lode when the ground suddenly cracked overhead and some stuff fell. This was known to the miners as a 'God send,' or warning; and examples of it have already been given in describing other accidents. These happened so frequently, however, that the men often ignored them; but it is significant that on this occasion all the survivors related how, on hearing the sound, they immediately made a dash for safety, and there is good reason for believing that those who were killed tried to do the same — showing that all were well aware of the potential danger of the place in which they were working. This 'God send' amounted to about a ton; but then, almost immediately after came an awful roar and crash, and the whole stull came thundering down in ruins.

The six who were at its eastern end immediately raced for the level and only just cleared their heels when the roof-stuff smashed down upon the stull, which itself then fell upon the other eight men, including Pollard, their leader, all of whom were instantly buried. This great collapse of ground drove before it a violent blast of air which whirled the men along as they ran. A stone struck Gregory on the shoulder; and Joe Williams, the rearmost man, had the rocks rattling at his heels. The tremendous air current caught a boy named Jimmy Tresawna and blew him like a feather four fathoms, whilst it also moved a stationary waggon, which was off its track, fully three fathoms and upset it upon a man's leg. Its effects were also felt some distance away. One man had gravel blown in his eyes; the flannel vest of another was torn off; a third suffered serious injuries by being thrown against the jagged sides of the level; whilst several others were much affected by clouds of choking dust. Trammers at the 358, high up in the mine, felt the ground shake under them.

The survivors waited until the ground settled, then shouted, but received no answer from the entombed men. One of them ascended to the 400, but found that that level had also been choked by the fall of ground. As there was a mass of stuff about 110 fathoms high above the stull[1] (all having apparently run together in the upper part from the 338) the men came up New East shaft and reported the facts to the agents. Rescue parties were at once organised and began to tunnel through from each end of the fallen mass of rubble in an effort to reach the buried miners. This proved to be slow and difficult work, as some of the obstructing rocks were very large, and the ground had to be timbered as they opened it.

For some time no indication was received that any of the entombed men still lived; but then, about three in the afternoon of the following day, the party driving through the sixteen fathoms of fallen debris from the east suddenly heard a voice calling "Praise the Lord!" They had then opened about three fathoms of ground, which consisted mainly of large rocks, with crevices between; and in one of these crevices a young man called William John Osborne, of Camborne, had been trapped alive. He had been lying there in darkness "praising the Lord" for more than twenty-four hours, with a piece of timber lying on his legs, which were jammed between the rocks. He told the rescuers there was no one else with him, nor could he hear anyone.

The relief party opened a hole, through which two small men managed to crawl over rocks and between broken stull timbers for about five or six fathoms until Osborne could see their light, but they were unable to get near enough to pass in a tube through which he could be given liquid food. Most unfortunately, it proved impossible for the rescue team to tunnel their way through to him till several days later, by which time his voice had fallen silent in death. His courage and steadfastness under the terrible circumstances in which he was placed were truly remarkable.

Soon after eight o'clock that day another voice was heard from under the ruins of the stull. It was that of Richard Davies, of Troon, who told the rescuers that he was unhurt, and that no rocks rested on any part of his body. He was then about thirty feet from the eastern party, and was able, after a while, to crawl some distance through the smashed timbers towards them. One of the rescuers, called Smith, then wriggled in towards him from the other side. Smith said encouragingly, "Les have your hand. I have got un now, Dicky. How es it so cold?" "No, both my hands are free," replied Davies. The other then realised that the hand he held was the hand of a dead man. Davies was extricated alive on Friday morning, largely through this own desperate efforts to get clear, as will be seen later.

Both rescue parties worked under appalling conditions. Apart from the great difficulty of tunnelling through the wreckage and fallen ground, they also had to contend with the stench from the bodies still trapped under the stull. One of the men had his shoulder injured while engaged in rescue work. By Saturday the relief corps at each end of the immense pile had driven a total length of about eight fathoms in a straight line by the side of the 'run.' By then, several bodies could be seen, the nearest being about 22 feet from the eastern 'spill' but at an angle, and it was impossible to reach any of them owing to the many barriers between. On Sunday the rescuers' efforts were further impeded by a 'surge' or minor run of stuff, which had to be cleared away before further progress was possible. However, at one o'clock on Monday morning fresh shifts were put on at both the eastern and western ends, and more rapid progress was achieved. By Monday night, however, the smell had grown so bad that it was thought the length of each working shift would have to be cut from six to four hours. Tuesday saw the eastern gang diverging north to reach the bodies that were visible, whilst the western men continued their straight drive. By next morning only about six fathoms of ground separated the two parties. The workers were allowed tobacco, disinfectants and spirits to enable them to endure the stench and fatigue; they worked in constant danger from the surging ground, as well as from the effects of the fetid atmosphere.

At midnight on Tuesday the body of Richard Jones was recovered by the eastern men and brought to surface through the Silver Valley shaft. The remains of James Adams followed on Wednesday afternoon, and several other bodies were found soon after. The body of William John Osborne was not extricated from the mass of rubble till the following Sunday night. His feet were crushed, death having resulted either from gangrene or loss of blood, some hours after he had told the rescuers that nobody was there except God and himself. The seventh, and last, body was not recovered until October 9 — twenty days after the accident; it proved to be that of Charles White, a 60 year old Camborne miner.

Richard Davies, the only man to escape alive from under the fallen stull, gave several graphic accounts of his experience. He described how he went down the mine at 7.30 a.m. with one of his partners, James Adams, the rest of the party having gone on before. They went up to the stope between the 412 and 400 levels, where the foreman, Pollard, asked him to help in cutting a prop. He took one handle of the cross-cut saw and another man the other, and they commenced sawing. Three other men were standing nearby. He had not been sawing for more than three minutes when he heard some timber cracking, and then there came a tremendous rush of stuff, which knocked him eight or nine feet away under the timbers at the bottom of the level. He was struck by debris on the head and legs. His comrades attempted to run to safety but they must have been knocked down where they stood and buried. Dick James shouted to Charley White, "Look out, Charley!" but the noise then became so terrific he was unable to hear any more.

Recovering from the sudden shock, Davies found he was lying face downwards, his head being lower than his heels. He could move very little, as a balk of timber lay across his body, whilst the space in which he was confined measured only about five feet long, two feet wide and three feet high, but the timber kept him down nearly flat. He remained in that position until Thursday midnight, but then managed to turn on his left side. A little later he faintly heard the rescue parties at work. Then, however, the timber above began to crack; putting up his hand he found it was quartering, and feared that the pressure would make it settle down on him. The rocks overhead were being crushed together at the same time, so that flashes of fire came from them, but the hope that the rescue party would come to his relief kept him from despair. At times, however, Davies wondered if he might perish of hunger or thirst before they broke through. He shouted at the top of his voice, but no one heard him, and also called out to find if any of his comrades were alive and near, but again there was silence.

Davies became cramped and sore, and could hardly move to hammer on the timber above with a piece of stone in answer to the rescuers' knocking from outside. The place was hot, close and dusty, and full of dynamite smoke from blasting by the relief parties. He began to fear that this blasting might make the earth run together again, but all through his ordeal kept a good heart, even when the smell of a nearby body reached him. After 'crying for mercy' for a while, he fell asleep, and on waking spoke to the rescuers, who told him it was Thursday afternoon — a day later than he thought. At six that evening he told them his name, which caused some surprise, as they had previously believed him to be Osborne. One of the men said, "Cheer up, Dick, old man, we will be there for you directly."

Knowing them to be so close, Davies then made a great effort, and after a long time managed to turn in the small space. He was then able to raise himself above the timber a distance of about ten feet. Here a plank and a fallen stull piece formed a kind of launder, with rocks overhead, and along this he crawled a distance of about thirty yards in the direction of the rescuers' lights, which could now be seen. Here further progress was blocked, but Smith crawled in an equal distance from the other side and tried to take his hand — only to find it was that of a dead man. Recovering from his thrill of horror, Smith passed him a hatchet, with which he widened the hole, and then crawled out after his rescuer, who had to proceed backwards, as there was no room to turn. He felt quite well when going out, but had to be supported when attempting to stand. They took him through the level to the winze at the 412, lashed a rope round his waist , and assisted him to climb to the 400, from where he was taken in the gig to surface.[2]

At the inquest held on John Henry Jennings, one of the victims, conflicting opinions were expressed as to the cause of the accident. Captain Thomas believed that the working party must have taken away some of the old props before putting in the new, thus weakening the stull and precipitating its collapse. (When the accident occurred the workmen had one of the new stull pieces which was to be inserted hanging on the blocks, trying to set it between some of those which were bent). The manager asserted that this new piece would not fit exactly, and suggested they must have taken away some of the old props before putting in the new, or else cut away the foot. The distance usually allowed for setting these baulks into the footwall was about a foot. He did not think the rock would be liable to splinter off. The distance allowed depended on the nature of the rock. James Johns, principal underground agent, thought, however, that some of the ground had given way after having 'been given vent' at the bottom. He could not account for the stull at the 400 coming away. No doubt the ground in the back of the stope had given way in consequence of the stull-piece breaking first. They had found the stull piece that they were repairing broken in pieces. William Sowden, one of the survivors, maintained they were doing nothing at the time which could have occasioned the fall; whilst as if a heavy fall or run of ground had occurred, and then a second one, followed immediately by the collapse. This view of the cause of the accident was corroborated by the fact that a large portion of the lode under the roadway of the 400 fathom level fell away at the same time, causing the collapse of the roadway at that level.

The Government Inspector attending the inquest posed a number of searching questions to the agents regarding the methods they had adopted for working the great lode. The most interesting and pertinent of them were: In such a large level, would it not be desirable to arch the roadways with masonry? Should not a roadway have been driven through the granite country rock, with cross-cuts taken from it to the lode, instead of having the roadway under the wall of the stope? Would not iron have been preferable to timber for supporting the roof in such wide workings? The agents gave detailed and reasoned replies to these

Another of J. C. Burrow's views of the 412 at Dolcoath
(Courtesy Royal Institution of Cornwall)

and other points raised; but one gets the impression that the techniques employed in mining this phenomenally wide lode were inadequate to cope with the immense weight and pressures there encountered. But tried and traditional methods die hard; and it is only fair to say that witness after witness testified to the general confidence felt in the security provided by the massive timbers of the 412 stull at Dolcoath.

The victims' names were:

John Pollard, chief timberman, Camborne.
William John Osborne, Camborne.
Charles White, Camborne.
John Henry Jennings, Camborne.
Frederick John Harvey, Camborne.
James Adams, Tuckingmill.
Richard James, Illogan Highway.

Whenever a piece of ground appeared dangerous and liable to fall, common prudence demanded that precautionary meaures should be taken, and this was usually done. Neglect to do so could bring disaster. An instance of this occurred at Ding Dong — that strange old mine situated in the lonely moorland heart of the West Penwith peninsula —

on May 1 1869. William Stone, 27, of Boswerthen, Madron, had worked in the mine for three months with a comrade on tutwork in the 70 fathom level. On the previous day, two other miners of much greater experience who worked in the same level but nearer the shaft, warned Stone that a dangerous piece of ground should be taken down, as there was a crack in it large enough for a man to put his hand in. Stone agreed with this, but said it might be left till Monday (May 8) when the captains would see it. Just previous to this he had removed ten or twelve barrows of stuff from the sollar in the back of the level, which weakened the ground and hastened the fall which afterwards took place. On Saturday morning Stone went to work as usual. He struck the ground with a hammer, which sounded 'drummy,' and remarked that it would have to come down. Between eleven and twelve o'clock about eight tons of rock fell away, and nearly buried him. He was still conscious, and gave directions as to the best way in which he might be extricated. They removed him to his home, where he lingered for two days before succumbing to severe internal injuries. At the inquest several witnesses proved that if Stone had required timber or assistance in securing the ground, he could have had it. The jury returned a verdict of 'accidental death'; but one of 'suicide' might have been more appropriate. Sometimes, of course, accidents of this nature were actually triggered off by attempts made to secure dangerous pieces of ground — the 1898 Dolcoath disaster might possibly have been caused in this way. In August 1864 a young man called Nicholas employed at Trevenen mine — a section of Trumpet Consols, lying a little to the south of Wendron — was discussing with the captain and his comrade means for securing the ground overhead, when it suddenly fell away, and he was crushed to death. His fellow workman was slightly injured, but the captain escaped unharmed.

Whenever rock falls took place, the cause was usually a simple and obvious one — cracked or weakened ground, excessive pressure from above or behind, or lack of proper timbering. Occasionally, however, something far more unusual was involved. A most interesting example of this was recorded at Tincroft mine, Illogan, on October 24 1877. Several instances of 'air explosions' had previously been observed here, the air in question being contained in 'bladders' in the rocks, which were very hard. After the ground adjoining these rocks had been stoped away the pressure of air behind was then sufficient to hurl them forward with great violence. On the day in question, a man and two boys were engaged at the 234 fathom level sending up tin stuff. The tramway in use was not an easy one, and in order to bring a full waggon from the mill (pass) to the plot, two men had to pull in front on a rope whilst a third pushed from behind. They trammed several loads without incident, and the boys were returning with an empty waggon, their comrade being a little in the rear, when the accident occurred. They had proceeded about twenty fathoms from the shaft when Phillips, behind the waggon, heard a strange noise, whilst at the same instant his candle was knocked out of his hand, leaving him in darkness. He called for help, and two miners came up (one being his own father) from whom he obtained a light. The three then advanced to a place about six feet ahead of where the candle had been knocked out of Phillips' hand. There they found the two boys, Sherman and Stephens, pinned under a rock of about a ton weight. It completely covered them, but their bodies could be seen through a cavity. The rescuers obtained further assistance and lifted one end of the rock. They first got out Stephens, who was insensible, but still breathing. Sherman was extricated with more difficulty; he had no visible injury, except to one leg, which was severed. He said he was dying, and lived for only an hour and a half, being in great agony all that time. Stephens died within a quarter hour of his release. Both were about sixteen years of age. The rock which killed them came from a stope in the back of the level about four fathoms above the place where they were working; the ground here was generally believed to be perfectly safe. About two tons of stuff came away with the rock. Blasting had recently taken place five fathoms away — too far distant, it was thought, to have loosened the rock. Samuel Martin, an agent, had inspected that part of the mine earlier in the day, and considered it secure. The general view was that the rock had been dislodged by an air explosion, which could not have been foreseen or prevented in any way. Accordingly, at the inquest on Stephens, the jury returned the rare and probably unique verdict that "the deceased was crushed to death by a rock falling on him, such rock having been loosened from the ground by an accidental explosion of gas".

Another rare (in Cornwall) type of gas explosion was caused by the accumulation of pockets of 'fire damp' or methane in underground workings, produced by the decay of old timbers. A spectacular example, which occurred in an unnamed Cornish mine, was described in the *Arminian Magazine* for November 1791. No less than seventeen men were killed by the blast, which also hurled the heavy wooden framework at the top of the shaft for some distance; it fell on a cottage, entirely destroying it and killing the poor man who lived there. A similar event was reported at Ding Dong during 1868 when workmen were reopening a section which had been abandoned about twenty years before. This was done to enable a rich underlying deposit in an adjoining part to be more effectively worked. The sections being recovered were known as Old Ding Dong and Ishmael's Mine, about 170 fathoms apart, communicating with each other by a level at a depth of 50 fathoms. Old Ding Dong was in fork to the 70; and in order to facilitate the draining of the Ishmael part of the 50; some feet below, it became necessary to put in a siphon, to convey the water to Ding Dong engine. Two workmen waded in through slime and water for that purpose, but had not proceeded far when a violent explosion accompanied by a blue flame threw them down and severely scalded them. A few days afterwards the managing agent, Captain Williams, caused a second explosion by inserting a candle fixed to the end of a long pole. This was even stronger than the first, but produced no injuries. After a short interval, Captain Thomas Daniel entered, carrying a naked candle, when there was a terrific blast which nearly cost him his life. No one was then allowed to go in until Davy safety lamps had been procured — one of the very few occasions when they were found of real service in Cornwall. Mr. Samuel Higgs, junior (who afterward contributed a description of the incident to the *Cornish Telegraph*) accompanied an exploration party into the level, carrying safety lamps, the elongation of whose flames surrounded by flickering blue haloes proved conclusively that the gas was fire damp. The peculiar freshness of the granite in the innermost backs indicated that slime and water had not entered them, though it had elsewhere risen 10 fathoms above the level, these being the places where the methane had collected.

References

1. Statements made by eye-witnesses as to the depth of ground which had fallen away vary considerably; the truth of the matter seems to be that no one really knew its extent, the section having been so shattered by previous 'runs'.
2. The death of Davies' widow, at the age of 91, was announced as recently as December, 1965.

A House of Water

The gaunt ruined engine houses which dot the countryside throughout the Cornish mining districts bear silent witness to battles waged long ago between the miner and his most ancient and implacable enemy — water. For his great ally in these stern contests was that tireless steam giant, the Cornish beam pumping engine, without whose assistance deep mining in Cornwall would have been impossible. But, inevitably, the victories gained proved only temporary. No sooner had the mines been 'knocked' than the insidious foe came creeping back into those subterranean recesses where for years — in some cases, centuries — it had successfully been kept at bay, flooding levels and drowning shafts to adit level, so that the deep caverns, once clamorous with the sound of hammer and drill, now lie fathoms deep beneath a still and silent flood.

But whilst it lasted, the struggle was intense and often exciting. During a period of exceptionally heavy rainfall, a much larger quantity of water than usual would seep through the porous or fissured ground into the workings, and then the engines had all they could do to keep pace with it. The wet winter of 1872 may be taken as a typical example. After months of very heavy rain, crisis point was reached in mid-February. All over Cornwall the pumping engines were working at far beyond their normal speed, with a consequent increased risk of breakages, whilst the saturated ground, if not soundly timbered, grew ever more unstable and prone to collapse. At South Condurrow, situated in the valley to the south of Camborne, one of the principal shafts, weakened by water, ran together for ten fathoms just after the men had come up from work on a Saturday night. This had the effect of stopping all work in the productive ground below the 40 fathom level for several months. North Treskerby, which lies nearly a mile north of Scorrier, also had to suspend operation, owing to the overflowing of the County Adit; the engine just could not cope, so it was stopped, and the water allowed to rise to adit level. As a result of this experience, the adventurers resolved to install a more powerful 80 inch engine forthwith. At Wheal Uny, south-west of Redruth, the water rose to the 90 fathom level; whilst at East Chiverton, two miles south-east of Perranzabuloe, following a series of accidents, it reached adit level. Basset and Grylls, in the Wendron district, suffered from a 'run' of ground of a serious nature. In the important Redruth and Camborne mining districts, most of the successful mines had been provided with ample steam power, and so sustained little damage or inconvenience. To add to the general difficulties, however, coal became increasingly scarce and dear, and in some cases wood had to be used for firing the boilers.

At no mine, however, was the struggle to keep the flood at bay fought with more heroism and resolution than at Mellanear, situated about three-quarters of a mile north-east-by-north of St. Erth. This mine was equipped with one 75 inch engine whose piston rod, on February 16, attained a speed of 280 feet per minute! Going at 14 strokes a minute, with 19 inch lifts, it raised a constant stream of 1,372 gallons every minute of the 24 hours! Despite this, the water rose to the 60, but was

Driving an end on the 340 fathom level, Williams' Lode East, South Condurrow, 1890s
(Courtesy Royal Institution of Cornwall)

then held. At 14 strokes a minute, steam was able to beat water; at 18 strokes the strife was equally waged; but if the engine stopped a short while — to pack the cylinder for instance — water had the advantage. The contest proved such a close-run thing that the adventurers, like those at North Treskerby, decided to augment their pumping capacity with a new 80 inch engine. The latter was put to work in March 1878, and christened 'Ellen' after a daughter of one of the directors.

A few years before this (January 1866) serious unemployment was caused by flooding at Great South Tolgus, lying just west of Redruth. Thirty men were discharged when the water rose so rapidly as to drown the lower levels. It was feared that some considerable time must elapse before they could be taken on again, as with the engine going at full power (ten strokes per minute) and consuming about eight tons of coal per 24 hours the water rose in one night by as much as four feet.

Even during wet periods such as these, the water rarely rose in the mines at such a speed as to endanger the lives of those working in them. Occasionally, however, as the result of a cloudburst occurring directly overhead, such torrents cascaded down the shafts that the men, unable to escape, were trapped and drowned in the workings. Such a mishap occurred in an unnamed mine in the parish of St. Martin-in-Meneage

Croust time at the 90 foot level, South Condurrow, circa 1890
(Courtesy Royal Institution of Cornwall)

during March 1824, when heavy rain caused such a rapid and unexpected inflow into the shaft that two men working there were drowned. An even worse accident of this nature occurred at Wheal Abraham and Crenver, Crowan, during the late October of 1806. After a 'water-spout' had fallen in the neighbourhood, streams flowed with such violence that the boundaries — protective walls — round the mouths of the shafts were broken down, carrying the 'country' with them. They also (stated the *Sherborne Mercury*),

> "choaked the adits, which forced the water back into the sump (or place where the fire-engine draws the water out of the deep part of the mine, and where the men generally work); forty or fifty of them made their escape up the ladders, but to prevent their breath being taken away by the violence of the water falling on them, threw their woollen shirts over their heads, and with difficulty reached the summit."

Five men were missing, presumed drowned; whilst the loss to the adventurers was put at between £5-6,000.

Less serious consequences attended a spectacular hailstorm which burst over Drakewalls Mine, near Gunnislake, in the Tamar valley, in July 1850. The morning had been extremely hot, and the downpour of rain and hail began about two o'clock, accompanied by fierce lightning and thunder. The hailstones were of almost incredible size, some being of four inches circumference, and beat so violently that over eighty window panes were broken in the engine and account houses. Such torrents of water ran over the ground that the roads were cut down in some places to a depth of five feet. Had the mine been situated at the bottom of the valley it would undoubtedly have suffered the same fate as Wheal Abraham; as it was, large quantities of rain and hail went down the mine, carrying with them much sand and dirt — so much so, that many of the men came up, fearing something dangerous might occur. This sand greatly impeded operations at the mine for some time after; but fortunately no other loss or damage was sustained. The adventurers at East Creber were not so fortunate when a rainstorm occurred in the Tavy valley during July 1830. The storm water caused the river to rise and flood the mine *via* its adit. Most of the miners managed to make their way to safety, but three working in the bottom (70 fathom level) were overwhelmed and drowned.

By far the most tragic of these floodwater disasters — indeed, the worst catastrophe known in Cornish mining history — was that which devastated the famous lead mine of East Wheal Rose, in the parish of Newlyn East, whose workings are situated in a large valley somewhat resembling an ampitheatre, surrounded by hills. Just after noon on Thursday July 9 1846, a dark cloud settled over the area and began to discharge itself in a torrential downpour, with loud thunder and vivid flashes of lightning. The deluge continued for more than an hour and a half, the fall being so heavy that eyewitnesses described it as like 'casks of water emptied from above'. Rainwater from the sloping hills poured into the valley with tremendous force, sweeping all before it, and cascaded down into the mine itself by the shafts, soon filling all the deeper levels. The great weight of water at surface simultaneously broke in the 'country', forming a large epit, the supporting timbers in the levels below having been torn down by the flood which rushed through the mine, and the soil, being very soft, giving way when deprived of its artificial supports.

Towards the northern part of the sett, the valley narrowed into a ravine, through which a stream, after passing the workings, ran towards the River Gannel, and thence to the sea at Crantock, about five or six miles distant. The flood rushed on, from south to north, towards this ravine, and directly over the mine. The valley floor resembled an inland sea, the narrow outlet being insufficient to free the accumulated waters. On the surface of the mine, all was chaos and confusion; below, in the dark depths, as the waters roared down the shafts and along the levels, where two hundred miners were at work, death and destruction were suddenly let loose.

As soon as the great rainstorm began, Captain Middleton, manager of East Wheal Rose, fearing there might be trouble, summoned fifty surface workers to watch the leats and prepare them for any emergency. In a matter of moments, however, the water was going down through the valley like a sea; so he then put three hundred men to save the timbers, barrows, and other materials, and to raise the protective walls surrounding the shafts. The steam whims, normally used for raising ore-stuff to surface, were put to work to draw men from the depths at Stephens's, Carbis's, Gower's, Davey's and Oxnem's shafts. However, the water poured down upon the sett in such broad and deep waves that all their efforts to prevent it from entering the workings proved unavailing. The flood, as it rushed towards the northern ravine, also deepened; and in this part, at Oxnam's shaft, it first broke into the mine. It soon broke down the defences at Magor's shaft, as well; and the sudden descent of this vast body of water sent a blast of air through the workings which blew out the candles, leaving the poor miners in total darkness.

Alarmed by this occurrence, those who were in the upper levels immediately ascended to grass, where they assisted the men trying to divert the water or dam it back from the shafts and footways. Those working in the deeper levels, or who, in ascending the shafts, met the cataracts falling from above, only escaped with the greatest difficulty, and many of them were trapped and drowned. As the kibbles descended in Gower's shaft, the drowning men caught hold of them, and were drawn up in clusters, like 'strands of onions'. One of the survivors declared that some of those who got into the kibble fell away again from exhaustion. Other miners caught hold of the chains, and were drawn up that way; one man arrived at surface with only one or two fingers hitched in the chain. At one time, six men were drawn up holding on by the kibble; and when it again descended to the 50 fathom level a miner named Harris and two boys jumped in, but the water was now coming down so forcibly that after they had been raised six fathoms the boys were washed out.

Down at the bottom levels, two little boys were said to have first given the alarm to some of the men working there, who immediately fled to the shafts. By this time the water had overtaken the lads — "and they begged pitiously for life; but, poor fellows, there was no arm to succour, and their wild shriek of despair was heard amidst the stunning noises of that awful hour." One of those who escaped on the chain "leaped at it on a venture and was saved by inserting one finger though a link and thus was drawn to safety on the surface." Another miner seeking to escape by the same means, unfortunately sprang into the descending instead of the ascending kibble, and was consequently plunged many feet under water, but held on with grim tenacity, and so was eventually drawn up to meet his anxious friends at the mouth of the shaft. One miner saved his life by placing his back against one wall of a narrow shaft and his feet against the other, so contriving to raise himself a distance of ten fathoms, the rapidly rising waters underneath goading him on.

In Michell's whim shaft, some men climbed the open shaft by hanging on to the casing, the water rising close to their heels as they ascended. Others reached grass by climbing for many fathoms against the cateract streaming down upon them, whilst some escaped through the manhole, from which the water had been diverted. Between the 50 and 40 fathom levels, one miner climbed fifteen fathoms by the pumps and rods in Michell's engine shaft. On learning how this man had made his escape, the Captain stopped the engine, fearing it might kill others attempting to climb up by this route, and it was not put to work again until they had ascertained that no more were coming up the rods. Some of those who escaped said that many more might have been saved, even from the lower levels, had they exerted themselves; but the sudden awareness of danger when the water first poured down and their lights were extinguished, seemed completely to paralyse their efforts.

James Hosking, a young miner from Newlyn East, who, with others, was working in a pitch at the 70 fathom level, graphically described to a reporter of the *Penzance Gazette* the scene of horror which ensued when the flood burst into the mine. He and his four companions heard a rush of water through a winze, of which they at first took no great notice; but in less than a minute this had so much increased that they abandoned their work, and soon realised the awful situation in which they were placed. The rush and fall of water; the gusts of wind roaring like thunder through the levels; the cries for assistance from their comrades trapped below; the terrifying darkness in which all were plunged by the extinguishing of the lights — these all added to the horror of their situation. The five miners, while escaping from the 70 fathom level, were breast-high in water. They hastened to a ladder which led to the 60 fathom level, and from there made their way to the Engine shaft, where further progress was arrested by the rushing flood, which was now fast gaining upon and threatening to engulf them. Terror-stricken, they hardly knew what to do. At length, two of the party persevered and got up the shaft against the stream, reaching 'grass' in a near-exhausted state, where they were led to the counting-house and given stimulants. Meanwhile the three remaining members of the party (including Hosking) made their way through the tributers' pitches for a distance of more than twenty fathoms, stumbling over several other miners who, weakened by fatigue, were groping about in the dark bitterly lamenting their fate and supplicating help — in vain. Some, apparently not striving to escape, "were on their knees, praying most fervently and devoutly to the Almighty — not to deliver them — but to have mercy upon their souls — thus awaiting the termination of their existence." Instead of giving way to religious fatalism of this kind, Hosking and his two companions fought their way up to the 40 fathom level, where they again went to the Engine shaft, and after great efforts, succeeded in making their escape.

Near Turner's shaft, in the southern part of the mine, Samuel Bastian was working with Samuel Wherry, aged 27, of Newlyn Churchtown, James Coade, 19 of Perranzabuloe, and several more. At about one o'clock the candles in their part of the mine were all blown out by a rush of wind, which alarmed them, and Bastian, with some of his comrades, managed to escape to surface, but Wherry and Coade were left behind. Reaching the surface, Bastian found that the water was running into different parts of the mine, but more particularly into Magor's shaft. The miners were escaping by the different footways (ladders) as best they could. Bastian went to Michell's sump shaft, to help the men up, and turn the water out of Engine shaft. Water was then pouring into the man-hole of the latter, but after he had diverted it from the opening, eighteen men made their escape there. Bastian went down again to within six feet of the 40 to see if he could find any more men, but failed to do so. Again ascending to grass, he put on dry clothes, and then went to the adit to dam back the water from its portal. Next morning about six o'clock he and others went into Gower's shaft, at the 50 fathom level, and after some hours of work, succeeded in recovering the bodies of his comrades. The water had been at the back of the level where they were found, and had drowned them.

A tremendous volume of water must have poured into the mine during the cloudburst. Michell's Engine shaft was 100 fathoms deep; and this and the other shafts were filled to above the 50 fathom level, this level itself being a mile in length. At the 100 fathom level, only one pare of twelve men were working; but at the 90 there were several pitches, and between that and the 80 were several more levels, all of which filled with water. Some hope was entertained that the air in some levels might have kept the water from penetrating to the backs, and that here some miners had possibly survived. In the hope of rescuing these trapped men, the two exceptionally large pumping engines were set to work as fast as possible, consistent with safety, in order to drain the workings. As a result, the long 50 fathom level was cleared of water by the following day. Captains Middleton, Michael Chegwin and William Long remained on the mine all night to keep the engines fully at work. Their efforts were rewarded when between four and five o'clock on Friday morning four men were brought up alive on the kibbles. They were Thomas Phillips, of Newlyn East; Edward Holman, of Perran; and Simon Harris and William Ellery, of Kenwyn. The poor fellows were utterly exhausted, and never expected they would have been saved. They had been trapped by the water in the tributers' pass in the 50 fathom level, 'there they had sought to make their peace with their Creater.' As soon as the pumps had reduced the water level a little, a rescue team went down into the mine and found them. They were the last to come out of the workings alive.

The adjoining mine of North Wheal Rose was also affected by the catastrophe. Here, two miners called Frederick Sanders and Nicholas Bennetts were working at the back of the 50 fathom level when the torrent burst in. Sanders was killed; and Bennetts, who escaped, related the story of his experience at the inquest held on his comrade at the house of Mr. Basset, innkeeper, at Mitchell, on July 10. He said that at about one o'clock their lights were blown out by a rush of wind, and becoming alarmed, they left their work and went down to a pass about seven fathoms below. Sanders then struck a light, and they went along the level to the Engine shaft, where the water was cascading into the mine, and saw there was no possibility of getting up. They therefore returned, and hearing voices down at the 60, drew up six men from that level with a tackle. The group was afterwards joined by two other men from the back of the 50. All then mounted to the 40 by ladders (presumably in a winze) and from there again went to the Engine shaft. By then, their lights had again been blown out, and they were completely in the dark. Sanders now attempted to get up the Engine shaft against the stream, and urged Bennetts to accompany him, but he refused, as did all the others. They never saw Sanders alive again. About ten minutes later they found the whim had been set to work, and six members of the party, at four different times, got to the surface by taking hold of the whim chain. The three others went to another shaft and escaped in a similar manner. There were twelve men altogether working underground in the mine when the water broke in; but Sanders was the only casualty there.

The scene at the surface of East Wheal Rose, when it became known that many men were missing, was pathetic in the extreme. Relatives and friends of these flocked to the spot; and on the Friday, when twenty bodies were taken up, the sobbing and crying among nearly 300 people who had assembled was most distressing. By Sunday, these hundreds had grown to thousands, as curious spectators poured in from surrounding districts. They saw but a wilderness of desolation and ruin. Marks of the descending torrent were evident in many places. In one part, a large boulder, of about 2-3 cwt., had been washed down several yards from the hill; deep furrows had been cut in the road and on the heaps of stuff brought up from the mine; and around Gower's shaft a vast deposit of considerble depth had been left by the receding waters, completely covering the site. The devastation was greatest, however, in Bishop's Land and in Oxnam's. The latter shaft was run together by the flood; and further to the south, where there had been no shaft, but merely the levels driven beneath, a great collapse of ground had taken place, the surface being sunk to a considerable depth. A number of men were put to work to fill the chasm. Dangerous cracks and subsidences were also visible in other places, hinting at the devastation that must have taken place below. The two great pumping engines succeeded in draining the mine to the 80 fathom level at both engine shafts by July 28. Thirty-five bodies had then been recovered out of the thirty-nine in the workings. It does not seem that the catastrophe can be attributed to any neglect on the part of the adventurers or agents. The East Wheal Rose management had widened the bed of the stream which flowed through their set to three or four times its natural extent; but the overwhelming flood which poured down from the hills on that fatal day was altogether beyond human anticipation. The only criticism expressed was of the failure of those at surface to send a warning below at the commencement of the great storm. However, in the confusion that prevailed, no one thought of doing so until it was impossible for them to go down without risking their own lives. It was, indeed, a tragic story, but one that should not be allowed to obscure the fact that East Wheal Rose ranks as one of Cornwall's truly great mines, being Cornwall's largest producer of lead, and employing, at the time of the disaster, a total of 1,266 persons at surface and below ground.

Some of the mines situated around the coasts had workings which extended under the sea, and these were sometimes subject to flooding by salt water. This could happen in two ways — by the sea, during stormy weather entering the adits on shore and pouring down the shafts; and by the pressure of water breaking down the roof above the submarine workings at points where these had been carried up too near the ocean floor. Rather strangely, flooding by ordinary seepage in such mines was never a serious problem; at Levant — the most famous of them — the mine was always dry and the pumping charges light. Indeed, an old Levant miner once told the writer that the further out she went under the sea, the drier she became, and this appears to have been a fairly general rule. However, Levant experienced plenty of trouble in other ways from Old Father Neptune, though the worst incident, luckily, did not take place until after the mine had been abandoned in 1930.

The history of this mine goes back to at least 1793, when its first known annual output was recorded. Hawkins stated in 1818 that in one part the workmen, tempted by a bunch of copper, had followed it five fathoms above the level, whose end was scarcely more than ten fathoms below the sea bed. "Not only the roaring of the sea in stormy weather, but the ordinary breaking of the waves on the beach is distinctly heard by the miners." The water entering here was salt, but there was so little of it that the whole was drawn to adit in a bucket by the labour of two men. In

J. C. Burrow's photograph depicting the Levant workings "half a mile under the sea" in the 1890s (Courtesy Royal Institution of Cornwall)

1852 the sea entered a winze over the 40 fathom level; whilst in 1869 this continuing threat to the mine's safety led to a crisis in its affairs. The owners refused to grant a renewal of the lease, alleging that at the 40 fathom level west the excavations had been carried up so close to the sea as to endanger Levant's security. This led to the winding up of the old company, which had worked the mine without a break since 1820, a new set of adventurers taking over in 1872.

More trouble occurred in 1906, when the sea entered the workings through an old shaft situated just above high water mark. The men, fearing for their lives, refused to go down; but the influx was quickly stopped by remedial measures. Levant continued in active production until 1930, though activity was somewhat restricted following the terrible man-engine disaster of 1919 (see pages 36-40). At some date subsequent to its closing the sea finally broke the weak spot above the '40 backs,' an event which must inevitably have resulted in a major catastrophe had the mine been still at work. As it was, when the adjoining Geevor mine wished to extend its workings westward in the early 1960's it realised that the flooded Levant mine would first have to be made secure and drained before this objective could be realised. This proved to be a prolonged and difficult operation, beset by initial failure; but eventually, in October 1965, the breach in the sea bed was effectively sealed, and work on pumping out and securing the mine from within could begin. The inspiring story of man's successful struggle to win back this mine from the sea has already been told in some detail in the author's *Levant*.

Mine flooding sometimes occurred through the collapse of an adit, making it impossible for the pumps to discharge water through the normal outlet. Such mishaps were not normally attended by danger, the water level rising too slowly to threaten the miners' lives, but the economic consequences could be very serious. In December 1874 an unsound adit, rotten in its timbers, ran together at Wheal Margaret, Lelant. For several days after the men continued to work as usual; but then, as the water began to rise, those in the lowest level had to leave their pitches. Wheal Margaret was connected undeground with two other mines, Wheals Mary and Kitty, which formed, together with Trencrom, the Wheal Sisters group. These also were affected; and as between them they employed a total of about 500 men, women and children, the prosperity of the whole district was threatened. Within three days the water had reached a depth of 50 fathoms in Wheal Margaret. At Wheal Mary, the deepest of the three, forty men were then unable to work, with twenty or thirty more from the other mines. Efforts were then made to clear out the water, by sinking shafts over the chokage. Through these unceasing efforts the adit was cleared, and in less than a week the water level in all the mines was reported to be falling.

Those detailed to carry out such repair work often ran great risk, for the water pressure building up behind the blockage made it liable to free itself spontaneously, and the pent-up flood would then come roaring out in a foaming cataract, sweeping all before it. An incident of this kind at Poldice mine, near St. Day and on the eastern flank of Carn Marth, was described in the *Mining Journal* during March 1872. Poldice, with other mines in that area, such as West Jewell, Wheal Damsel and West Damsel, were drained by the Great Adit (sometimes known as the County or Gwennap Adit). The manager of Poldice, finding that a choke in this adit near the abandoned Wheal Damsel was threatening to flood his own mine, instructed two men to build a dam to keep back the water. Whilst they were at work in the adit, north of the blockage, Captain Johns, of West Jewell, who wished to inspect the position of the intended dam, went down to the site, accompanied by another miner. Realising that the dam was to be built to the north of one of the West Jewell lodes on which the adit was extended about seventy fathoms west, he wished to select a different position for it so that access to the lode might be preserved.

Coming up to the level, he told his companion that he would go in to examine the lode. Just then the man noticed that the water issuing from Wheal Damsel was dirty, indicating some disturbance. Knowing that no one was working in that section, he concluded that the chokage was yielding to the pressure of water, and said to Captain Johns, "Don't go far, I think that we are in danger." Captain Johns walked in about seven fathoms, but was then recalled urgently by his companion, and returned to him. They walked back to the two dam builders, by which time the adit was nearly full to the back. The four men then half-walked, half-swam before the stream till they came to a cross-cut, at the right, into which they went a few fathoms, and so came to a shaft in Old Wheal Jewell, down which the water fell 'with a roar like that of the Falls of Niagra.'

Thinking the shaft would soon be filled, they climbed up through it, they hardly knew how, about six fathoms, without any ladder or rope, when further progress was stopped by a sollar or stull. Perched in that uncomfortable position for two hours, their fears eventually subsided, as the water did not appear to rise up the shaft. However, getting down again looked like being a difficult matter. If they slipped, it would be into the yawning gulf beneath; and if it was the highest man who fell he would carry all the others down before him. They agreed to tie together all the cords they had with them, and fastening the top end, use the line as a guide or stay in their descent. When one went down, the air being bad, the candles above went out. One of the candles was sent down by the cord, re-lighted and drawn up. Fortunately, all came down safely. The party next had to press through the stream, now somewhat reduced in volume, to the adit. They then found some boards and placed them across the adit to divert as much of the stream as possible from the shaft, so making it less difficult for them to reach the footway. By this they made their escape with thankful hearts. They had certainly had a wonderful escape. If Captain Johns had not taken his companion's advice to leave the level quickly, he would have been suffocated, as it was only two or three feet high, whilst if the men had fallen from their perch in the shaft, certain death would have ensued. When the two dam builders went in afterwards to resume their work, they found the water had entirely ceased to run, and, concluding that a new chokage had taken place, refused to remain in the adit for fear of the probable consequences. The accumulated water in Wheal Damsel was said to have been about 3,000 cubic fathoms, so they certainly had grounds for apprehension.

In the richer mining areas, the mines were often grouped very closely together — so much so, that cases sometimes occurred where the adventurers of one sett were accused of poaching upon the preserves of a neighbour. In such a situation, the workings of adjacent undertakings could accidentally intersect one another, an event resulting in nothing worse than strained relations between the parties involved if both mines happened to be in active production; but should one of them be disused and flooded, then a major catastrophe might well ensue. The picturesque term given by miners to the reservoir impounded in the shafts and levels of an abandoned mine was 'a house of water.' The accidental tapping of these pent-up floods was fatally easy in the days when inaccurate dialling (surveying) and imperfect plans were all too common, and when miners did not have the diamond drill to probe the nature of a suspected piece of ground.

When a 'house of water' was known to adjoin a working mine, efforts were sometimes made to remove the danger by tapping the reservoir and draining it away — a highly dangerous operation. On May 11 1801 a party of miners at Rosewall Hill mine, just west of St. Ives, were holing into old workings for this purpose when the ground suddenly gave way, and three men working at the bottom were instantly drowned.

In such a case as this, the workmen could at least be prepared for serious consequences and take all due precautions — which, however, seems not to have been done, as no miners should have been in the deeper levels whilst this work was going on. In general, however, these disasters were quite unexpected, and the casualties resulting from them often high. Near Horrabridge, in Devon, is situated a mine called Furze Hill Wood, which had a somewhat unsuccessful career as a tin producer between 1862 and 1877, the recorded output for this period being only 196 tons of black tin and two tons of arsenic. Further up the hill to the east lay the abandoned workings of Old Furze Hill Wood mine, whose exact whereabouts, or, indeed, even existence, was unknown to those engaged in the newer concern. The oldest inhabitant in the neighbourhood could not remember this ancient mine being worked, nor could they recall hearing any traditions concerning it from those of an earlier generation. The picturesque hill on whose side both lay contained two shafts of Old Furze Hill Wood, one being 40 fathoms and the other 60 fathoms deep. In addition, there was a large number of shallow shafts, together with broken ground, showing that the workings had been quite extensive. It was believed that these workings did not go below the adits, which were quite dry. The shafts of the new mine were sunk on a lower level than those of the old one, and cross-cuts to reach the lodes were not made until a depth far below that of the known workings of the old mine had been attained. However, as events were to prove, the ancient workings extended well below the adits, and in these parts a considerable body of water had collected.

The men on night core at Furze Hill Wood on May 11-12 1866 noticed that the ground was getting a little 'fairer,' but attached no importance to it as an indication of possible danger. The next core consisted of eight men and two boys, who went down at 6 a.m., and would have come up again at noon. However, at eleven o'clock, while Henry and John Fox, father and son were driving east of the 40 fathom level, a body of water unexpectedly burst out of the ground where they were working and at once swamped that level. It then rushed into a winze and down another shaft into the 54 fathom level, the bottom of the mine, and in scarcely two minutes flooded the whole of the workings. Several other men besides the Foxes were working at the 40 fathom level, and four miners were engaged in a stope nearly down to the 54 fathom level. Amongst these at the 40 were two boys clearing away rubbish close to the footway winze. Whilst so employed, they received a hurried warning from a miner called Yeo that water had broken loose, and he told them to make their escape as fast as they could. Without making further enquiries the two lads rushed for the ladder and ascended to grass. Yeo then went back in the level intending to warn others of the accident, but was himself overtaken by the torrent and shared the same fate as those he had sought to save.

As the boys reached the mouth of the shaft they were met by Captain Doidge, the resident agent, who was about to descend. They told him what had happended, and he immediately went down the shaft until stopped by the water. Although the captain got down only five minutes after the first breaking-in of the water, he found that it had already filled up the 54 and 40 fathom levels, and the whole of the stopes, winzes and cross-cuts in the mine, and reached 5 fathoms above the 40. Here he stayed some time hoping to render assistance to any who might have gained the shaft before the water trapped them. But this proved a vain hope; and at last, after receding step by step as the water rose higher, he returned to surface.

Eight miners — nearly all the shift — died in the inundation, the only ones to escape being the two lads warned by Yeo. Their names were:

Henry Fox, married, 45, of Buckland Mitton.
John Fox, 15, his son.
William Elford, married, 39, of Buckland Milton.
Michael Yeo, married, 27, of Buckland Milton.
Silas Pike, single, 22, of Horrabridge.
Benjamin Gorman, married, 37, of Horrabridge.
Henry Thomas, single, 20, of Horrabridge.
Thomas Wooten, single, 24, of Buckland Monachorum.

In order to escape, the Foxes and others in the 40 fathom level would have had to get through the ladder winze, and then traverse sixty or seventy fathoms to the main shaft. Those in the stope, near the 54 fathom level, had no chance of escape once the water poured down upon them both through the winze and shaft. The presence of the water in the mine prevented any immediate steps being taken to recover the bodies, but the engine was kept at work pumping out 160-170 gallons per minute. Despite this, the water rose steadily till the evening. The bodies at Furze Hill were not, in fact, recovered until after several days of pumping. Captain Doidge had a narrow escape from becoming one of their number; for whilst on his way to descend the shaft, he was detained in conversation at the account-house, and so was met at the shaft's mouth by the boys with news of the accident, otherwise he would hve been below when the flood burst in.

On February 11 1857 a fatal accident occurred in some of the old workings of Boscean mine, St. Just. It appeared that a run of ground had previously taken place in a level, causing the water to be dammed up, and all operations were suspended until means could be found to drain it away. Various plans had been tried without success, the intention being, if possible, to draw off the water through a pipe, at the same time taking care to secure the ground with timber. That morning Michael Davy, with John Semmens and his son were working at this task, and towards noon Captain James Trezise went down to see how they were getting on. After suggesting they should put in another piece of timber, he left them and went to the further end of the level and had just begun to return when he heard a noise like the rushing of wind. Before Captain Trezise could get back to the crosscut in the level he was thrown down by the force of the stream which had broken through the fallen ground, his mouth being filled with gravel and slime, and it was with the utmost difficulty he escaped with his life. The younger Semmens dragged himself to safety by struggling desperately along with the help of a rope through from one to two fathoms of slime, geat quantities of which were forced down his throat. He saw his father borne along by the stream and grasped him by his clothes, but was compelled to let him go to save himself. Davy was also drowned in the torrent of slime. An attempt was immediately made to recover the bodies by driving from another shaft lower down the hill, the distance to be covered being 30 fathoms or more. This was attended with great difficulty, the level being only 3½ feet high and proportionately narrow, in addition to which the agents found the men very reluctant to volunteer for this dangerous and unpleasant work. Large crowds of sightseers visited the mine during the following week-end, and great excitement prevailed in the district. It was not until Monday that the bodies were reached and brought to grass — Davy with scarcely a mark or bruise upon him, Semmens with a leg broken — 'and both looking quite natural and as if in a sweet sleep.'

One mile south-west of St. Day, near the centre of the Carn Marth district, lies the Cathedral mine, which in 1881 was the scene of a fatal inundation. During the previous forty-five years it had been worked at intervals by three different companies, the last of which began operations by sinking a new shaft to the east of the old workings, and also put down an engine shaft sixty fathoms below the adit. On the evening of January 26, James Mathews of St. Day, who, with a boy, was driving the western end of the 50 fathom level, drilled two holes and fired them. Whilst waiting outside for the smoke to clear, he heard the rush of water, and at once ran with the boy to the shaft. On reaching it Mathews cried out as loudly as possible to the other men in the mine to be quick for their lives, and hurriedly scrambled up a loose ladder about six feet high (kept there for moving about when tramming was in progress) so gaining the fixed ladder above. Mathews then looked back and saw his young comrade, Ferril, take hold of the loose ladder and endeavour to follow him. He called out "Are you all right?". The lad replied "Yes, all right," and Mathews' candle then going out, the latter climbed on, but did not see or hear anything more of the lad. It was supposed that Ferril, not having sufficient strength to climb up as he did, was overtaken by the water and drowned. When Mathews reached the 40 fathom level the water was close at his heels, but he gained on it at the 30, and reached the surface safely. Two men and two boys were working in the eastern end of the 50; they either did not hear Mathews' warning, or failed to reach the shaft in time, and were 'drowned like rats in their holes.' Three other men were in the bottom of the shaft, ten fathoms below the 50. They were supposed to have had a terrible death, as it was believed that there was a plat of waste stuff or deads near the shaft at the 50, waiting to be drawn to suface, and that all this crashed to the bottom of the mine with the influx of water. Soon after escaping, Mathews again descended with Captain Davey, the agent, and found the water still at the 30, but there was no sign of any of the eight missing boys and men. It was a long time before their bodies were recovered. Six months after the diaster it was stated that the engine, which previously could fork ten fathoms in twenty-three hours, was not then doing 1½ fathoms, showing conclusively that there was a connection with some very extensive old workings. Launders were being erected and other work carried out to prevent surface water going down the old mine.

The names of the victims were: John and William Blackler (brothers) St. Day; Joseph May, married, Cusgarne; Richard Oates, married, Little Beside; George Richards, single, Carharrack; Richard Bennetts, boy (he lived near the mine, and this was his first day underground); William Northy, boy, Todpool; and J. H. Ferril, boy, St. Day. The Blacklers and May were sinking in the shaft; whilst the others (except Ferril) were working in the eastern end of the 50.

Fortunately, not all the inundations caused by the holing of underground reservoirs resulted in such a heavy loss of life. The *Mining Journal* of February 24 1838 recorded that whilst several miners were employed in an adit at Balmeneer mine, in Wendron, a quantity of water from the old workings burst in upon them, drowning one poor fellow called Harvey before he was able to escape. A very similar mishap occurred at Blencowe Consols tin mine, at St. Stephens-in-Brannel during April 1872. Two miners, George Kendall, 49, and Thomas Allen, 15, died when water from an old level broke into the adit and filled all the lower parts of the mine. On February 8 1842 a great body of water broke away in Wheal Providence mine, Gwinear, and poured into a level in which Henry Whitford, with one of his sons, was working; the son escaped, but the father was drowned, his body not being recovered till nine days after.

Several near miraculous escapes occurred when Wheal Creber, lying two miles south-west of Tavistock, was flooded in May 1869. (It is interesting to note that one part of this mine, the Georgina lode, was worked from the Tavistock canal tunnel, which leads into the Tamar valley at Morwellham.) Water from old workings broke in above the western level at seven o'clock in the morning. A miner named Bowden saw his young son washed past him towards the shaft, through which the boy escaped to surface, believing that his father had been drowned. He had seen the older man get behind a piece of timber in the level, and feared he must have been swept away from this refuge by the rushing water or else, holding on tightly, had been engulfed by the rising flood. Two other men, Jenkins and Mitchell, were trapped 120 fathoms below the surface in the eastern level, but it was felt in their case that there was some hope of survival.

The pumps were accordingly kept going; and during the afternoon men who descended the mine heard noises coming from the level in which Jenkins and Mitchell had been working. In the evening a short lighted candle placed upon a piece of wood was floated under the rock into the place where the poor fellows were trapped. Shortly after the wood was returned without the candle, proving they had taken it and were still alive. As soon as the water had got low enough, a rope was passed into them, and one after another they made their escape, each fastening the rope round his body under the armpits and floating out upon a piece of wood.

At noon the following day, two brave rescuers named Tor and Vinton very courageously got into the water and swam into the level where Bowden had been working., They found him alive, and by means of a rope was drawn out to the shaft and assisted to surface, 'where, after being mourned as dead, he was now most fervently congratulated upon his miraculous escape.' He was, however, very weak, and had sustained some head injuries. When the water rushed in, after telling his son to escape, he took shelter in a waggon, which the water turned over, making it a place of refuge for him, Jenkins and Mitchell did not know that anything had happened until they found the water was rising in their level and had effectually cut off escape. Their candles continued to burn, showing the air was good, but they feared the water might rise higher or that the engine might stop. They watched the water, and saw it was at a standstill, then it rose again half an inch, but afterwards gradually sunk until they were able to make their escape.

They were less fortunate at the Grambler & St. Aubyn mines, near St. Day, when a great volume of water from a long unworked section rushed into the workings in August 1875. For some time past the 25 fathom level had been driving to communicate with this old flooded mine. The ground was rather fair; but as soon as the miners holed to the reservoir the water burst out with great violence, and rapidly filled all the bottom levels. Most of the miners managed to escape, but a man named Pope, his son, and another man were drowned, a fourth being injured in the rush to get away. This was the elder Pope's first day in the mine, where he had gone to assist his son. It was said to be evident he knew nothing of the whereabouts of the old workings, although there were maps and plans on the mine showing their position, and it was known they were full of water. The mines thought the water was several fathoms distant from them. In a report of the accident, it was mentioned that, when driving towards old flooded workings, the practice was to keep a long borer in front to discover when the partition was cut; it had not been ascertained whether this precaution had been observed in the present case.

Whilst considerable risks had sometimes to be taken in mining, the occupation being by its nature a dangerous one, the bounds of prudence and common sense were sometimes so far exceeded as to make accidents almost inevitable. As an example may be cited the inundation which took place at Great Work, Germoe, on Christmas Eve, 1891. It was known that all the ground in which this mine had been set to work was honeycombed to shallow depths by those shrewd and industrious explorers, the old tinners. Though they could not get very far below an adit, they delved the ground above and got at the tin in an wondrously persevering way. The resident agent, Captain Josiah Thomas, having 'a warning knowledge of masses of accumulated water (was) very careful to ensure vigilance and discretion.' He seems, in fact, to have expressly forbidden any mining operations in parts known to be dangerous; but just how his instructions were observed will appear in the sequel.

At a point where two miners called Johns and Berryman were at work, some 'weeping of the ground' had been noticed, and additional watchfulness was enjoined upon them. On the morning preceding the mishap, when the pare resumed work, the agent again impressed upon them that a considerable body of water lay at the back. However, it sometimes happens that water in considerable quantities intrudes without there being any huge and dangerous reservior behind waiting to break through and unleash destruction in the mine. As a result, the men often ignored such warning signs, believing them to be of no significance. It seems fairly certain that this is what Johns and Berryman must have done, preferring to trust to their own judgement rather than follow Captain Thomas' injunctions. Exactly what happened could not afterwards be ascertained. Either they were picking away at the slender barrier between themselves and a column of water pressed on by other ponds, or blasted nearby and shook the ground; whichever it was, there must have been a sudden avalanche of rock, mud and water which overwhelmed the two men, making it impossible for them to escape up the ladders to safety; and so they perished, it may truly be said, by their own hands.

The most dreadful of all the disasters caused in Cornish mines by the accidental holing of flooded workings was that which took place at Wheal Owles, St. Just, on January 10, 1893, when twenty miners lost their lives. Wheal Owles sett lies a little to the north of St. Just Churchtown, and consists of a long, narrow strip of ground bordered on the north by Botallack, on the south by Boswedden and Boscean, and on the west by the Atlantic Ocean. In Nancherrow Valley stands the fine engine-house of old Wheal Drea, that part of the sett from which the floodwater came; whilst the Wheal Edward and Cargodna sections border the steep, grass-covered cliffs. A short distance off stands the engine-house of West Wheal Owles. Below this, and part way down the 300 feet high cliffs, is the 'Square,' or Cargodna Shaft, protected on top by a low collar. It was this shaft that the miners descended, singing hymns, on the morning of the tragedy as they went to work, many of them never to emerge again.

The mine is quite an old one, and was re-started in 1810 and again in 1834. Boys and Grouse were amalgamated with it in 1837, Parknoweth in

1857, and Drea a year or two later. In 1863 Wheal Edward was re-opened, followed in 1870 by Cargodna. Disappointing developments led to Owles, Grouse, Boys, and Cargodna being closed in 1878, activity then being concentrated on Drea, but in 1884 this section became poor, and was abandoned. Cargodna was then re-started and remained in production until the mine was flooded. Wheal Owles thus worked continuously from 1834 to 1893, producing in that time 8,450 tons of black tin, mainly from the inland sections, and 340 tons of seven per cent copper ore.

In 1893 the Wheal Owles sett consisted of several shafts with underground workings on several lodes, some being connected, others not. The shafts were known as Buzza, Wheal Boys, Cargodna, Corpus Christi, Wheal Drea, Wheal Edward, Flat Work, Wheal Gendal, Wheal Grouse, Wheal Owles, West Wheal Owles, and others. Cargodna shaft, commenced about 1883, was the only one then working, the remainder being full of water to adit level. Wheal Drea lay about 400 fathoms south by east of Cargodna, and was sunk on the same lode, which ran north-west by south-east, with an east by north underlie. The northerly workings at Cargodna extended under the sea, but had been idle for two or three years. The 30 fathom level of the southerly workings intersected a cross-course about 80 fathoms from shaft, which bore south-east and north-west, underlying north-east, several intermediate levels following the cross-course to the south-east from where they cut it.

The northerly workings on Wheal Drea cut the same cross-course, but more to the south-east than those on Cargodna, and the levels followed its course to the south-west. Thus, the two sets of levels approached each other on the same vein; but this was not shown to be the case on the working plan. The Cargodna levels were reckoned from adit, whilst those on Drea were reckoned from surface; consequently the 65 in the first and the 148 in the second corresponded in depth respectively; and it was the holing of the 65 into the 148 which brought about the inundation. The accident was thus caused by an inaccurate plan, which resulted from the surveys over a number of years having all been plotted to the same magnetic meridian, that of 1841, in which year the plan was originally prepared. This error led to the Wheal Drea workings being shown too much to the south and the Cargodna too far to the north, as well as being apparently on different veins and going in different directions.

Mr. Martin, the Government Inspector of Mines, who drew up a report on the disaster, happened to visit Wheal Owles a few weeks before the tragedy, and examined the plans. He drew the attention of Captain Thomas Tregear, the chief agent, to the fact that they appeared to be working between two ranges of old flooded workings, and in no very great width of ground, and mentioned that they would need to be very careful. Captain Tregear replied that the manager (Richard Boyns) was 'most particular' about the plans, and allowed no one but himself to interfere with them, as he was rather 'plan-proud.' Feeling uneasy about the position, Martin requested a Mr. Stokes to go thoroughly into the plans; the latter did so, but found no reason to doubt their accuracy.

It was a great pity that Martin's suspicions did not lead to a more intense probing of the situation. Perhaps if he had been aware of several incidents in the past when Owles had blundered into the workings of neighbouring mines, pointing to serious errors in her own plans, this would have been done, and the calamity avoided. Around the year 1867, for example, a breakthrough was made between Owles and Boscean, as a result of which the management of the latter mine was charged — falsely, as later events were to prove — with erroneous dialling, and obliged to forfeit their Goldings section, valued at £1,200, as compensation for their alleged 'trespass.' Again, in 1875 Wheal Owles actually admitted having made an encroachment on Botallack, and ceded a part of Truthwall sett in Buzza by way of settlement of Botallack's claim; whilst in 1882 Owles holed into flooded workings of Boscean mine, a disaster being only narrowly averted.

Those who worked in Wheal Owles just prior to the flooding were totally unaware that their operations were attended by danger. Captain Tregear, the underground agent, stated afterwards that he had not the least idea that their workings were anywhere near the 'houses of water' known to exist in the older parts of the sett. In fact, the plans showed them to be going *away* from the area of possible risk; but what no one knew was that those plans had been inaccurately kept. The map indicated at least ten fathoms of solid ground between them and the flooded workings of old Wheal Drea; it showed also that the Cargodna vein (the only lode then being worked in Wheal Owles) on which they were driving south had never been driven on from Wheal Drea. In both these particulars it was completely in error.

Trusting to the plans, Captain Tregear felt himself to be as safe in the levels of Wheal Owles as in his bed; and all the miners there fully shared his confidence. All, that is, except one. This man, called Thomas Henry Lutey, had what appears to have been a premonition of coming disaster; and in the days just prior to the holing he used to alarm his comrades by rushing through the workings crying "Water! Water!" in a terrified voice. The other men were put to some trouble to quieten his apparently groundless fears, but they took no notice of this 'warning,' and went on with their work just as usual. On the morning of the accident, a young miner called Johnny Grenfell, of Tregeseal Cottages, had a strange experience, which was afterwards interpreted as a 'token' of impending disaster. Reaching the mine, he found he had left his underground clothes behind, and returned home for them. His mother asked him in a thoroughly frightened manner why he had come back, adding, "I believe something is going to happen, for it's bad luck for a miner to return from mine before he starts to work." Johnny nevertheless collected his clothes and retraced his steps to 'bal,' leaving his mother in an uneasy and anxious state of mind till he came back after the disaster, in which he experienced a hair's-breadth escape from death.

Thursday January 10 1893 was the monthly 'measuring day' at Wheal Owles; and when the forenoon core went to work at eight o'clock they blasted almost at once so that the smoke could clear from the levels before Captains Tregear and Legge, the underground agents, began measuring their 'bargains.' About a hundred men were employed in the mine at this time, of whom forty were in this core. The pitches being worked were in the 45, 55, 65, 75 and 85 fathom levels. There were five other levels below the 85, but these were then idle. The tributers who ordinarily worked in the 105 level were engaged in dressing the stuff they had brought to grass the previous Saturday, and to this circumstance owed their preservation.

The blasting carried out by the men just after going down must have broken the thin rock wall which alone separated the workings at Wheal Owles from the great house of water in Wheal Drea in the 65 level, and the flood, acting under tremendous pressure, came bursting through into the doomed mine. Those working at this 65 level were: Mark Taylor (married); John Taylor (single); Edward White (married); William Eddy (single); James Rowe (single); James Edwards (married); William Davey (single); and William Roberts (single). Some were working at monthly wages and others by contract, and all of them were drowned. No witness, therefore, survived, to tell the dreadful story of what happened at this place where the rock barrier broke away, and the torrent came sweeping in, carrying all before it. It might have been thought that all the miners in the lower levels would have shared their fate; for the water, reaching the rearward end of the 65, poured down the shaft in a thundering cascade, filling the deeper workings at a tremendously rapid rate. And, indeed, nearly everyone down there was drowned, without a chance of survival. All those in the 85 perished, their names being: Richard Williams (married); John Oats (married); Thomas Allen (single); William John Thomas (single); John Grose (widower); Thomas Grose (single); Lewis Wilkins Blewett (single); and Charles Thomas (married). From the 75, however, there were, miraculously, some survivors, but several others were drowned. Those who lost their lives were: James Williams (single); Peter Dale (single); James Thomas (single); and Thomas Ellis (married). They were all tutmen, and had been working at their pitches at a distance of about 70 or 80 fathoms from the shaft. Although they must have received warning of the disaster from the crash and roar of the inrushing water, they had not sufficient time to reach the shaft and ascend the ladders to safety.

Thomas Henry Lutey — the miner who had experienced a premonition of the disaster — and his brother Richard were both at the 75 tramming. They had brought a waggon to the shaft, emptied it, and turned to go back through the level, when they met the water rushing out. They at once made for the ladderway alongside the shaft, groping their way in pitch darkness, for the blast of air caused by the holing had blown out their candles, and started desperately climbing to surface. Richard had to drag his brother up the ladder at one point clear of the raging water, and both had a very narrow escape from death. Thomas never fully recovered from the shock of this experience. A resident at St. Ives informed the writer that he remembered Mr. Lutey quite well in his later years, walking along the roads with a shuffling gait, his eyes always fixed on the ground, as if he were expecting the earth to open under his feet. He never worked in the mines again, and earned his living hawking oranges in the St. Just district.

The other men in the 75, Richard Blewett and William Charles Grenfell, both fillers, happened to be only about ten fathoms from the shaft when the water broke through. They managed to fight their way out of the level and followed the Luteys up the shaft to safety.

The most dramatic series of events connected with this tragedy, however, occurred at the 55 fathom level — that is, the one immediately above the level where the water came in. With the story of what happened here, the name of James Hall will always be linked. It was he who made the communication between Drea and Boscean in 1882; and he now emerges as the great hero of the later disaster — the man who, by his coolness of mind, steadiness of nerve, indomitable courage and intimate understanding of the mine, saved not only his own life but those of no less than five of his comrades as well.

James Hall was a genial personality known to everyone in St. Just by the friendly soubriquet of 'Farmer.' An experienced miner, he had worked in the Wheal Owles sett for 17 years, eight of them in the Cargodna shaft. He afterwards expressed the opinion that he had had a narrower escape at the time of the Drea-Boscean holing than during the 1893 disaster, but it is doubtful if those he rescued at Cargodna on the latter occasion would have agreed with him on that point.

'Farmer' Hall went to work that morning as usual in the 55 accompanied by two boys — John Grenfell and Walter Oates. Nothing unusual occurred until nine o'clock, when they heard a rumbling sound, which Hall at first thought sounded like a stull falling. He paid little attention to begin with, but when the sides of the level began to shake and gravel ran down, he at once realised that something serious had occurred.

Calling to the boys to come from the stope at the back and run out of the 55 as quickly as possible, he got down himself, and they quickly followed — jumping on top of him in their excitement. Hall then gave warning to those in the end — George Toman, of Carn Bosavern, and John Lutey, of Kelynack. As soon as they were down in the level, their candles were extinguished by a strong current of air, and they had to feel their way in starting for the shaft. Because of this handicap, it looked as if they might not reach it in time; but then Hall had an inspiration. Finding an empty tram waggon, he put Johnny Grenfell into it, intending to push the tram along the rails, which would thus guide them along the level. Lutey thereupon exclaimed, "Farmer, I have a wife and seven children!" so Hall put him into the waggon too, and telling Oates and Toman to catch hold of either side of him, he set it in motion. Their speed may be estimated from the fact that in their rush for the shaft, they overtook James Williams in the darkness, and told him to run before the waggon, which he had the greatest difficulty in doing, his alarm and terror being heartrending. The danger for all of them indeed, was appalling; for besides the possibility of collison with unseen obstacles on the level, there was also the risk of misjudging the distance to the junction, and so going headlong into the shaft.

To make matters worse, young Grenfell, unknown to Hall, jumped out of the tram before reaching the end of that nightmare ride; and when, on nearing the shaft, Farmer called out to him, he shouted back that he had fallen into an eighteen feet deep plot. There was no other way out but by climbing over the loose stones, which he did, and when nearly at the top, Williams pulled him up by one hand, remarking that he "felt no heavier than a pound of candles."

As they were about to take the ladder in the shaft, Hall found that Walter Oates and George Toman were missing. The air current was now coming in irregular gusts, enabling them to strike and protect a light. Placing one candle against the pump, Hall went back into the level to look for the two men. Twenty fathoms in he found Oates, and several fathoms further off saw Toman going in the wrong direction, stooping as if on all fours. He directed them to the shaft, and then retraced a further thirty-two fathoms of level looking for more stragglers. Right at the end he came across Richard Blewett, of Bosorne, standing motionless, and called to him to hurry for the ladders. Blewett, however, did not move, saying he was waiting for his son, but when Hall told him his boy had gone up, he made his way to the ladders.

Back at the shaft, Farmer tossed in a stone to discover how far the water had risen. Not hearing any splash, he concluded it to be still a good way off; and then this intrepid man went down the shaft seven fathoms (three fathoms short of the 65 level) and heard voices, which must have been those of the unfortunate cousins, John and Mark Taylor, and of Edward White, calling out piteously "Bring us a light!" James Hall replied "Make for the shaft!" thinking the light he had left on the pump would guide them. But there was no response; and by a second stone thrown into the depths Farmer could tell that the water was now within twelve fathoms of where he stood. This was dangerously close, so he hastened back up the shaft.

In ascending, he saw no indication of life anywhere until he encountered Captain Tom Tregear at adit level, who was on his way down to investigate the disaster. Captain Tregear kept on descending until he reached the 35 fathom level, where the rising water stopped him. Farmer had not come up too soon.

A miner called B. Hosking, who also escaped from the 55, although apparently not with James Hall's party, proved doubly lucky in eluding death that day. He had been previously working in the 65 fathom level (where the water broke through) having been engaged there right up to the previous day. However, on the Tuesday morning some repairs were needed to the tram-road at the 55, and he, with another man, went to attend to it. But for this circumstance, he would have been working in his usual place at the 65, from which escape was impossible.

Among those in the 45 level that morning was Alexander ('Sanders') Rowe. He had begun his mining career at the age of ten in Wheal Owles, and later worked in Brazil and the United States. Whilst in the former country, he had experienced a severe earthquake shock underground, but the noise of this was nothing near so loud or appalling as that which fell on his startled ears on the present occasion.

"I had commenced work about half-an-hour," Rowe stated afterwards, "when I heard an unusual sound, like that caused by a tram-haul, or when a huge mound of rubbish falls away. That gradually increased until the noise was louder than 'ten thousand thunders.' I was drilling a hole when I heard it first, and William Richard Thomas was sitting down on a plank having a 'touch-pipe.' 'Will Rech' exclaimed "What was that?" and I answered "It's water!" Both of us made all haste to the ladders and what we hoped was safety. Those longed-for ladders were about three hunded feet from us. My light had gone out the moment we heard that strange language of the waters, but fortunately my comrade's remained burning till we reached the shaft and had ascended to the 25 fathom level. Mr. Thomas was greatly excited, and by the merest chance I saved him from falling into the shaft. Coming through the level, I was once knocked down by a sudden and strong blast of air, and for a moment gave myself up for lost. However, I made another attempt, and reaching the ladderway was the first to get to surface and the blessed sunshine. On the way up we heard heart-rending appeals for assistance, but these ceased at the 25 fathom level, where my comrade's light went out."

Rowe's story was confirmed by Thomas, who added that when they reached a spot eight or nine fathoms from the top, the ladder shook violently under their feet and the pumps rattled, indicating a second great convulsion somewhere. They reached grass one and a half minutes before any of the others, and scarcely dared to hope that more had escaped. "I shall remember the shock as long as I live," he stated. "We were singing carols, together with a good many of those who are now in the mine, as we descended, and the sadness of that so presses on the mind that I fear I am not thankful enough for my own escape."

James Bottrell, of Botallack, was also working in the 45 that day, but thirty fathoms further in. He had started work at 6.15 a.m., and after blasting one hole, he and his comrades were using hammers in the drift when they heard an unusual sound. Bottrell estimated the time then at 8.45 or 8.50 a.m. It was the loudest and most appalling noise he had ever heard, and his light was extinguished immediately. Dropping their tools, they hurried back through the level. Bottrell heard Michael Harvey and Thomas Angwin crying for help from the bottom of a winze where they were working. He went to their assistance and started to pull them up one by one from the winze, which had become a veritable death-trap. He hauled Angwin out first; but when the nearly rescued man was within two fathoms of the top, the rope became jammed in the standard and the trees, or, to use the miners' expression, 'got jammed in the biggs.' Angwin then climbed up hand over hand the remaining distance, and helped Bottrell to free the rope. Harvey was then drawn up. All this had taken five minutes to perform; and five minutes is a terrifyingly long time under such circumstances as these. Bottrell and his comrades then made all haste out of the level. One candle, almost by a miracle, kept alight till they reached the shaft. Had this light gone out, none of them, probably, would have survived. On taking the ladder, the men encountered a tremendous blast of air coming up the shaft, impelled by the rapidly rising waters below. Bottrell said he had never experienced anything like it above ground, his hat being immediately blown off and the light put out. He heard no cries, only the roaring of the water and the wind. He was the seventh survivor to reach grass.

Several strange and tragic stories connected with the disaster remain to be told. One is of the two boys who changed places. It appears that a lad named Chenhalls had intended to go down the mine to work that day for the very first time; but another boy, with whom he was friendly, wished to go in this place. They decided the matter by tossing a coin. Chenhalls lost the toss, but won his life, for the lad who went in his place was among those who perished.

Another remarkable incident of this kind is related of a miner called Thomas. This young man was engaged to a local girl, and their wedding day had been fixed for January 10 — the day of the disaster. Had matters gone according to plan, therefore, he would have been above ground preparing to lead his bride to the altar at the moment the water broke in, and so preserved his life. However, it so happened that the Vicar had another wedding ceremony to perform that day, and because of the clash in his engagements, young Thomas and his bride-to-be agreed to postpone their own nuptials to a later date. So it was that this unfortunate young man came to be underground, working as usual, on that fatal morning, and was drowned, turning what should have been a day of joy for his bride into one of grief-stricken anguish and mourning.

A curious story which got into print at the time of the flooding and afterwards developed into a kind of legend, though entirely without foundation, concerns one of the two boys then working underground, who was supposed to have saved his life by swimming. His name was Lewis Blewett, and he had been working with eight others at the 85, where the falling cascade of water made escape by swimming or any other means absolutely impossible. Yet the tale of his marvellous swim to safety is still told, as though it were fact.

The two agents, Captains Tregear and Legge, had a remarkable escape from death. As already mentioned, it was measuring day at the mine, and they were due to go down soon after the men to measure the bargains. They left the account house together to walk to the shaft on the cliff, but on the way met Newton, the pitman, who told them that a pump at West Wheal Owles had split in the lift. Captain Tregear stayed to discuss this with Newton, while Captain Legge went on as far as the shaft collar where he remained waiting for his colleague, as they were in the habit of measuring the bargains together. But for this delay, they would have been at the 85 fathom level when the inundation occurred, from where there was no escape.

As they were about to descend the shaft, they heard some men coming up, who proved to be Rowe and Thomas, the first of the survivors, who told the horrified officials of what had happened below. Captain Tregear then descended the shaft to ascertain the extent of the disaster. On the way down, he met James Hall, who being somewhat more short-winded than his comrades, had fallen behind, and was now resting at adit level, exhausted and without a light, having dropped his candle as he climbed up the shaft.

The holing which had taken place between Wheal Owles and Wheal Drea was at a place almost directly below the road running in front of Wheal Drea burrow and engine-house. Soon afterwards, a large and dangerous subsidence occurred here, the ground collapsing to a depth of twenty feet. This was said to be due to the outflowing of water from the flooded Wheal Drea workings, the unsupported ground then collapsing to adit level. As Boscean and Wheal Drea had already been connected by an earlier holing, the latest accident meant that these two mines, and

Wheal Owles, were all joined underground, and that one immense lake of water ran through their workings. This pool extended for a mile and a half in length, stretching almost from the sea to beneath the Wesleyan Chapel at St. Just Churchtown. As the depth at Wheal Owles was 125 fathoms below sea-level, and the water rose within half-an-hour to two fathoms below the 30 fathom level in both shafts when the inrush ceased, this meant that the pool had in that short time attained a depth of 95 fathoms in the mine.

An enquiry into the cause of the disaster resulted in a prosecution being brought at Penzance the following April against Captain Richard Boyns, the aged and much respected purser of Wheal Owles; who had directed the mine's affairs since 1855 and had been associated with it for the whole of his long working career, the charge being that he had failed to keep an accurate plan of the workings, in accordance with the nineteenth section of the Metalliferous Mines Act, 1892. His plans showed the 65 fathom level in Cargodna and the 148 fathom level in Drea to have been 18 or 19 fathoms apart, whereas in fact they had come very close together. The plans also indicated the Wheal Drea and Cargodna lodes as two parallel and distinct features, though they were actually one and the same. The Bench found defendant guilty of failure to make any allowance for magnetic variation when drawing his plans, the result being that they were wrong 'to the serious extent of considerably over one hundred feet in the distance shown... between the present and an older set of workings.' Because of the defendant's good character and other mitigating circumstances, a nominal fine of only £15 was imposed. Such was the tragic end to the career of one of Cornwall's most distinguished mining officials. Indeed, Captain Richard Boyns deserves almost to be numbered among the victims of the disaster; for the flood destroyed his name and reputation as it snuffed out the lives of the poor miners underground.

As a result of the inundation, the pumping equipment on Wheal Owles was quite incapable of draining the flooded workings, whilst the neglected and probably collapsed condition of the old adits presented another great obstacle to the re-opening of the mine. Apart from the question of providing employment for those thrown out of work by the stoppage, a strong feeling existed in the district that the mine should be cleared, if only to recover the bodies of the twenty victims. Proposals for establishing a new company to re-work Wheal Owles were actually issued later that year, but proved abortive. The mine had been the only one making profits in St. Just, whilst the prospects were known to be excellent. The disaster was thus, in every way, a most unfortunate one for the district. Whether the immense body of water in the sett will continue a permanent obstacle to its re-opening remains yet to be proved.

A very dramatic rescue of men trapped by water in a flooded mine took place at Wheal Reeth, Germoe, on Saturday January 23 1937. About half-past four that afternoon, when a dozen miners were underground, a wall of rock separating Wheal Reeth from the old Wheal Boys shaft caved in, and water came rushing into the workings. A sudden blast of air and a terrific roaring sound warned them that something dreadful had happened. Those who were working in the bottom level near the shaft gallantly struggled up the ladders with a terrific weight of water pouring down upon them from the level ninety feet above so as to leave the cage free for the escape of others who they knew were behind them. So great was the volume of water that they had the utmost difficulty in ascending against it, but their self-sacrificing action unfortunately proved of no avail, as those in the rear were unable to reach the shaft and make use of the cage.

Six miners altogether were trapped in this way by the rapidly rising flood. One of them, C. Bowden, 23, of Godolphin, was working in a stope above the 310 fathom (bottom) level when he felt the blast of wind, which seemed at first like the bursting of an air pipe. Realising from the roar which followed that something serious had taken place, he very bravely resolved to try to warn two of his comrades, and called Semmens and Weeks, who were working at the end of the 310. Accordingly, he descended to the level, but found that water had already come up to the rise leading to his stope. He knew that the level sloped down towards the shaft, so there could be no escape that way. He called out to Semmens and Weeks, and told them that their only chance was to get into his stope. They climbed up into the stope which rose about twenty feet above the bottom level. At the end there was a rise connecting the 220 feet level above with the bottom level, and water was pouring down this in cataracts past the mouth of the stope. So great, indeed, was the quantity of water running along the 220 that the rise could not take it all, and so it rushed on and down the main shaft. The three miners remained in their stope watching the water rise and hoping it might abate. After a while it lessened, and they heard Semmens' father and other men shouting above. These rescuers lowered a rope down the rise until it was opposite the mouth of the stope. Weeks grasped it, and was hauled up, followed by Semmens and Bowden. When Bowden reached the 200, however, he was surprised to find that Semmens was not there. He had, in fact, lost his hold and fallen several feet down the rise. His father, Mr. A. Semmens, the shift boss, saw his son lose his grip on the rope, and was himself lowered into the blackness to search for him. He found the young man lying almost unconscious on a pile of ore with rising water all around. But for his father's prompt action Semmens would certainly have been drowned. The rescue party who volunteered to go down after these three miners had found great difficulty in getting into the 220 level because of the water. As soon as they could, they penetrated to a rise — that is, a small shaft for bringing up materials from the level below. This was the rise which cut across the mouth of the stope in which Semmens, Weeks and Bowden had taken refuge.

The three other men trapped below suffered a far worse ordeal. Their names were David Sedgeman, 40, of Perranuthnoe; G. A. N. P. Williams, 21, of Long Rock; and John Bates, 23, of Helston. At the time of the accident Bates heard a shout, "Run for your lives!" but as he began to do so was struck in the back by a terrific inrush of water and almost knocked down. He seized an air-pipe and kept himself up until he was able to scramble into a stope where he found the other two men. Their position was a most perilous one. They climbed into places they would never have dreamed of entering, spurred on by dread of the ever-rising water. Then, after a while, they noticed it had ceased rising, and realised there was now no danger of it overtaking them.

Meanwhile, at surface, the greatest efforts were being made to rescue them. Captain Herbert Bennetts, the manager, assisted by Mr. R. King, H.M. Inspector of Mines, worked incessantly throughout Saturday night, Sunday morning and afternoon, and then spent most of Sunday night underground. The miners followed their example, working laborious shifts with only a short rest spell in the drying house. Every endeavour was made to reduce the water level in the mine. Two Cornish pumps were kept going constantly, with four electric ones working below the surface. However, the water fell with maddening slowness, and although Monday morning brought an improvement, this was not maintained. In an effort to pierce through the floor of the 220 level, diamond drills with operators to work them were borrowed from neighbouring mines.

During Monday it had become possible for men to get down to the bottom level and wade for increasing distances along it. However, there was a V-shaped dip in the level making a deep pool between the rescuers and the stope where the three men were imprisoned. At one time, a miner succeeded in wading to within 25 feet of the deepest part of the sump; if he could have crossed the centre, he would have reached rising ground, making it then an easy matter to get to the men. But as the water was up to his neck he was forced to return. Another rescuer made six attempts to get through, but proved equally unsuccessful. At surface, the anxiety and tension had been hourly increasing. Fears that the men might not survive their ordeal grew stronger, and those were increased by false rumours that one of the pumps had failed.

However, the moment of release was not delayed much longer. The water level fell rapidly, enabling about a dozen men to form a chain and wade neck high through the pool to guide the imprisoned miners to the bottom of the shaft. They were inspired to make this brave attempt by the example of Clifford Bowden, who, carrying a flask of hot coffee and a torch, swam through icy cold water in the dark tunnel to his imprisoned comrades, and then swam back to report to Captain Bennetts that they were alive, after which he collapsed. But for his plucky action, the men might have remained entombed throughout another night. Bowden thus played an important part in the rescue of both groups of trapped men, and was the hero of the occasion.

The first to be brought to surface at seven o'clock was Williams, followed by Bates and Sedgeman. Although they had been imprisoned for about fifty hours, they were in astonishingly good health and spirits. Sedgeman gave a graphic account of their experiences to a reporter of the *Royal Cornwall Gazette.*

> "The time dragged slowly, and at one time we began to fear that we might not be able to get out. We sang hymns for a time, and the boys prayed for deliverance, and that their parents might be cared for if they could not be rescued. I kept up a continual tapping with the men above, and how long we were there I had not the faintest idea. It was a great joy to us when Bowden, who had swum through the tunnel, shouted to us from below. They persuaded us to come through the water and got us up to the 220 level through a rise. We could never have got up through the main shaft."

Bates confirmed that they had had no idea of the passage of time. They huddled together and must have dozed for short periods. They had no food, their lips swelled, and after a while they became too stiff and sore to move. The sound of their rescuers tapping from above put new courage into them, however. After the air in the stope became exhausted they kept themselves alive with compresssed air used for driving the drills. Said Williams: "The memory of the inky darkness of those hours with the water almost swishing around us will be always with me."

Whilst the men were still entombed, an urgent message was sent to Devonport for a team of divers, but their services were not required, the miners being released a few minutes before their arrival. The accident resulted in no damage or unemployment at the mine, which had a work force of about 170 men.

Disasters caused by holings into flooded workings have been all too common in Cornish mines, as the foregoing examples show. A much rarer type of inundation, resulting from the influx of slimes from surface, still remains to be described. ('Slimes' is the miner's term for liquid mud or silt produced during the stamping and dressing of ores.) One of these slime pit accidents occurred at Porkellis United Tin Mines, in Wendron, on the morning of August 4 1858. At the southern part of this sett was an old shaft which had been sollared over for some forty or fifty years, and then covered with stones to a considerable depth. The surrounding surface area was concave, forming a depression, and on it had accumulated a large quantity of slimes — the refuse from stream works — to a depth of two or three fathoms. For a week or two previous to the accident tributers had been working too close underneath this mass of superincumbent mud, the danger being increased by the fact that the 'country' rock consisted of porous, decomposed granite.

On the fatal day, more than fifty miners were engaged underground in different parts of the workings — mostly at the north, and so at considerable distances from the treacherous old shaft — when a sudden rush of wind gave warning of a calamity. Most of them got safely to 'grass;' but seven miners were overwhelmed by the inrushing slime after the ground had collapsed about a hundred fathoms from the ends where they were working. Their names were: Dunstan (two); Sincock, Ching, Penlerick, Andrew and Combellack. They included three shaftmen who were believed to have been working below the 60 fathom level. All were in the deepest part of the workings (65 fathoms) at the northern section of the mine. The slimes and refuse, breaking through the sollar, poured down the old shaft, through a 24 fathom cross-cut, down another shaft, and into a 35 fathom cross-cut, rushing on northwards with a roaring noise described both by witnesses at surface and those who escaped from below as being like thunder. All lights were instantly extinguished, and the men had to grope their way in darkness from the levels and ends to the shaft. It was thought the seven who were lost had been trying to escape in this way when overtaken by the rushing flood of slime. Estimates varied as to the quantity of refuse which ran into the mine. One account says the slimes at surface occupied an area "of about a quarter of an acre diameter in every direction" — whatever that may mean — and another that they measured 30 fathoms in length, 20 in breadth and three in depth. Something like 2,000 square fathoms must have fallen in. In about an hour, the mine was filled from its lowest depth, 65 fathoms, up to 24 fathoms. One curious incident related of the disaster concerns two men working in a rise at the back of the 15 fathom level in the western part. They remained wholly unaware of the accident and their danger until warned by two miners who reached them from another level, so enabling them to affect their escape.

Thirty years after the accident, another strange story was recalled by a writer in the *Cornish Telegraph.* The mine had by then changed its name to Basset and Grylls:

> "It is related, on good authority, that one aged miner, rather than entrust his earnings to his wife, carried £40 in a belt, and this amount he took underground with him on the day of the catastrophe. This man was urged by his comrade, a youth, to make all haste to surface, as strange sounds denoted that something serious was amiss. The elder of the two hesitated, and finally consented to go. But too late. He was caught by the descending flood, and was drowned, his youthful companion barely escaping."

His remains, and the belt of gold, lie in the depths of the mine to this day.

In the Tamar Valley, several mines were worked below the bed of the river; and where the workings had been carried upwards too near the bed a risk of flooding existed. Several mines were drowned in this way by the river bursting in, the most spectacular of these incidents occurring at South Tamar mine on Sunday August 31 1856. The South Tamar (known to the miners as Cowis mine) lies on the Devonshire bank of the river about two miles above Cargreen in the parish of Bere Ferris. The village of Bere Alston, where many of the miners lived — it then had a population of 2,000 — lay three miles north of the village of Bere Ferris. Formerly there had been extensive smelting works in the area for lead, silver and tin, but these were closed two years before the accident.

The South Tamar mine ran south under the river, extending backwards for over half-a-mile, and in following the lode a level had been carried into the sett of Furzehill or East Tamar mine. About a quarter of a mile distant, and in nearly the same direction, was Witsam mine, and half-a-mile from that Lockeridge mine; whilst westward of all lay Tamar Consols, or South Hooe mine. South Hooe also ran under the river and was much deeper than the South Tamar. About thirteen years before as the men were rising towards the river bed in South Hooe, a large 'pebble' was removed, and the water suddenly rushed in through the aperture, partly flooding the mine; but the effect was not serious, and the hole was speedily plugged.

South Tamar employed over 290 persons, the wages amounting to nearly £1,000 per week. The mine was very old, and once formed part of the ancient Bere Alston mine, worked, according to some accounts, as early as the reign of Queen Anne, or even of Queen Elizabeth, and had yielded very large quantities of silver. Operations ceased when the workings became too deep to be carried on with the primitive machinery then in use, but were resumed in 1845, and had continued on an extensive scale ever since. The mine had proved profitable, the shares, which had cost the adventurers £1 1s. 6d. each, having returned in profits more than double that amount. The bottom was 120 fathoms deep, the shallow level immediately under the river bed being at 30 fathoms. The mine extended a little more than half-way under the river between Holo's-hole and Cargreen, the excavations running for more than two and a half miles. At some earlier period the mine had been worked up very close to the river bed in following the ore. Adit level of the shaft was between three and four feet above high water spring tides.

In the river bed, about half-a-mile from the engine house, there was a 'slide' — a section of soft ground running down through the whole depth of the workings — and it appears that this, living up to its name, ran inwards at the time of the accident after having been undermined from beneath. Its collapse produced a depression in the river bed measuring ten fathoms by four. When it fell there was a spring tide, which would have added another six feet depth and weight of water to what it normally had to bear, this probably being a contributory cause to the disaster. Five months previously, a miner named Robins, employed at the Tamar Consols (South Hooe) stated publicly that the mine was in danger from this slide, and was discharged in consequence. Two other men working in the South Tamar itself entertained such misgivings as to its safety after some ground had fallen away that they refused to continue there. It seems clear from this that the management had not been paying sufficient attention to the security of the workings, and that by taking precautionary measures the mine might have been saved.

About eight o'clock on that fateful Sunday evening two engine-men and two watchmen on duty at surface were startled by an explosion whose effects resembled an earthquake shock, a mile away the sound was likened to that of thunder. Recovering from their fright, the men went to investigate the cause, and found that the trap-hatches on some of the covered shafts had been blown up by the air, which was issuing from them with such force that they were obliged to beat a precipitate retreat. Later, it was discovered that the explosion had resulted from the mine having become inundated with water which had burst in through the bed of the river. Mr. Wolferstan, the managing agent, who resided at Plymouth, was immediately informed of the occurrence, but nothing could be done that night, owing to the lateness of the hour. Next day, however, the full magnitude of the disaster became apparent. It was estimated that the water rushed in with such rapidity through the huge aperture left by the collapsed slide that the entire mine was completely filled in five minutes. From the South Tamar, the water had swept on with terrific violence into the East Tamar mine, which was partially inundated; but from some mysterious circumstance the level was so choked that the pumps were able to keep it at bay. The general opinion was that the South Tamar had been irredeemably destroyed, though a 'practical man' who had been engaged at the Thames Tunnel when a similar accident occurred there, estimated that the water could be pumped out from the South Tamar for £1,000.

On the Monday morning many of the men proceeded to their work as usual, and were astounded to learn what had taken place — "but the loss of their labour was mitigated by the feeling of thankfulness at the escape from the terrible death which, had the accident occurred on any other day, must inevitably have overtaken them. It was touching to witness the joy evinced by the poor fellows in the shaking each other by the hand at finding they had been miraculously saved."

The district round about was stunned by the news. Less than a fortnight afterwards Bere Alston was described as almost a deserted village. Already two publicans had made arrangements to leave, one for Plymouth and the other for Tavistock. As for the miners, fifty were preparing to emigrate to Chile, thirty to New Zealand and fifty to America, whilst many of the shopkeepers had already left or were arranging to do so. The rest of the miners had gone into other districts to seek employment. It seemed as if a fatality was attached to the area, for the local fruit crop had failed that summer, resulting in a loss of £3,000. The Earl of Mount Edgcumbe, who was Lord of the Manor of Bere Ferris, would lose £500 a year in dues through the closing of the mine. The value of submerged and irrecoverable machinery was put at £30,000. In December, the materials at surface were offered for sale, including a 22″ horizontal engine, 24″ pumping, stamping and crushing engine, 26″ pumping and drawing engine, and 28″ horizontal stamping engine. No effort was ever made to rework the enterprise. Wolferstan gave it as his opinion that they had tapped the stream at the 30 fathom level three years before; since then they had come under the 102; the water had percolated through the cross-course (slide), sapped its base, and it had dropped with the weight of water. Just a few months ago the silver-lead ores discovered and laid open were valued at £20,000. When the water came in, 120 tons were broken and lying underground.

Blasting Accidents

The use of gunpowder for blasting rocks in mines was first introduced into this country around the mid-seventeenth century, but at least fifty years elapsed before the new technique became widely adopted. This was particularly true of Cornwall, the reason probably being that here the 'mines' still consisted largely of stream works or very shallow pits and 'coffens.' But, once accepted as a most valuable means of enabling mineral lodes appearing at surface to be pursued to considerable depths

"Gunpowder, Cap'n! There ain't a man had more experience widdun."

The hazards of gunpowder (Courtesy Rigby Ltd.)

underground, the tin mining industry began to develop on a scale never known before, giving much greater employment and producing far more wealth for lords and adventurers than was previously ever dreamed of. Unfortunately this welcome access of prosperity was accompanied by a terrible increase in accidents, as miners were maimed, blinded and killed by the exploding charges they had themselves laid and fired in the confined underground workings. From being a pleasant, safe and healthy occupation, mining had been transformed into a dangerous and sickly one, carried on at increasing distances from sunshine and fresh air, amidst flying rock fragments and the foul thick smoke of gunpowder. For something like two hundred years this terrible tale of carnage and suffering was continued, its effect almost resembling those of a long drawn out war of attrition. Eventually, the invention of improved explosives and the rigorous enforcement of safety measures brought this unhappy epoch to a close, so that today blasting accidents are almost unknown.

The traditional method of using black powder was to drill a hole of the required depth by a 'boryer' beaten with sledgehammers, which was then cleaned with a wooden swab-stick and charged. For inserting the powder, an iron tamping-bar was used, having a concave or spoon-shaped end; and this tool, when being rammed in, sometimes struck sparks from the rocks, resulting in a premature explosion. During the eighteenth and early nineteenth centuries the great majority of blasting accidents were caused in this way. The remedy — a simple and effective one — was to sheathe the bar in copper. Sir Rose Price proposed this innovation in 1814, his ideas being enthusiastically taken up and developed by Dr. J. Ayrton Paris, who in 1817 published a monograph on the subject. To drive home the frequency and dreadful consequences of accidents produced by the dangerous blasting methods then in use he included a catalogue of over eighty which had occurred principally in the Hundred of Penwith. The list would have been more valuable had the accidents been dated, and if it were free from the suspicion of duplicated entries. Nevetheless, some interesting conclusions may be drawn from a perusal of its grim details. Perhaps the most significant of these is the comparatively high ratio of mishaps causing blindness, shattered limbs and disablement compared with those of a fatal character. However, the nature of the injuries sustained was often so crippling or disfiguring that death would have seemed a kinder outcome. Most, if not all, of these accidents were caused by the use of iron tools. The Rev. William Hockin, Rector of Phillack and Gwithian, who collected over half the accidents listed by Dr. Paris, stated that in every one the common iron tamping bar had been used; most of them occurred when laying the second layer of tamping.

The method of inserting the charge was as follows. After the powder had been put into the hole, a long round iron rod — it could sometimes be of copper — called a 'needle' or 'neele' by the miners, was pushed down through the charge to the bottom, the tamping laid on the powder and made firm with an iron mallet and flat-ended ramming bar, the needle then being withdrawn, leaving a long, narrow orifice in the compacted material. Into this hole was inserted a rush packed with powder, the end of which would then be ignited with a touch-paper. The iron needle naturally presented the same hazard as the iron tamping bar. A third way in which premature explosions could be produced by iron tools occurred when it became necessary to clear out a hole which had misfired, as the detonation of even a small quantity of residual powder could produce very damaging results to the unfortunate miners involved. Some of the old blasting practices, however, were comparatively safe. One such was the use of powder-filled paper cartridges in overhead holes, where loose powder would simply have run out; and the substitution of the needle by a tube of quills, inserted one into another, and filled with finely crushed powder.

Needle, rush and quill were all rendered obsolete by the invention of the Bickford safety fuse around the year 1830. This consisted of a small quantity of powder wrapped around with thread, and its slow burning properties gave the miners plenty of time to reach shelter before the explosion took place. Its use reduced, but by no means eliminated, blasting accidents underground; for the fuse did not always burn at a uniform rate, and miners were sometimes killed by returning too early to a hole which they believed had misfired when in fact the explosion had only been delayed. A further great advance came somewhat later in the century with the invention of dynamite first of the modern high explosive agents.

But the old-time Cornish miner had to work without the benefit of such aids and refinements. With his iron tamping bar and needle his safety margin was narrow indeed, and accidents were consequently all too frequent. Several of these occurred in the year of publication of Dr. Paris's pamphlet recommending the use of copper tools, and so served to underline his warnings in the grimmest possible manner. On Friday June 20 1817 the *Royal Cornwall Gazette* reported that on the previous Monday.

> "... another dreadful accident by the use of iron tamping-bars, took place at Dolcoath mine. Two men named John Allen and Francis Harris, having been employed in the dangerous experiment of tamping a hole with a common bar, the charge prematurely exploded; when Allen was killed on the spot, and his companion was so shockingly mutilated that but little hopes are entertained of his recovery."

Small wonder the *Gazette* expressed concern at the frequency of this kind of mishap; only about three weeks before, John Edwards, of the parish of St. Erth, had been killed and his son temporarily blinded through the same cause in a mine near St. Ives. In this case, the powder and quills, together with a little rubbish (for tamping) had been put into the hole, and the iron tamper applied; but the hole had not been properly swabbed.

In spite of such examples as these, iron tools continued to be used in some Cornish mines for more than half-a-century afterwards. It is difficult to account for this wilful disregard of personal safety except by attributing it to the miner's innate conservatism, and, perhaps, to a feeling that he, the practical man, knew far more about such matters than learned experts who had probably never once been below 'grass' themselves. Whatever the reason, those who persisted in such a known folly were sometimes called upon to pay a terrible price for it. On May 13 1873 John Moyle of Carnmenellis and Thomas Bolitho were preparing a hole in the 50 fathom level at Wheal Buller, about a mile south of Redruth, Moyle tamping and his comrade standing a little to the rear. Moyle had got about half-way through his task, using an untipped bar, when Bolitho suddenly heard an explosion, and saw that his comrade had fallen into a hole twelve fathoms deep. He procured assistance, and within ten minutes the rescuers reached the place where Moyle lay. He was on the ground, bleeding and bruised, and cut about the head. He appeared to be in great pain, and died within an hour. At the inquest, the jury returned a verdict that Moyle had been "accidentally killed by being precipitated a depth of ten fathoms, in conseqence of an explosion of powder."

Miners at Wheal Trenwith (Noall collection)

In addition to accidents definitely ascribed in published reports to the use of iron tamping bars, it seems highly probable that a large number of others listed simply as 'premature explosions' were due to the same cause. When there was no surviving witness, the facts could not with certainty be ascertained. On April 5 1821, as John Chenale was preparing a hole for blasting in Wheal Rock, near St. Agnes, the charge prematurely exploded, blowing him to atoms. A miner called Woolcock received a fatal chest injury by the premature bursting of a rock at Wheal Trenwith, St. Ives, in November 1828. Sometimes it happened that several persons were killed and injured in one of these accidents. On May 26 1840 John Polglaze and George Trenowth were killed and Benjamin Geary severely injured at the Charlestown Mines, St. Austell. A similar accident occurred at Wheal Pembroke, near Par, in December 1830. Three men, R. Barry, B. Warwick and J. Cook, were preparing a hole for blasting when a premature explosion killed the first two and broke the other's thigh. Two men tamping a hole at Wheal Fanny, Illogan, on April 22 1817 were so severely mangled when the charge went off that little hope was entertained of their recovery.

Miners sometimes died indirectly as the result of a powder explosion rather than from the effects of the blast itself. Take, for example, the sad

The little-known mine of Wheal Gorland, in Gwennap
(Courtesy Royal Institution of Cornwall)

case of James Berriman, who was killed at Wheal Unity mine, location unknown, during the late summer of 1823. A sudden explosion of gunpowder having blown out his light, he was proceeding to another part of the mine to obtain one when in the darkness he fell into a shaft and was drowned. Equally unfortunate were two young miners called Nicholas Grenfell and Henry Chappel who met their deaths at Wheal Owles, St. Just, on February 25 1842. After a hole had been blasted, they went back to their pitch to resume working, but were suffocated by the poisonous fumes which had not had sufficient time to clear.

A somewhat freakish accident at the Mutteral part of Wheal Gorland, in Gwennap during October 1835 resulted in the death of a tributer called Joseph Hichens. About one in the morning he and his comrade lit a train to blast a rock, and then went up on the stull which they believed to be a place of safety. The charge exploded, but a fragment of rock struck the stull, which collapsed. Hichens fell about fifteen feet, and received such serious head injuries that he died soon after. His companion escaped with minor abrasions.

Whilst on this theme of unusual gunpowder explosions, mention must be made of a very singular case of alleged murder, said to have been perpetrated at Crown Dale mine, near Tavistock, during blasting operations in 1804. It appears that three miners — James Matthews, his son-in-law John James, and Simon Pryor — were working together in a shaft about 22 fathoms deep. Pryor, who was employed by the other two as an assistant labourer, descended by windlass into this shaft one night and bored a hole for blasting, being afterwards drawn up again by Matthews. James then laid a match to the train and called out to his comrades to pull him up. Matthews and Pryor wound up about five fathoms of the rope, but then Matthews suddenly let go the windlass and told Pryor to do the same. Pryor, knowing well what the consequences must be to the man down below, refused; whereupon Matthews threatened to knock his brains out if he did not obey. Pryor again refused; and this time Matthews struck him on the right arm with a pick hilt, which made him quit his hold, and James was precipitated to the bottom, his skull being so dreadfully fractured that he died two days after. Whether his death was caused by the fall or by the explosion, or a combination of both is not stated. No explanation is given either for Matthews' strange conduct in this affair; one can only assume that his desire to kill his son-in-law was the result of a family quarrel.

Pryor subsequently related what had happened to his brother, who was a smith at the mine, and to a few other men; but they all agreed to conceal Matthews in a small room behind the smith's shop until a coroner's jury had returned a verdict of 'accidental death' on the murdered man. Pryor himself was induced to conceal the crime out of consideration for Matthews' large family. He did not see Matthews again until sixteen years later. Matthews was then living at St. Agnes and Pryor at Redruth; and when the two men accidentally met the latter felt so troubled in conscience for his part in concealing the crime that he at once made a deposition on oath before a county magistrate. As a result, Matthews was committed to Bodmin gaol in February 1821 to await his trial at Exeter during the next Assizes. This came on in March; when the Grand Jury threw out the bill against him, "the evidence not being entitled to sufficient credit."

The introduction of the safety fuse during the 1830's brought about a great improvement in working practices, since it gave the miner more accurate control over the timing of explosions, thereby enabling him to get well clear of the danger area before the blast took place. Regrettably, however, it did not eliminate such accidents altogether, since matters unconnected with the fuse itself could still go wrong and lead to fatal consequences. On November 22 1838 Richard Hosking lit a safety fuse in South Crofty mine, Roskear, and his comrades raised him by a rope to a plat high above the danger zone; but just as he placed his foot on it the board unfortunately slipped and precipitated him to the bottom of the winze close to the burning fuse. Escape was impossible, and the explosion took place almost immediately, the poor man being so much injured that he died three days after.

It requires no great exercise of the imagination to realise the horror a man must feel when trapped and unable to escape from the vicinity of a burning fuse. Most of those who have found themselves in such an awful situation have not lived to tell the tale; but one who did survive, and of whose experience a particularly graphic description has been preserved, was James Grenfell, of St. Just. In October 1838 he was engaged with his son, James Grenfell the younger, and another miner called Nicholas Bowen in cutting down the famous Crown engine shaft on the cliffs at Botallack mine. They had prepared two holes for blasting, and Bowen and the younger Grenfell retreated into a level about six fathoms above the stope, leaving Grenfell senior to light the fuses and follow them. Both fuses were ignited, and Grenfell ascended the ladder to join his comrades in their refuge; but just as he was about to step from it into the level the ladder gave way, and he fell into a place about seven feet below the burning fuses. The ladder having fallen into a sump, his retreat was completely cut off, and only a frightful death appeared to await him. By the dim light from the sputtering fuses he found the lift of pumps through which water was drawn from the sump, and grasping it with all his strength, awaited his fate. To use his own words, "I knowed I must be blow'd to pieces, but that wasn't hafe so dismal as to think about my wife and cheldurn." The first thundering explosion soon followed; and much to his own surprise, Grenfell found himself still alive and uninjured. But his ordeal was not yet over. Only one of the holes had gone off; and through the miserable gloom he saw fire spouting from the remaining fuse. The second blast followed; but, miraculously, he survived that also. Almost covered in attle, still clinging to the pump, deaf and speechless from the noise — he could scarcely believe himself alive.

His son afterwards described the incident to a *West Briton* reporter, who set it down in young Grenfell's own West Cornwall dialect:

> "When I heerd faethur screech, and he and the ladder fale away, I knowed 'twas all ovvur; he must, thoft I, be killed in one of these here three ways. — Ef he's gone to bottom, every lem es brock. — Ef ennything life lie es left, he must be drowned in the sump; and ef he shud be catch'd up by the stage where we belong" — *i.e.*, the stage on which they stood to work, and which they had just left — "the two holes must blow un into a thowsand pieces. — Oh, dear! Oh, dear! I faeld down pon my knees, and all that I cud pray was — Oh, Christ, save faethur. Nicky was standing up, and I said to un — oh, Nicky, pray for faethur. Nicky kneeled down, but he dedn't pray, I reckon, for when the holes went off, he said — 'He's out of pain or he's in the sump swemming.' My lighted candle was on my hatcap — I catch'd hould ov the lift, slidered away from flanch to flanch, and was down pon the stope like lightning. The place was full of smok, and not a lem nor nothing human cud be seed. At laest up agenst the lift I seed faethur's head and shoulders. The attle was to his brist, and hes face in a dismal shape; hes eyes were uppun, but he cudn't speak. — O, help me, Nicky, help me, doey, to clear away the traed from faethur. He's glazing, said Nicky, but he caen't be alive, you know; twud kill a thowsand cats ef they'd ben there. — Oh, clear away quicker! quicker! Nicky. Oh, my dear faethur! caen'ty speak, faethur?"

After several more appeals of this kind from the son, the father's lips at last quivered, and then words came, faint but distinct — "I believe I'm saved, Jimmy, and I baen't hurt much, I reckon." When Jimmy heard his father speak, he tore away with his hands at the attle, and eventually freed the trapped man, who was brought to surface 'deaf as a haddick,' but apart from that, and a few small cuts, none the worse for his amazing adventure.

Another wonderful escape occurred at East Lovell, roughly two miles east of Wendron, during the early morning of September 7 1832. John Wearne had been working in a winze adjoining the engine shaft 'last core by night' boring a hole for blasting, and having lit the safety fuse, was wound up some distance in a kibble by his son. However, as he was stepping from this into a ladder, his hand slipped, and he fell several feet into the shaft. As luck would have it, he landed on the fuse, accidentally knocking out the 'snoff' before the fire had travelled very far, and thus averted a calamity which must have proved fatal to him. However, he did not entirely avoid injury, for the fall had knocked him insensible, his head also being cut, shoulder bruised, and collar-bone broken. John

Treloar, who was working near rushed to his assistance, although quite unaware that the 'snoff' had been extinguished — such is the bravery of our Cornish miners — and with the help of others drew the injured man to surface.

Another courageous action was performed by an unnamed hero at South Crofty on November 1st 1862. With a miner called Hosking he was at work on a swing-stage stripping down the sides of a shaft; they had charged a hole with powder, and Hosking's comrade then ascended to the brace by a rope, leaving him to ignite the fuse and follow by the same means. Hosking succeeded in climbing a short distance, but then missed his hold and fell ten feet down the shaft. "His comrade then, with the praiseworthy and unprecendented intrepedity of a modern hero, descended instantaneously by the rope, and snatched the snuff from the fuse before it ignited." *(Cornish Telegraph.)* By this daring act Hosking was preserved from certain death, as in another moment the whole burden must have exploded around him. He had, however, been greatly injured by the fall about the head and limbs, and little hope was entertained of his ultimate recovery.

When two pares of men were rising and sinking towards each other underground, it was essential that the closest liason should be maintained between them when blasting, otherwise fatal consequences might ensue. On October 31 1857 William Skewes and Richard Edey were in the back of the 50 fathom level of Craddock Moor mine, in St. Cleer, preparing to hole through six feet of ground in conjunction with John Jiles and John Waddleton in a winze above. Waddleton went below to make arrangements for firing, when it was agreed that it should be done simultaneously on a signal being given by the party who were first ready. Those beneath gave the signal, and without answering it the other pare fired their hole. The consequences were fatal to Edey and Skewes, who were both struck on the head by rock fragments. Edey's head was nearly blown off and his comrade only survived a few hours. At the inquest, held in the Cornish Arms inn, St. Cleer, the jury, in returning a verdict of 'accidental death' on both victims, severely censured Waddelton, to whom great blame was attached for not adhering to the agreed blasting procedure. One cannot help wondering, however, whether the pare in the 50 had in some way misunderstood the signalling arrangements, but as neither survived, their testimony on this vital point is not available.

Fooldhardy conduct by miners when engaged in blasting operations was sometimes the cause of serious accidents. On March 1 1842 Samuel Prisk, aged 38, with a comrade, was firing a hole in the Consolidated Mines, Gwennap. Prisk having lit the fuse, his companion retired for safety into a pit four feet deep situated about 25 fathoms distant from the hole. Prisk himself then retreated to the edge of the same pit, but instead of getting into it, stood outside, as he had done on previous occasions without injury. He had been there about a minute, and had just remarked to his comrade that he feared the fuse had missed, when the charge exploded, and a flying stone hit him on the head, fracturing his skull and knocking him into the pit. He died on the following day from the effects of the blow.

Panic or confusion among the men could have equally fatal consequences at such times. At Providence and Trelyon United, near St. Ives, John Ellis and James King were charging holes in the lower part of the mine at about 1.30 p.m. on April 9 1878, King being about three feet above Ellis, whilst a third miner called Hall, who was helping, stood just a little behind. Everything was ready for blasting, and each man supplied a candle to the end of the safety fuses. King had been told by Ellis that Hall was going to fire at the same time as they did, and replied "All right." King's fuse ignited a little earlier than he intended, however; and being frightened and confused, instead of descending and running out through the level, as he should have done, ran into the place where Hall's hole was exploding. After the blast, King was found lying on his back, his head resting on his shoulder; a little blood flowed from his mouth, and there was a cut on his chin. He was groaning, but could not speak. The unfortunate man died whilst being brought to surface. It was believed death had been occasioned by a shock to the system.

Providence Mines, circa 1880 (Noall collection)

In an earlier chapter an instance was cited of rocks exploding underground through the bursting of air pockets trapped behind them. Another remarkable example of this occurred on July 2 1874 at Carn Brea mine. James Richards and James Davey were working in the 180 fathom level, where they shot a hole which went off quite satisfactorily. They then prepared to bore another hole; and had been down two minutes setting the borers ready, but had not actually commenced drilling nor used any powder, when the ground on which Richards stood flew all about the two miners. The previous hole had thoroughly heaved its burden, whilst no others had been bored in that place, the ground being perfectly solid. Davey, who was standing about three feet away from Richards, received no injury, but as the ground commenced cracking he feared for his life, and ran up the ladder as fast as possible. Thoroughly frightened, he stayed in the upper level for ten minutes, but recovering himself, went back to his comrade, and found that several men were already with him. Richards — a lad of nineteen — had been badly cut about the abdomen; they got him speedily to surface, but he died soon after. One of the miners who went to his assistance had been working about nine fathoms off when the accident occurred; he heard the ground burst, but it was not like an ordinary explosion, as it cracked several times. Another witness stated that he had often known ground to burst up in this way, more often after than before a hole had been fired.

Gunpowder accidents sometimes occurred 'at grass.' On Dolcoath it was the practice to stock powder in barrels in a powder house from where it was served out on Monday mornings to the various 'pares' of miners who stored it in their chests or lockers, of which there could be as many as forty in one room. On August 30 1865 William Bryant asked his 13 year old son John to collect 15 lbs. of powder from the powder house and deposit it in his chest, giving him the key to this chest for the purpose. Between nine and ten that morning John invited another 13 year old lad, Benjamin Rogers, of Camborne, to go with him to the Wheal Harriet section of the mine; he was then walking towards the building where the miners kept their chests with a large powder can on his back, and said he intended to put off some powder. Rogers refused to go with him, and half-an-hour later heard an explosion. The blast was also heard by Francis Osborn, a surface worker, who ran to the locker house where it had occurred, and on looking through the open door saw a boot and a piece of a leg. He went in and found John Bryant with one leg in part of a chest and the other outside. He carried out the boy, who was still breathing but died soon after. A part of the roof of the house, which consisted entirely of timber, had been blown away, and the rest was on fire. At least twenty chests had blown up, and there were further explosions later. At the inquest, William Bryant said he had never seen his son meddle — *i.e.*, play about — with powder; John had taken out powder for him the previous week. He had seen powder spilt in the locker house when powder was taken from the larger cans to be put into the smaller ones for use. Near the door of the house were several large stones, whilst John had hob nails in his high boots. From the evidence given it is difficult to tell whether this was a true accident, caused by ignition of spilt powder on the floor, or by John's 'meddling' with the dangerous substance; for children working on the mines were sometimes known to put off small amounts of powder for the pleasure of listening to the noise. (see page 171). The jury returned a non-committal verdict to the effect that "the deceased was killed by an explosion of gunpowder."

During the 1860's the Swedish chemist Arthur Nobel, founder of the Nobel prizes for physics, chemistry, medicine, literature and peace, invented a new explosive, dynamite, which proved extremely suitable for use in mining. Its active ingredient was the highly explosive liquid nitroglycerine (75 per cent) rendered safe and convenient to handle by a mixture with Kieselguhr (25 per cent), a siliceous diatomaceous earth which served as an absorbent base. In subseqent years dynamite was largely replaced by gelatin-dynamite, in which gun-cotton took the place of Kieselguhr, and by other even more sophisticated explosives. High explosives require a different technique in use from gunpowder, as they are not readily detonated by a flame, and a small percussion cap or detonater has to be secured to the end of the safety fuse and buried inside the explosive cartridge. The cap originally contained a mixture of fulminate of mercury and potassium chlorate, but other chemicals are now used.

Properly handled and used, dynamite is an extremely safe explosive; but, inevitably, accidents did occur. What may have been the first fatal casualty caused by dynamite in Cornwall took place at Dolcoath mine on August 15 1872. Dynamite had been introduced into the mine about eight months earlier; but it appears that none of the agents gave the miners any instructions regarding its use, and they had to find out themselves how it should be employed. On the day in question a lad named Joseph Trythall was working with two other men in the 278 fathom level on tutwork, whilst his brother John was with others in a nearby stope. Just after midday William Henry Eustice, Joseph's comrade, came and told John that a hole had gone off and hurt his brother, and that he needed a light. John went immediately with one and found Joseph in the end with his head between his legs. He appeared much injured about the face and head, and a large pool of blood lay on the ground. He was brought out alive, but died two days later. At the inquest — opened on the 19th and adjourned to the 24th — Eustice said he had been working in Dolcoath on tutwork for the past seven months. At the last setting day Joseph

Trythall, Samuel Roberts and himself took a bargain in the 278. On the 15th they went down in the forenoon core to bore a hole in this level. Ten days before, Trythall, a man called Edwin Rule and himself had bored a 2 feet hole there, which they charged with gunpowder and fired, but it tore only to a depth of eighteen inches. The same day they put in dynamite on the remaining six inches, and, not having the usual percussion cap, covered it with a small quantity of gunpowder, into which they inserted the safety fuse and a little fine tamping, which Eustice pressed down with his finger. The fuse burnt, but the charge failed to explode. In that state the hole was left until the day of the accident, but then it was decided to bore a fresh hole about six inches south of the old one. However, when they reached a depth of about eight inches the old hole exploded. They were using a steel borer, but Eustice thought no fire had been struck, as the hole was wet. Eustice was holding the borer, with Trythal and Roberts striking. The explosion destroyed all the new hole and all save the back of the old one. Trythall received severe head injuries, while Eustice was hurt in the leg, hand and face. Eustice was at a loss to explain the accident. He had been blasting holes with dynamite for the previous four or five months and believed he had used it correctly on this occasion. Captain Stephen Williams, agent for the sale of dynamite, gave evidence to prove how safe dynamite was. He stated that a case of the explosives had been thrown from a height of 130 feet, but although the box itself broke in fragments, the dynamite did not go off.

The coroner described dynamite as "a preparation of nitro-glycerine and powdered silica, in the proportion of 75% of the former to 25% of the latter; in this form, the nitro-glycerine was no longer dangerous, and the material might be handled freely; it would not explode by fire alone, nor when accidentally subjected to percussion; its explosion was produced by a percussion cap, which acted by percussion and fire — the combination of the two producing the effect, neither alone being effective."

The jury returned the following verdict in this historic case: "That the said Joseph Trythall, on the 15th day of August being engaged, with other persons, in a certain mine called Dolcoath mine, boring a hole for blasting purposes, it so happen that another hole which had been bored and charged near the same place several days before, but had misfired when attempted to be put off, suddenly and unexpectedly exploded, by means whereof the said Joseph Trythall's skull was fractured, and other serious injuries were sustained from which fracture and other injuries he lingered and languished until the 17th day of August instant, when from these causes he died; but how or by what means the said hole exploded there is no evidence to show."

The element of mystery attending this first Cornish dynamite accident could not be explained until some years later, when further experience with the explosive led to a better understanding of its peculiar qualities. In the meantime, other men had to die because of the general ignorance on this subject. Two of these accidents occurred at Botallack; and as a result of the second of them a theory was evolved to account of the inexplicable way in which this supposedly 'safe' explosive sometimes behaved so strangely out of character. In the first accident, which occurred around 1874, a miner blasted a hole with powder. The effects proving unsatisfactory, the same hole was charged with dynamite. This did not explode. The man drew the charge and began to drill another hole near the unsuccessful one. There was a sudden explosion which broke one of the legs and tore away part of the foot of the other; he died later from his fearful injuries. The second accident took place on May 16 1877. During the morning, Thomas Bone, 35, and Peter Henry Wearne were working about twenty fathoms from the bottom of Durlo shaft in the eastern part of Higher Botallack. They had blasted a hole with powder the day before, but the explosion only caused a crack in the ground, 'refusing to heave its burden,' so that they tried a charge of dynamite. This did not go off, and they condemned the percussion cap as defective. The dynamite was taken out, a fresh cap affixed, and the charge replaced in its hole. The cap now exploded, but not the dynamite. The hole was cleaned out with a swabbing stick, and they began to drill a new hole in the same burden. Bone was stooping down, his back towards the country, and turning the borer between his legs. Wearne was striking the borer, standing a little in front and at Bone's side. In an instant there was an explosion which shot Bone forward several feet into the level. Wearne was 'peppered' in the face by small stones, but Bone received terrible injuries to the lower part of his body. So great was the pain that he could not stand, and an improvised stretcher of planks was made to convey him to surface. Securely strapped with his face to the longest plank he was hauled 300 feet up the shaft, and from there removed to old Boscean account house, where he lay in a critical condition. It was presumed that nitro-glycerine had been washed out of the dynamite in the first hole, which then ran into the crevices caused by the first imperfect powder explosion, and was ignited by concussion in boring the second hole. The miners alleged that it had frequently happened that nitro-glycerine had washed out from dynamite charges and made pools of water impregnated with the dangerous liquid; on throwing a stone into this water the pools would explode. It will be remembered that water was present in the hole which unexpectedly exploded at Dolcoath in 1872; indeed, the circumstances attending all three accidents were remarkably similar, and indicated the same common cause.

A somewhat similar accident to these took place at Crenver and Abraham mine in Crowan on June 10 1873, though the cause in this case appears to have been somewhat different. William and James Pope, brothers, were working in the 135 fathom level preparing a hole for blasting. They put some dynamite in the hole, lit the fuse and retired; but finding it had not exploded, William Pope went back at the end of half-an-hour and pulled the charge out by the fuse. James was not present when this was done, but his brother told him it had come out whole. The hole was then charged a second time, but again missed fire. This charge was removed in the same way, but it did not come out whole. As their supply of caps had run out, no more dynamite was tried, but they made an effort to bore the hole larger. As soon as the borer touched the bottom there was an explosion, and both men were struck in the eyes with gravel. William Pope's right arm was also burnt, and he told his brother he had been "struck in the bowels." Both men then ascended to surface, where William walked unassisted to the dry and changed his clothes. While here, he told another miner that the hole had exploded when he was cutting it down, despite his having swabbed it out two or three times before using the borer. This miner then accompanied him to his home where he died soon after from injuries to the bladder. Captain Paull, an agent of the mine, saw the injured man on the evening of the accident, when he explained that he had been cutting down the hole to insert a powder bag — a substitute for the dynamite which they could not use owing to the lack of caps. He thought the borer had flown out and struck him sideways. Next morning Captain Paull found the borer still jammmed in the hole. It was thereupon concluded that the dynamite must have 'smuttered' away, some of it getting into the crevices around the hole, and so causing the explosion. Captain Paull thought it would not be safe, judging from what had happened in this instance, to use a steel borer in a hole where dynamite had previously been inserted. James Pope told the Government Inspector who enquired into the case that he had not squeezed the cap on the end of the rod, nor had they used any tamping. He added: "If I had found the hole misfire twice, and I had swabbed it out three or four times afterwards, I should not have been afraid to have bored it as he did, but it will be a lesson to me in future."

Following a blast, the concentration of dynamite fumes in unventilated workings could prove just as deadly as those of gunpowder. On the evening of September 9 1892 Thomas Whear and James Parsons went into the rise at the 240 level at East Pool to blast four holes. They had previously fired eight holes in this rise and waited three-quarters of an hour for the smoke to clear. On entering, they still found a lot of smoke there, and retreated sixty fathoms to the cross-cut, waiting another half hour. When this had expired, they went into the rise again; there was then no smoke, only a little smell. Whilst charging the four holes Parsons became giddy, but Whear did not complain. Whear was handing up the 'primers' from below. Eventually both men lost consciousness. A trammer working with them later went in and found Parsons still breathing, but Whear was not. After some delay caused by a broken knocker line, both men were brought to surface. Parsons was found to be suffering from acute ashma caused by inhaling noxious fumes, whilst Whear appeared to have died from the same cause.

Though still in a very weak state, Parsons was able to give evidence at the inquest on his comrade. He stated there was a $2\frac{1}{2}''$ pipe at the bottom of the rise to admit fresh air from the compressor for the boring machine and to ventilate the level. It was regulated by a tap. The pipe was not closed off after the machine had finished work, but a plug, with a hole in it, inserted in the end. Whear had inserted the plug and turned on the air, but the end of the pipe was later found to be partially buried in stuff blasted down by the earlier explosions. They cleared this before going out again to the cross-cut. One of the rescuers, a man called Trevillion, stated, however, that when he went into the level the air was turned off. The inquest was remarkable for the strange conduct displayed by the foreman of the jury. He demanded, and secured, the withdrawal of Captain Penhale, one of the agents, on the grounds that his presence would 'intimidate' Parsons. Soon after this, he rose to his feet, and pointing his forefinger at Parsons, exclaimed "There's not enough ventilation in that rise, and you know it, and you ought to complain!" This produced protests from some of the jurymen, one of them saying that the foreman should have more consideration for Parson's weak state. Unabashed by this remonstrance, the foreman turned his attention next to the doctor: "Now, sir, on your honour as a gentleman, do you mean to say that all the nutrition is in the air, after it has been squeezed in that pipe?" Dr. Tabor: "It remains in the compressed air, and on expanding resumes its normal condition." The Foreman: "Then I beg to differ from you, sir!" (Laughter.) He also crossed swords with the Government Inspector on the ventilation question, and was rebuked for his attitude. A verdict of 'Accidentally suffocated' was returned after an exhaustive enquiry.

Another case of asphyxiation by dynamite fumes was attended by highly unusual circumstances. A young man called Joseph Rodda, who operated a boring machine in West Frances, one of the mines of the Basset group lying in the valley between Carnmenellis and Carn Brea, went underground at eleven o'clock at night on February 22 1881 to begin work in the 132 fathom level where the afternoon core had blasted some hours earlier. Reaching the level with his comrade, he went into the end, passing a locker which contained a supply of dynamite. His comrade, who was behind him, saw fire issuing from the box, and shouted to him to return, at the same time running himself for safety. Before Rodda could escape, however, an explosion took place, which killed him — not by injuries from the blast but, rather strangely, through suffocation by the fumes.

As time went by, dynamite was supplemented by other new explosive agents, some possessing the virtue of being smokeless. Gelatine, for example, acquired considerable popularity; but its use led to one of the most tragic, and mysterious, blasting accidents known in Cornwall. This took place on August 13 1920 in Levant mine, which only the previous year had suffered the appalling man-engine disaster. Four trammers went down to the 190 fathom level west of Skip shaft, to tram stuff from the previous shift's blasting to the shaft. They were sitting down in a corner, one of them being near a tin in which miners kept a stock of gelatine. As they were talking, there was a sound as if something had dropped on the tin. The explosion followed immediately after. One of the four was killed outright, but the other three — who included two brothers — were still alive when rescue parties reached the scene. Some of the latter had come from their workplaces half-a-mile away on hearing the blast. The injured men were got to surface, but two died on the way up, and the last — the elder of the two brothers — soon after at Penzance Infirmary. The three dead comrades were laid side by side in the same building, below the account house, which had been used as a mortuary in the previous contingency. The accident could not be satisfactorily explained. The manager believed that one of the men had taken the tin to see what it contained, but could not say how it exploded. About another fifty sticks were exploded by the intense heat as they fell out of other tins broken by the concussion.

Powder Mill Safety Fuse Works and Dynamite Factory Explosions

Whilst Cornish miners were being killed and maimed underground by gunpowder explosions, some of their womenfolk ran equally grave risks in factories established in various parts of the county for the production of this dangerous commodity. Indeed, the making of gunpowder — and, at later periods, of safety fuse and dynamite — became quite an important auxiliary industry, so great was the demand from the mines; but, despite all precautions, a severe toll of life was exacted from those engaged in it. A celebrated gunpowder works was established at Cosawes Wood, near Penryn, in the early years of the nineteenth century. Soon after — to be precise, on July 31 1809 — a serious accident occurred there, forerunner of a number of others. One of the carpenters had been instructed to make a small alteration to the machine that worked the sieves, and the man in charge of the sieve house made preparations to remove all the powder then under process, as a precaution, but was prevailed on to let it remain on being assured by the carpenter that only a wooden mallet would be used. Soon after, however, the neighbourhood was alarmed by an explosion; and the manager, on going to investigate, found that the carpenter and the other workman, with two women, had been blown about twenty yards from the ruined house. The workmen and one woman survived only a few hours; the other woman languished until the following morning, when she too died. Another man and a girl, who were working in an adjoining building, escaped unhurt, though they were only a few yards from the seat of the explosion. The other buildings and mills, being all sited in a valley, and about fifty yards distant from each other, with banks of earth between, received no damage. Whether the accident was caused by the carpenter using his axe, which was afterwards found in a field of oats at a short distance, or by a tobacco pipe concealed in his pockets, could not be ascertained; but from his confession, made before he died, it was supposed from the latter. When the Cosawes Wood powder mill, then owned by Mr. Gill, blew up again on August 23 1813, the results were less serious; no lives were lost and only one man was slightly scorched.

Another powder mill explosion took place near Ponsanooth just after midday on February 17 1826. In this case, the mixing house, where the ingredients were compounded, was blown up; and of the four persons working there, one man and one woman each received fatal injuries, whilst two other men escaped almost unharmed. Although at that period it was often found difficult to account for accidents in powder mills, this one was attributed by the *Royal Cornwall Gazette* to an old woman who had been roasting potatoes some distance from the works unknowingly bringing a spark into the mill on her clothes. This was seen almost immediately on her entrance, but before it could be extinguished, it fell, and the explosion instantly followed, no doubt from the ignition of powder dust lying on the floor.

One of the largest powder mills in Cornwall was situated in Kennal Vale, near Ponsanooth. It remained in production for a great many years, and the following description was published in the *Cornish Telegraph* during 1887, by which time the works had probably been developed to their fullest extent:

> "Kennal Vale itself, one of the loveliest spots in Cornwall, is very little known. It lies between Perranwell and Penryn and extends from Devoran to a little above the village of Ponsanooth, a distance of about five miles. The most picturesque portion of the vale is in the possession of the Gunpowder Company, and is, of course, rigorously closed against the public. The fame of the valley, however, is so great that the proprietors receive numerous applications for permission to view it, all of which are firmly but courteously refused. The road from Ponsanooth to the factory is extremely pretty, and before reaching the works the magazine and the saltpetre refining house are seen on the right. Just inside the saltpetre house is the manager's house, beautifully situated, and a little beyond are the Company's offices. These buildings extend practically across the valley, which at this point is narrow, and mark the point beyond which the public cannot go. A good idea, however, of the beauty of the valley is obtained. The portion in the possession of the Gunpowder Company is about a mile in length, and it increases rapidly in steepness towards the head. Down the vale rushes a fine stream of water, and its power is utilised in driving all the machinery of the factory by means of water wheels, of which there are a large number...Looking on the beauty of the machinery and the singular peacefulness of the spot, it does seem incongruous that such a death-dealing agent should be manufactured there."

The peace of Kennal Vale was on several occasions shattered by explosions at these works. One such occurred on February 16 1839; but although the report was heard for many miles round, no lives were lost. Two men were killed in another mishap during the following year; whilst a few weeks afterwards (on January 8 1841) another mill in this valley exploded at seven in the morning with a most tremendous concussion, a large quantity of powder being stored in it at a time. The only man there was decapitated, his head being blown to a considerable distance, whilst other parts of his body were found among the branches of a tree. Another man living nearby escaped with trivial injury, but several trees were uprooted by the blast. The cause of the disaster was not known.

A tremendous explosion rocked the Kennal Vale mills, then owned by Messrs. Sampson and Lanyon, in January 1847. The blast occurred in the stamping mill, a new building, which was blown to atoms, except for part of a wall, a small piece of which was left standing. Two men, named Martin and Dunstan, working in the mill, died in the accident. Stated a contemporary newspaper: "A number of persons, on hearing the report, congregated around the spot from the neighbouring village of Ponsanooth, and great was the lamentation among them, it not being known what family had been bereaved of its members." The bodies of the two workmen were, however, soon found in a dreadfully mangled condition. Part of Dunstan's body was blown into the water; his arms and one of his legs were torn off, his face frightfully disfigured, and the whole remains in such a mangled state that they had to be taken up in a cloth. Martin's body also presented a shocking appearance, the skull being entirely blown off. Both men were married, but left no children; a brother of Martin had perished in the last explosion at the mill. The victims were interred in Stithians churchyard two days later when "a vast concourse of deeply affected persons followed their remains to the grave."

Shortly before eight in the morning of November 7 1887 the people in the neighbourhood of Penryn were startled by a tremendous explosion, whilst at Camborne, where it was also heard, the inhabitants attributed it to gunfire from the fleet practising along the north coast. The blast had, in fact, originated in a building at Kennal Vale, where boxes of powder were placed two at a time in a press worked by a water wheel. Henry Thomas went into the press house that morning to change boxes on the press, which was being operated by William Dunstan, the only other man there. Ten minutes after he had left the building was completely wrecked by the explosion. Dunstan was killed; whilst another man who had apparently been working nearby was found lying injured in a leat. The dead man had been wearing the mill clothes supplied by the company — made of white woollen — and slippers. Thomas was similarly attired, and all the normal safety precautions appear to have been observed. The press had also been recently overhauled, and was working perfectly. However, from evidence given at the inquest, the cause of the accident could be deduced with a fair degree of certainty. After the two boxes had been placed on the press by the two men, the operator would put on the top block, and start the press by moving the handle connected with the water wheel. This handle was situated inside the house. After working the press up, the cock would be turned on which let the ram down, the boxes subsequently being taken off the press and placed on the raised platform in front. The assistant helped to load the press again, after which he went away. The pressman would then open the compressed boxes of mill cake with a wooden mallet, and their contents would be placed in barrels. It took about half-an-hour to make one press of powder. The pressman would have to steady the boxes until the press took its bearings, which would take about a minute, and from then until the full pressure was applied thirty minutes was required. From this, it could be inferred that when the explosion occurred, one lot of powder was in course of being pressed, whilst the first set of boxes was being opened by the pressman. The wheel-ruts made by carts coming and going to the house and the platform from which they were loaded were always kept damp; but it was believed that on this occasion the barrels of powder, instead of being lifted bodily into the cart were dragged over the floor, and that the friction thus created caused the explosion. This was the first accident which had occurred at Kennal Vale for twenty-eight years, when two persons were killed within a month of each other.

One of the most dreadful of all Cornish powder mill explosions was that which took place at the safety fuse and powder works of Messrs. Davey, Brothers & Co., at Nancekuke, Illogan, on September 9th 1862. The works were situated on the hill about half-a-mile west of Porth Towan, the blast originating in the drying house. A description of the process of manufacture, given at the time by Mr. Thomas Davey the principal owner, is interesting and worth quoting:

> The drying house contains at one end steam kettles in which the saltpetre was put for solution with water. When dissolved, necesary quantities of sulphur and starchy matter were added, and the whole mixed by means of a stirring apparatus. The mixture would then be in a state of wet paste, and this was placed on a perforated brass plate over which brass rollers revolved, to press the paste through the holes of the plate, and thus it was made to form grains or strings, which fell on an endless canvas, which conveyed the granular powder into the drying room, which formed a continuation of the building. The powder was thus conducted to the extreme end of the drying house and fell off the moving canvas on to canvas frames, and was distributed by persons employed in different parts of the room for the purpose of drying. The temperature of the powder in the wet state would not exceed 100 degs., the temperature of the room being only about 70 degs. The powder while being dried was placed on frames near steam pipes heated with exhausted steam from the engine. The time required for the drying process varied from 24 to 48 hours according to the state of the atmosphere.

At 11.30 a.m. that fateful morning Mr. Tonkin, the foreman, and Mr. Morcom, the accountant, passed through the drying house, where everything appeared in order, and had just reached the sifting house, some distance from the dry, when the latter blew up and almost instantly exploded the sifting house. Tonkin immediately ran into a room where materials were weighed and shut the door; but the door, roof and window were blown away, and he escaped through the fire by clambering out of the window with his face and hands burnt but otherwise not seriously hurt. Morcom ran into the open air amidst falling debris, but was uninjured.

All the dry powder had just been removed from the drying house which contained only about 15 cwt. of wet powder. The dry, mill house and sifting house were completely destroyed by the explosion, but the engine house, boiler house and machinery remained comparatively uninjured. 'The Works,' according to the *Cornish Telegraph*,

> "presented striking and most melancholy evidence of the tremendous force of the destructive material which has occasioned this catastrophe. The drying house, charcoal mill and the house where the powder was broken after being dried were a mass of blackened ruins, a great portion of the walls, which were of considerable thickness, being blown down and all the woodwork charred and much burnt. The roofs of the buildings had been blown off, evidently with tremendous force, the debris being scattered to a considerable distance around."

Four women were killed instantly by the blast and two others died later of their burns. The names of the victims were:

Betsey Haughton, 50, a widow with three sons.
Harriet Johns, 28.
Mary Johns, 31, sister of the above.
Hannah Reynolds, 16.
Elizabeth Thomas, 16.
Mary Andrews, 20.

At the inquest, the jury, according to the custom of the time, viewed the bodies, and found them "all burnt, blackened and swollen in such a manner as to be utterly unrecognisable, especially the four last" — those who had been instantly killed.

Giving evidence, Thomas Davey stated that the dry powder required a temperature of 800 degs. to ignite, whilst a much higher temperature would be required to ignite it in the wet state. He believed it was the wet powder which had exploded, and put forward the view that the accident might have been caused by a lightning flash entering through an open window:

> "The weather at the time was close and sultry, and I was told there was a slight shower of rain and a flash of lightning... I do not think that any of the unfortunate victims could have caused the explosion unless they had purposely set fire to the powder with a match, but all of them were remarkably well behaved and steady."

Had the calamity indeed been occasioned by lightning, as seems probable, it must be classed as one of the most bizarre of its kind on record. The jury, however, declined to theorise on this interesting point, and returned a simple verdict of 'accidental death.' It was mentioned that there had been an explosion at the works three months previously, when a woman entered the boiler house, contrary to orders, there setting her clothes on fire and in her fright igniting something which communicated with the dry and caused the blast, but no one was injured on that occasion.

Another important group of powder mills was situated at Herodsfoot, about five miles south-west of Liskeard. Known as the East Cornwall Gunpowder Works, these were the scene of a disastrous explosion at 9.15 p.m. on April 26 1850. Its effects were plainly felt at Liskeard; whilst sightseers were 'afforded a grand but an awful evidence of the tremendous power of gunpowder,'' and ''found a spectacle of devastation and wreck such as (those) who have not visited the spot will be totally unable to conjure up in their imagination. Large buildings were not only levelled to the ground, but every stone and every vestige of their foundations removed to a distance of many yards. Large trees were not only torn up and broken in pieces, but every fibre of their composition *brackled into fringe*.'' (*West Briton*.) The destroyed buildings comprised a drying house, sizing house, and a graining and glossing mill. Other mills and buildings at a considerable distance were shattered and unroofed, and doors and windows in every part of the valley exposed to the blast, destroyed and unhinged.

A few minutes before the disaster, the manager's son, Mr. Lobb, had parted from Joseph Pengelly and Samuel Truscott, who were then going on their nightly round of inspection with a lantern. Both these young men were killed in the disaster; and from the position in which some of Truscott's remains were found, it appeared that the explosion commenced in the drying house. This was a large building surrounded by rows of steam pipes heated by a boiler in a nearby house. This dry had contained 37 cwt. of powder in a partially dry state. About twenty yards distant stood the sizing house, where the gunpowder was sized, or divided into grains of different sizes by sifting; here were stored about two tons of undried and unsized powder. Fifteen yards from it lay another building which housed two machines for polishing and corning the powder; Pengelly's body, in mangled fragments, was found between these premises. Besides its valuable machinery, the polishing mill held about 13 cwt. of powder; and all these three buildings were totally destroyed. The pressing house, which contained a considerable quantity of mill cake, fortunately escaped with minor damage. Above these buildings were the pulverising mills holding a small quantity of powder which did not ignite. Higher still, in a commanding situation, stood the manager's house, which suffered considerable blast damage; the manager himself, who was in bed in one of the front rooms, received severe facial injuries from flying glass. Some distance above his house was a magazine containing over forty tons of powder in a finished state, packed and awaiting shipment; the door was blown in; but as it lay at least two hundred yards from the scene of the explosion, was somewhat sheltered from the direct blast, it sustained no other damage. Even without the addition of this large magazine, the shock produced was a tremendous one. At Lostwithiel, eight or nine miles distant, the effect was like an earthquake.

The Herodsfoot works were the scene of a number of other gunpowder accidents. In February 1857 a workman called Truscott placed some powder under the granite roller, resembling an apple pound, for grinding. It was customary to allow the roller to perform a few revolutions before the operator approached it, but Truscott neglected to observe this precaution, and when the powder exploded he was dreadfully scorched. Enveloped in smoke, he ran into a ditch, but died of his injuries soon after, leaving a wife and nine children to deplore his untimely end.

Seven months later (September 25th 1857) Samuel Hoar and three other men were killed by an explosion in the breaking house. At the inquest, which was attended by some of the proprietors of the mills, a lengthy investigation failed to ascertain the cause of the disaster, but the jury gave it as their opinion that "more powder was in the breaking house than was necessary for keeping the various Mills in regular working, to the danger of the men in the breaking house, as well as the other men on the Works, and to the inhabitants around."

In December 1866 a man called Veale was filling wooden boxes with powder in the press house to take the place of those already in the press when an explosion took place at the press. Veale, described as a steady and industrious workman, was badly injured by the blast, and died twelve hours later.

The grim catalogue of disasters continued. In May 1876 three men were killed and almost every building destroyed; whilst on October 14 of the same year two more workmen lost their lives. These men, called Roskelly and Stephens, were employed in the house used for breaking up the powder. As a safety measure, the Company had abandoned the old method of breaking it by hand, and substituted grooved rollers. However, during the process of breaking, the grooves became choked, and it was necessary periodically to clear them. The two men were doing this, using a copper chisel, when the explosion occurred. It blew the roof off the building and inflicted such frightful injuries on them that they died soon after.

The St. Allen Blasting Powder Company's works, situated in Bishop's Wood, about four miles from Truro, acquired a very bad reputation for accidents in the 1860's. On April 14 1864 two young women called Grose and Reynolds were killed; on February 5 1866 two men, Sweet and Thomas, received fatal injuries; and on October 16 1866 a young man named Rouse was badly hurt and lost the sight of one eye. The most spectacular of these blasts, however, took place on November 26 1868.

Between three and four that afternoon the residents of Truro and surrounding districts were startled by three loud detonations in quick succession, followed by two others of lesser intensity. Windows rattled, doors closed, and articles of furniture were moved, whilst the inhabitants rushed into the streets, thinking there had been an earthquake. However, from elevated vantage points a vast column of smoke was seen to be rising from the site of the St. Allen works, which indicated the true cause. A great many people at once hastened to the scene to render what help they could. However, their services were not required, as no casualties whatever had occurred among the employees.

The operations were carried on in a number of buildings well separated from each other. These were of wood, with stone ends, except the engine house, magazine, stables and office. The explosion had originated in the sulphur grinding house by, it was believed, the presence of a piece of iron among the sulphur being ground. The burning sulphur ignited the woodwork, and despite the efforts of the workmen the flames quickly spread to the adjoining saltpetre and sulphur stores. The trees overhead also caught fire, and the burning embers were carried some distance by the wind. Realising that all efforts to contain the fire would now be ineffectual, the men sought places of safety; and it was well that they did so; for scarcely had two minutes elapsed when, in quick succession, three charge houses, each containing about five hundredweight of powder, the dry-house and packing house exploded. All were completely destroyed, not a vestige remaining of the packing house. The stables, office, cooperage and engine-house were much shaken and partly unroofed. Trees were uprooted and large branches torn off by the blast. A large iron water wheel near the sulphur house was blown out of its bearings and broke to pieces.

The invention of the safety fuse proved a great boon to the Cornish miner, but the manufacture of this product proved a dangerous occupation. One of the worst fuse factory accidents took place at Tuckingmill on April 29 1872. The factory involved was that of Messrs. Bickford, Smith & Co., and employed about a hundred young women and girls, for whom the work of spinning the thread which encircled a small quantity of gunpowder was well adapted. Major Bickford and Mr. Smith had given years of thought and attention to safety measures at the works, and as a result no serious accident had previously occurred there. However, the day preceding the disaster had been a Good Friday; and advantage was taken of the holiday to stop the engine which powered the machines so that its boilers might be cleaned. When the women returned on Saturday they could not resume their usual work, and so were put to cleaning up their respective compartments and machinery. This meant the careful sweeping of every crevice and a general tidying up, so as to be ready to resume production on Monday. Half-work of this boring kind induced at least one of the girls to leave her own compartment and gossip with her neighbours — an infringement of the rules. There were about five of these rooms under one roof, consisting of a reeling mill on the ground floor and spinning mills on the first floor. In the latter, small quantities of gunpowder, finely ground, were run into machines and spun with threads to form a small coil. At the end of the day, all unused gunpowder was collected and returned to one of the overseers, who then stored it in an isolated magazine.

The spinning room contained eight pairs of spinning apparatus, and was well lighted by three windows on each side. The girls had ample room to move all round it, between the machinery and the walls, except in one corner, where the staircase head lessened this space. At the corner opposite had been temporarily placed twenty or thirty coils of manufactured fuse, each weighing about twenty pounds. These were to produce grim and fatal consequences when the accident took place. At that time, most of the girls were cleaning the machinery, but one or two stood in the corner farthest from the door, chatting. To go from here to the door, round one side of the room between the machinery and wall, they would have to pass the corner where the safety-fuse was stored. But there was a more direct way for those used to the place; for with the machine idle it was possible to stoop and thread one's way among the upright spindles to the door. The windows, too, could be opened out in a moment, for they swung by hinges at the top, enabling the ground to be reached by a jump of about ten or twelve feet.

Thus, in case of emergency, the factory was by no means a death-trap; but the various means of escape that existed were not used by the girls when the crisis came. This may have been the result of fear; but a much more likely explanation seems to have been the lack of any fire-drill or similar measures. So, the reporter of the *Cornish Telegraph* was able to write his horrifying description of "the poor girls, who one moment are recounting, with laugh and joke, the incidents of the Good Friday holiday, the next are a panic-stricken herd, and the next are senseless and dying."

The accident was ascribed to the dropping of a part of one machine, which struck a spark which ignited a small quantity of gunpowder dust in a crevice in the floor, and so led to the firing of a pile of safety-fuse. This suddenly blazed up; the upper floor filled with dense, choking smoke, and the stampede began. The girls nearest the door succeeded in escaping unharmed; but those who followed, being less nimble or not so well placed for gaining the exit, were burnt as they passed the fuse in the corner. In this way, about ten managed to get clear. Then, one girl fell — probably overcome by the fumes — followed by two or three others, their bodies blocking the escape route. One girl, retaining her senses, rushed over the prostrate forms of her companions, broke down the partition by the stairs, fell into the staircase and was saved, though seriously injured. Three or four others could not imitate her desperate leap for life, and collapsed. Altogether, eight young women perished — the cause of death in each case being suffocation.

The alarm being given, a hose was quickly fetched and a stream of water directed on the building. Previous to this, however, the repeated enquiry was made — are all the girls safe? The answer was — yes. Then someone discovered that a spinner was missing, but almost immediately she presented herself, and the other girls who had escaped said that all were safe. Some efforts were made to get into the room within two minutes of the outbreak being discovered, but the dense fumes made this impossible, and one man who tried to enter the first floor door staggered back and fell senseless. As smoke continued to pour out, the windows and roof were broken to give the water more effect. Nearly half-an-hour passed in this way, the fire-fighters having no idea there was anyone trapped inside. Then it was discovered that three young women were missing. Instantly the room was entered, and one after another of the pathetic heap of bodies lying there dragged out. Eight of them proved to be dead, but a ninth recovered after being given medical aid. The victims were:

> Mary Ellen Sims, a spinner, and Louisa Ann Sims, a reeler, her sister, both of Beacon.
> Emily Climo, a spinner, Camborne.
> Emily Carah, a reeler, Camborne.
> Eliza Ann Marks, a reeler, Camborne.
> Annie James, a reeler, Camborne.
> Ellen Goldsworthy, a spinner, Beacon Hill.
> Martha Towan, a reeler, Camborne.

Several girls were also injured, one of them, Fanny Bennetts, of Park Bracket, being in a serious condition.

When a hole was fired in a mine, using only a small quantity of black powder and fuse, the smoke generated was so pungent that some time was required for it to clear before anyone could work in that part again. The deadly atmosphere produced by the burning of a large quantity of fuse in a room measuring 27′ x 21′ x 15′ with the windows closed and no other outlet for the fumes but through a doorway and down a staircase, can readily be imagined. Everything in the room bore traces, not of fire, but of the densest smoke and fumes; the wonder was that any had escaped alive.

> ''In a lofty and spacious warehouse'' (wrote the *Telegraph*) ''the sides of which were lined with thousands of coils of a material which is known all over the world where mining, quarrying, and submarine blasting are known — lying on straw in three irregular rows, sister at the feet of sister

— were eight young women, swathed in homely, serviceable shrouds, and only the faces and hair uncovered for identification. — young women, who, but a short time before, Good Friday past and Easter festivities at hand were either singing merrily at their light toil or chatting and joking about the amusements in store. One minute brightness and hilarity! A sudden alarm! and, within the next sixty seconds, some of them dead to this world, and to all its joys or miseries. No sermon could preach as those upturned faces — some tranquil, and as if beaming with health and beauty, some distorted and disfigured — must have preached to the most unimpressible beholder."

At the inquest, Sarah Ann Cock stated that she was in the spinning room at the time of the accident, cleaning the machinery:

"In the morning Ellen Sims had unscrewed one of the arms." (This was forbidden by the rules.) "I saw her do it. As she was taking it off the machinery, it fell out of her hand on the floor on some powder dust. There was scarcely any powder dust on the floor, as I had assisted in brushing out the room myself on Thursday. A little powder dust might have remained on the outside of the machinery, and which might have been brushed down that morning. I saw this iron arm fall to the ground, and immediately an explosion took place."

Charles May described how he went to the head of the stairs and heard a groan. Rushing into the room and stooping very low, he found two girls, one lying across the other. There was then so much smoke that nothing could be seen. Neither of them was quite dead. One survived, but the other died in his arms shortly afterwards. Not a hair of either was singed. They were within four feet of the door.

The jury returned a verdict of 'accidentally suffocated by a fire caused by a piece of iron which accidentally fell from the hands of Ellen Sims, and which ignited some powder dust." They expressed a decided opinion that no blame was attributable to the proprietors of the works, who had done all they could to observe good regulations and ensure the safety and comfort of the people they employed. All this may have been true; but one would have thought the practice of allowing finished coils of fuse to be left lying about the spinning room a censurable matter. However, there is no doubt the factory had a good safety record, as during the previous forty years only three other deaths had occurred there.

An accident of a different character affected the safety fuse works of Messrs. Brunton & Co., at Pool, on April 10 1861. In this case, the premises were wrecked by an explosion the nature of which could not be explained. The walls of the fuse room were blown down, one of them being carried right across the high road that passed up to the railway. The roof was hurled into a garden, the western end of the building being left a complete wreck, whilst the blast shook the roofs of adjoining premises, breaking a large number of windows, and shattered the manager's dwelling house. Two girls and a man died in the explosion. Their bodies were placed in coarse sacks, which the coroner's jury were afterwards obliged to inspect.

> "On opening the mouth of the first of these was seen a fearful object, which was the remains of Ann Hancock; the skull was charred and black and all the flesh and skin of the face appeared to have burnt away. The other poor creature, Elizabeth Blight, was so black that nothing could be seen but her teeth which presented from their extreme whiteness a very striking appearance."

William Sleeman, the male victim, had been killed by the roof falling about him and his body showed no marks of fire.

The wrecked Penhallick Safety Fuse Works, which stood near the old Pool station of the West Cornwall Railway, was soon rebuilt and production resumed. In 1864 Messrs. Brunton decided to extend the factory, and purchased assitional property for that purpose; but on April 27 1865 another dreadful explosion occurred, resulting in the total destruction by fire of the new building and the death of two more young women. The manager was then Mr. P. A. Renfree, of Redruth, and the workforce comprised thirteen women and girls, two men and a boy. At the building's western end, on the first floor where the explosion took place, were the fuse, winding, varnishing, tape and machine rooms, besides a fitting up shop. The safety fuse was made of jute and flax threads, tape, gutta percha and gunpowder. During the manufacturing process a constant stream of powder ran through the tube at the end of which it was caught and wound about in the threads. Five girls were working in the winding room, which was separated from the fuse room by a wooden partition, the other six being in the rooms below. The foreman (Phillips) and his assistants, together with the boy, were in an outhouse placing fuse in tin boxes which were to be packed in casks for use abroad. At about 3.30 a slight report was heard, and the building was soon in flames. All the women and girls, except two, made their escape; but Elizabeth Vivian, 29, of Illogan, and Ellen Opie, 20, of Pool, who had been attending to the machines, were not so lucky. They were heard to shriek; and from the position in which their bodies were afterwards found it appeared they had tried to get out through the windows, but failing in the attempt were burnt to death. Two other girls received slight burns.

The fire attracted the attention of a large number of miners who at once rushed to the spot. The boiler was made safe and water brought from various places, but when the flames reached the lower floor 5,000 coils of fuse caught alight and the building was completely destroyed. When the bodies were dug out of the ruins they could not be identified except by measurement. The inquest failed to elicit any cause for the accident, but the jury, in returning the usual verdict of 'accidental death,' added a recommendation that in future the girls should change their shoes downstairs.

A disastrous explosion occurred at the Unity Fuse Works, near St. Day, on February 20 1875. This factory had been established in the neighbourhood many years before by Messrs. Hawke, but was later acquired by Sir. F. M. Williams, M.P., who modernised and improved it. At the time of the accident the place consisted of a group of buildings enclosed within a courtyard, the entrance to which was always kept locked. The chief buiding was the factory itself, attached to which was the boiler-house. The other edifices, of which the most important was the tarring shed, lay around the sides of the enclosure. To reduce the risk of grit being brought into the buildings, they were connected with each other by brick-laid pathways. The fireproof powder house stood outside the courtyard, but only a small quantity of powder was kept there, the magazine being fully half-a-mile distant.

The factory contained two floors, the ground floor being divided, like Caesar's Gaul, into three parts. The smallest section, adjoining the boiler house, housed the little engine by which the machinery was driven. At the other end was the store for manufactured fuse, its capacity being a ton and a half. The middle and largest section was used for the preparation of the fuse in its earlier stages. A flight of stairs, with a door at its head, led to the floor above, where the filling and finishing processes were carried out. This floor consisted of one large room containing a number of machines carefully boarded off to leave a clear passageway, whilst the windows and door were kept unfastened.

On the morning when the accident took place, Hamlyn, the foreman, with twelve women and girls, were engaged on their various tasks when the powder in the upper room, which did not exceed twenty-seven pounds in weight, suddenly exploded. There were at least three separate explosions as the powder in different parcels ignited. These not only shook the building to its foundations, but set it on fire, and in a moment it was filled with dense and suffocating smoke. Hamlyn fell unconscious with his right arm under the crank of the engine, by which it was severely injured. One of the girls, called Stephens, was hurled from one end of her compartment to the other; and the others were stunned. By the time they came to themselves the smoke made it almost impossible for them to find the door. One did so, and made her exit over the courtyard wall. Another was rescued by a man called Pooley, who rushed to the scene on hearing an explosion, and thought he was saving his own daughter. Others were brought out by Hamlyn, who quickly recovered his senses, and utterly disregarded his own injuries in attempting to save his companions.

Those on the upper floor were less fortunate. Hamlyn shouted to them to throw open the windows and jump. But the sad story of Tuckingmill was again repeated here. The only girl to be seen was Margaretta Long; and though she got to a window she appeared too bewildered to open it, and continued her ineffectual struggles until she was enveloped in flames and all but suffocated. In desperation she dashed her hands through the glass, cutting them badly, and leapt into the arms of Hamlyn who then, with others, helped to put out the flames in which she was still wrapped. Not only were her clothes nearly destroyed, but her hair was blazing.

Nothing could be seen of the other workers in the upper room, and the fire had now obtained such a hold that it proved impossible to rescue them. Efforts were accordingly directed to putting out the flames and rolling the barrels of safety fuse out of the store. Fears were entertained that the boiler might explode, but this danger was averted by a man called Whitford who pluckily attached a rope to the safety valve, which was then kept open. By early afternoon the fire had been extinguished, but nothing then remained of the building save four blackened and shattered walls. A search for the bodies was begun; and the sickening stench which pervaded the place afforded grim indications of the state in which these were likely to be found. When discovered they were merely blackened, shrivelled fragments of headless and limbless trunks. At first it was thought that these were the remains of only three persons; but further examination showed that what had been taken for part of one body was really portions of two.

The injuries and shock sustained by Margaretta Long in making her desperate leap from the burning building proved fatal, and she died the following day. Before then — though fearfully bruised, cut, burned and blinded — the eighteen year old girl was able to give a description of the scene in the room when the explosion ocurred. She herself was 'scoring' fuse, and a young girl called Pooley 'winding' to her. The room was instantly filled with smoke, and though she heard a few groans she saw nothing more of her other companions Mitchell, James and Davey. Pooley was struck down at her feet and lay there crying and helpless, whilst she herself entirely lost her presence of mind. Unless they had been too severely stunned to recover in time, it would have been quite possible for the girls to have saved themselves by crawling along the floor past the boarded-off machinery to the door. They appear, however, to have been quite overwhlemed by the suddeness of the catastrophe.

The dead were:

Ann Davey, 37;
Elizabeth Jane James, 29;
Christinana Mitchell, 17;
Elizabeth Ann Pooley, 14;
Margaretta Long, 18.

As the bodies of the first four could not be separately identified, they were buried in a common grave. At the inquest on the victims, it was disclosed that one girl had been found to be wearing boots with metal nails; this was contrary to the rules, and had most probably been the cause of the explosion.

All the factory explosions so far described were produced by gunpowder. Towards the end of the 19th century, however, a very large establishment for the manufacture of the more powerful explosive nitro-glycerine, was set up among the sand dunes near Hayle. Several accidents occurred here. In September 1894 James Perry, of Gwinear, and Samual Craze, of Hayle, were blown to pieces; and in October 1899 a lad named William Harvey died, the explosion on each occasion occurring in a mixing house. The worst of these blasts, however, took place on January 5 1904. At that time some six hundred men and women were engaged in the various buildings of the National Explosives Company scattered over a wide area among the dunes. The explosion took place at 10.55 a.m.; and immediately all these employees rushed into the open, where they saw a dense cloud of smoke and dust rising high over the scene of the disaster, which gradually floated away on the light breeze seawards. Windows everywhere were shattered by the blast; but the manager prevented panic by quietly going about the task of finding out exactly what had happened. Mounting the sandhills, he found that two huts sited in a hollow and sheltered by several marram-covered dunes, to reduce the effects of blast, had completely disappeared from the danger area.

It was at once apparent there had been loss of life, as four men had been at work there — three in one hut and one in the other. Ther first of these huts housed the plant for washing and filtering the nitro-glycerine, whilst the other was the precipitating house. The buildings were connected by a conduit, consisting of a leaden pipe sheathed in a wooden case, which carried the nitro-glycerine from the filtering to the precipitating department. For hundreds of yards round the devastated area lay chips of the wooden structures, which had been reduced to matchwood. The long grass had been scorched on the surrounding dunes, and the sand had taken on a deeper red-brown tint than usual. But the grimmest sight of all was afforded by the fragments of clothing scattered around, and the severed limbs of human beings. The victims were Andrew Curnow, 45, Connor Downs; William Cliff, 20, Gwithian; Walter Luzmore, 28, Copperhouse; and Simon Jory, 27, Hayle. A Swede, named Oscar Sjholm, was badly injured. It was remarkable that so few lives had been lost. In the depression where the two sheds stood were several other buildings, including the laboratory, where two chemists were at work. The windows were blown in, the walls considerably shaken and the roof torn half off, while practically all the glass instruments were smashed, but the occupants escaped with a few slight scratches and cuts. A large drying shed about a hundred yards from the huts had practically collapsed. The walls had caved in and the roof seemed ready to fall, so that it was feared that the materials stored here would give rise to a second explosion. As relatives of these employed at the works swarmed to the scene to ascertain what had happened, steps had to be taken to keep these anxious crowds out of the grounds, in case a second disaster did occur.

The shock of the explosion was felt with terrific force at St. Ives, across the Bay, where it caused the greatest consternation. Some attributed it to an earthquake, others to a gas explosion, whilst a few believed it was Judgement Day! But a glance in the direction of Hayle Towans, where a cloud of dust and smoke could be seen, soon showed the true cause. Private houses and public buildings were shaken to their foundations, and a large number of windows broken, including the plate glass fronts of many shops. The fine east window of the Parish Church was also smashed, the falling fragments narrowly missing a lady arranging flowers at the altar. At Dr. Best's surgery in Tregenna Place about sixty bottles of drugs and acids were blown on to the floor, and most of them broken. Several roofs and ceilings also fell. Carbis Bay and Lelant felt the shock severely; and at the latter place terror-stricken people rushed hither and thither in wild alarm, some shrieking, others crying, some thinking it was an earthquake, others that the dissolution of the Universe was taking place — and several pious folk were found kneeling in prayer!

At the inquest on the victims, Captain Thomson, H.M.'s Inspector of Explosives, gave it as his opinion that the blast originated in the precipitating house, and was due to Luzmore allowing the heavy lead-lined lid to fall into the tank in which the nitro-glycerine was flowing. He recommended that the lid be made lighter, and that lead cups to catch the drainings of nitro-glycerine be removed. It was officially stated that 4,000 lbs. of the liquid had exploded — a fact which sufficiently explains the widespread damage caused.

The sand dunes at Perranporth provided another suitable site for a dynamite factory; and the Nobel Company established one there, which was the scene of a disastrous explosion in January 1902. This happened when explosives were being trammed; two brothers named Menadue and a man named Bown were killed and other workmen injured. A horse and cart were destroyed. The three men were blown to pieces, whilst a driver was hurled some distance, but although shaken was able to walk home. The shock was felt over a considerable distance. This was a large works, employing hundreds of hands; but when its closure was announced in 1904 a great feeling of relief was experienced at Perranporth, which was then trying to develop itself into a holiday resort.

The Engine House

So great has been the rate of technological progress during the present century that it has become somewhat difficult to conceive just how dependant men were upon the steam engine in the early and middle phases of the Industrial Revolution. Instead of a ubiquitous electric grid pumping power into the remotest corners of the land, every factory and workshop then had to provide its own energy requirements; and, save for the fortunate few who were able to harness the force of a nearby stream, this meant installing a steam engine. It was somewhat unfortunate that this almost universal application of steam power should have taken place at a time when the conception of officially enforced safety measures was still at an embryonic stage, and when, too, those responsible for the maintenance of such engines often displayed the greatest carelessness and ignorance. As a consequence, the industrial history of this whole period is darkened by an endless succession of boiler explosions, resulting in serious destruction of property and a truly appalling loss of life. Wherever steam was used, these disasters occurred. The most shocking of them took place in factories, where a bursting boiler might bring a large building crashing down in ruins, killing scores, maiming and scalding many more. It is an almost forgotten thing now, this frightful and tragic catalogue of disaster and suffering, yet deserving of a mention in any survey of the period, for men should never lose sight of the high sacrifice that progress has so often entailed.

As one of the cradles of the Industrial Revolution, Cornwall was the proving ground for some of the earliest experiments in steam; whilst in the heyday of its mining prosperity the number of engines at work here ran into hundreds. The first 'fire-engines' used for draining the mines worked on the atmospheric, or vacuum system, for which only a low steam pressure was required, and were, therefore, despite their primitive construction, comparatively safe in use. With Trevithick, the apostle of high-pressure steam, there came a radical alteration in the picture. Engines multiplied in numbers; their efficiency also increased to a remarkable degree; but, most lamentably, this new access of power brought with it a fearful number of explosions – so much so that one gains the impression that the engineman in his boiler house constantly ran a far graver risk than the miner in the most dangerous underground workings.

The fatalitites resulting from such explosions were usually limited to the engineman himself and any individuals who chanced to be in the boiler house at the time. Generally, there were very few of these; though the practice of the miners changing their clothes 'on the boiler' at mines where a suitable 'dry' had not been provided certainly added unnecessarily to their number. Even when there was no loss of life, considerable damage often resulted to the engine and its house; and, in some instances, where insufficient auxiliary pumping power existed, the flooding and suspension of the mine could be an even more serious consequence.

In the early days, an aura of considerable mystery surrounded boiler explosions. Whilst an examination of the shattered remains sometimes afforded valuable clues as to what had occasioned the disaster, there were many others in which the cause was less apparent; and quite fantastic theories - myths, one feels, would be a better term - were invented to account for them. The most popular and persistent of these was the idea that under certain conditions water could generate an explosive force comparable with that of gunpowder, which was then capable of bursting the strongest boiler. Such mistaken views were fondly cherished by many of Cornwall's leading mining engineers, and, by encouraging the belief that they need look no further for an explanation, led to a tolerance of practices which allowed the dismal sequence of disasters to continue.

This point was made abundantly clear during a discussion held by members of the Mining Institute of Cornwall at Redruth on February 25 1879, on the subject of 'Boiler Explosions.' The debate centred around a paper on this theme written by the distinguished engineer, Mr. Loam, expressing what may be called the 'classic' view of the matter, his opinions being strongly supported by the 'old school' of mine captains, and equally powerfully criticised by the younger and more scientific engineers present. This is not to say that there was not a certain amount of common ground between them. In particular, all agreed that a frequent cause of explosions was lack of 'feed' - water supply - to the boiler, which resulted in overheating and rupture of the tube. Captain Teague, the chairman , and a traditionalist, stated in his introductory remarks, that if he believed explosions took place from any other cause than want of water, he certainly should never enter a boiler house again; and a little later remarked, "it is always my first safeguard when anything is considered wrong, 'now you must try yours cocks and while the water is flush in the pipes there is no danger, but the moment the water is gone, I am gone too' " - a sally which produced much merriment in his audience.

Captain Teague's view on explosions was thus a simple one - though he accepted Mr. Loam's 'exploding water' theory as being valid also. Now, the great attraction of the 'lack of feed' argument for mine captains, engineers and boilermakers alike was that is enabled them to make the poor engineman a scapegoat - often a dead one, at that, and so unable to reply - for their own mistakes and shortcomings. If the wrecked boiler were worn out, or had been badly constructed, then by charging the engineman with neglect in keeping up his feed, they were themselves exculpated from blame. Should the evidence be crystal clear, however, that the feed *had* been kept up, then the accident might be conveniently explained away by the exploding water theory, or something equally fanciful. Thus, the true cause of these accidents all to often remained hidden, and measures to prevent their recurrence were seldom applied.

In a paper read for him at the meeting, Mr. Henry Miller had some scathing comments to make regarding the views which Loam had propounded. "I think it is a pity," he wrote,

> ".... that such exploded theories respecting the disasters which happen to boilers should be promulgated by any engineers. Investigations of explosions by the various Insurance Companies and Inspection Associations have cleared away many mysteries which were formerly allowed to enshroud them. It has been shown, over and over again, that all explosions are really due to simple causes, and we have little difficulty, when the fragments of a boiler are available, to account for its failure. Such peculiar theories only encourage careless people to work bad or weak boilers, as if such were accepted as correct, they could fall back on them in case of disaster. A large proportion of the explosions which have occurred in Cornwall have arisen from collapse of flue tubes owing to *their originally being too weak* for the regular working pressure. In many instances the occurrence has wrongly been attributed to deficiency of water, and undeserved blame cast on those in charge of the boilers.
>
> "The mystery, which...formerly encompassed such explosions was entirely cleared away in Sir William Fairbairn's experiments on the collapse of tubes. There is now no difficulty with makers who understand the matter in rendering their boilers amply strong in the tubes, and thereby preventing total collapse. Explosions due to rupture of the tube caused through overheating of the plates when the water supply is deficient are easily accounted for. The furnace crown is softened by the overheating, and its resisting power so reduced that it is depressed or forced down by the pressure, but frequently the plate is so ductile, or at such a high temperature, that it stretches sufficiently to allow great alteration of the form without fracture and explosion. With large tubes unstrengthened by hoops or flange seams at the joints, the danger of extensive rupture with explosion when the water becomes deficient is much greater than with small tubes, as the crowns of the former being comparatively flat, slight overheating so reduces their strength that they easily yield to the pressure, and as the plates are not much softened, rending at the seam of rivets or even in the solid plate is probable, as also the extension of the collapse beyond the furnace part of the tube where it was first developed. The hoops or flanges now adopted by the leading makers confine the injury, and prevent the entire collapse of the tube in case of deficiency of water. It requires no explosive force, as described by Mr. Loam, to produce such a collapse and rupture as occurred in the tube of the boiler at West Tolgus. The tube was really *too weak for* the *ordinary load* in the safety valve, and

> thus had little margin of strength. Hence with slight overheating the pressure could easily depress the crown, and the circular form once lost, sudden and total collapse would rapidly follow."

Mr. John Hocking (who read Mr. Miller's paper) gave it as his own opinion that plate tubes (*i.e.,* tubes unstrengthened by rings or other supports) were not absolutely safe even when covered with water. Questioned by Captain Teague, he agreed that trouble could arise where there was a group of boilers by one boiler 'stealing' water from another, and thought this might be caused by gravitation, if they were not all the same level, or by one of the fires being too strong, so leading to overheating and a collapse tube.

Captain Teague – perhaps unwittingly – drew a grim picture of the conditions prevailing in some Cornish boiler houses at that period. "I

"What steps would you take if steam pressure went up to two hundred pounds?"
"Longest ones I could, Cap'n."

More of Pryor's pertinent humour (Courtesy Rigby Ltd.)

have seen boilers so leaky that they had to put fire-bars to stop it. How often does one encounter boilers with the plates fractured over more than a foot in length directly over the fireplace and leaking like baskets? Some present have seen plates so fractured that it has been hard work to keep up the feed.'' Small wonder that explosions were of commonplace occurrence when such a state of affairs existed.

For an early example of a Cornish boiler explosion one may cite that which took place at Wheal Golden, a silver and lead mine in Perranzabuloe, on November 14 1820. The *Royal Cornwall Gazette* attributed the accident to the boiler 'being overcharged with steam;' and its effects were certainly spectacular. The roof was blown off the engine-house and a boy attending the engine was hurled to a considerable distance, but received little injury. A man was also slightly hurt; but there being few persons near at the time, these were the only casualties. Less serious results attended an accident at Polgooth mine, about a mile south of St. Austell, in January 1824. Despite alarming rumours which at first circulated, it was later established that not one house in the neighbourhood had been damaged, whilst the engine itself was soon back at work again 'sinking the water regularly' in the shaft.

Although, as already mentioned, deaths caused by such explosions were generally not high, exceptional circumstances sometimes produced a grievous casualty roll. Probably the most tragic occurrence of this kind was that which took place at the United Hills mine, in the parish of St. Agnes, on February 3 1830. The weather at the time happened to be bitterly cold. The Swanpool, near Falmouth, froze over - a most unusual event - and large numbers of people went skating on it; whilst at Sithney, near Helston, two bullocks were given to the distressed poor of the district. About eight o'clock that morning Jane Goyne, a poor half-frozen bal-maid, left off her work of ore-dressing at the United Hills and crept into the boiler house to warm herself, together with several other workers who were also suffering severely from the bitter weather. After she had been there about five minutes, James Sampson, the engineman, asked Jane's elder sister, Elizabeth, to fetch a pitcher of water for his breakfast. This Elizabeth refused to do, probably not relishing the idea of going outside again in the freezing wind; but Jane good-naturedly took up the pitcher instead and left the house. This involuntary act of kindness saved her life; for she had not gone many yards when she heard a loud noise, and looking back, saw a cloud of steam ascending to a great height in the frosty morning air. Frightened by the sight and the rushing of the steam, she fled to a safer distance. When Jane left the house, her sister, with a number of other persons had been standing near the fireplace. The engineman had just put coal on the fire and turned the gauge cocks to check the feed, then remained standing where he was, taking no part in the general conversation. That picture of the scene inside the engine-house just half-a-minute before the fatal explosion must have remained etched on Jane's mind for the rest of her life; for she never saw Elizabeth or any of the others alive again.

James Hocking, a miner, was one of the very few actually inside the building who survived. He happened to be standing in the engine-house doorway leading to the boiler-house when the boiler burst. Pulling some clothes that were hanging nearby over his head, he thus gained some protection from the clouds of suffocating steam and dust. When the rush of steam abated he looked about and saw two men emerging from a large cupboard where they had taken refuge; one was unhurt, but the other had been badly injured. Hocking assisted in the rescue operations as soon as he could. Altogether, nine men, a boy and a girl were in the boiler-house at the time, and one man (Hocking) in the engine-house. Of these, nine were so dreadfully injured by the steam, scalding water, and blows from the stones and bricks scattered in every direction, that they died within a few hours, whilst of the remaining three, one or two were thought unlikely to survive.

Richard James, one of the captains, ran from the account house to render assistance. At the inquest on the victims he gave a gruesome description of the state in which the dead and dying were found. All the victims were dreadfully burnt and bruised, so much so that they could scarcely be recognised. Some were so scorched that the skin of their hands fell off, and when picked up, was not unlike dry leather gloves. He testified that the boiler had not been in use for more than two or three days after having undergone a thorough repair at the Redruth hammer-mill; it burst in the bottom of the tube in a place apparently as strong as any part of it. He agreed that no blame attached to the engineman, who was fully competent, and could offer no explanation of the accident.

The correspondent of the *Royal Cornwall Gazette*, however, believed that it had been caused by the tube in the boiler, in which the fire was made, being of an oval instead of a round shape. In a round tube, the pressure was equal in every part, but in an oval one it was unequal, acting more in one place than another both internally and externally. By reason of its construction, an oval tube was partly pressed in, whilst a round one would be uniform strength. It was the inside part of the oval tube into which the fire was put that burst, and not the case of the boiler.

The victims of this tragedy were:
William Endey, of Illogan, aged about 32, married.
William White, of Illogan, 30, married.
James Sampson, of St. Agnes, the engineman, aged about 60.
Richard Treglown, of Illogan, 32, married.
James Champion, of St. Agnes, 27, married.
James Peters, of St. Agnes, aged about 22.
James Whitta, of St. Agnes, 20.

A lad named Wills, of Illogan, 15.
Elizabeth Goyne, of St. Agnes, aged about 20.

The badly injured were a man named Tyrrel, of Redruth, and two others called Willoughby and Haughton, both of Illogan.

A large number of people were also involved in a boiler explosion at Boiling Well mine, near Hayle, in February 1858, though the fatalities were not so heavy. The accident occurred between six and seven o'clock, killing the 'engineer' (? engineman) and a woman, and severely injuring six or seven others, two of whom were not expected to recover. The engineer was found buried in the ruins of the house, whilst the poor woman lived only about two hours; she was a widow, and left a family of three children entirely unprovided for. It was believed there had been some defect in one of the plates of the boiler.

The boiler-house at Buller and Basset United Mines (about two and a half miles from Redruth) also appears to have been crowded with miners when a similar disaster occurred there on May 13 1863. About two o'clock in the afternoon Frederick Uren, aged 33, George Teague, 19, and eight other men were changing their clothes in the house when one of the two boilers 'blew out' and the water and steam rushing through the bottom flue scalded four of them, Uren and Teague being so severely injured that they died soon after. During the inquests, it came out that the miners had always been accustomed to 'change on the boiler' — a practice condemned by the foreman and some jurors. As a result, it was announced that a changing house would be provided for them.[1]

Two men also died when the boiler at Wheal Tolgus, near Redruth, burst with a tremendous explosion at about six o'clock in the morning of July 25 1835, whilst several others received serious injuries. About a year previously (February 1834) there had been a spectacular explosion at Great St. George mine, in the parish of St. Agnes, when the boiler of the South-engine burst with a deafening noise at midnight, carrying away the roof, throwing down the walls of the boiler-house, and scattering the materials about in every direction. James Phillips, the engineman on duty, was killed, being found buried beneath a part of the wall. A fatality also occurred when the boiler of Pendeen Consols exploded on July 8 1861, the victim's name being Charles Jenkin. The man in charge of the pumping engine at nearby Levant also died when one of its boilers burst on September 2 1859. This man, called Edwards, had just tested the feed, and was turning to go out when the boiler exploded around him and burnt him so badly that he died the following day.

An interesting but tragic explosion occurred at East Boscaswell (Old Wheal Hearle) on May 14 1873. On the previous evening, Joseph Wearne, a miner aged 46, came to the engine-house to learn to work the engine, as he proposed becoming an engineman himself. Alfred Ernest

Williams happened to be on duty at the time, and Wearne remained there with him throughout the night until one in the morning, when the accident took place. The engine had been put to work at six in the morning of the 13th, and was stopped for an hour at eleven, as there was no work for her to do. Williams put her to work again a little before twelve, when she worked quite smoothly. About an hour before the accident Wearne had made up the fire, whilst Williams had tested the feed about an hour-an-half earlier — that is, around half-past-ten — and found sufficient water in the boiler. The mouths of the feed pipes were a little corroded, and Williams did not know when they had last been cleaned. It was usual to try the feed-gauge when the fire was made up, but it could not be ascertained whether Wearne had done this at midnight. Williams, in fact, should have checked the feed every half-hour, especially seeing the engine was working very fast, but had deputed this task to Wearne, who had had only three weeks' experience as a trainee. Neither of the regular enginemen, however, had been authorised to depute any responsibility to him.

About one in the morning the two men were sitting side by side in the engine-house when Wearne rose up to look at the fire. As he opened the door leading into the boiler-house, Williams heard a noise, like that of escaping steam. He rushed to the boiler-house door, which had closed, and after some difficulty opened it and brought his companion out, Wearne could stand but not speak, and was scalded a little about the face and hands, appearing otherwise uninjured. The engineman put him to lie down, and went for assistance, but Wearne died within a quarter of an hour. At the inquest, Williams stated that his comrade's death had been caused by the boiler tube bursting and throwing a quantity of steam over him. He added that the feed-rod had been bent for some time, and believed there was some obstruction in the pipe. This would have prevented sufficient water entering the boiler when the engine was working at high speed.

John Davey, joint engineman with Williams, described how he went to the boiler-house the following morning and saw the tube broken and hanging down. Henry Harvey, a boiler maker, who was sent to repair and examine the burst boiler, found that the plates were perfect; but the feed-hole, through which the water came in, had become so corroded that it would just take his finger, whereas it ought to have been two and a half inches in diameter. Despite this, it was his opinion that the disaster had been caused by the feed-hole not being worked sufficiently to keep water in the boiler. The jury returned a verdict of accidental death, adding that the explosion was caused by an insufficiency of water in the boiler, 'but there is no evidence to show if the desceased had neglected to examine the state of the water at the time he had last made up the fire.' Following the Government Inspector's report, the mine manager was convicted of failure to comply with the regulations concerning the steam and water gauges, but not fined, this being the first prosecution of its kind. The case must, indeed, be considered quite an extraordinary one; for whilst the engineman, on his own admission, had not been blameless, it was the manager who was brought to trial – an outcome quite contrary to what might normally be expected!

Another accident involving the death of a trainee engineman took place at Wheal Busy, a mile east of Scorrier, on February 11 1860. James Phillips, the engineman on duty, had taken his seventeen year old son to assist him that evening in working Harvey's engine. About half-an-hour before the accident he went into the boiler-house and ascertained that the water was up to the top cock. He then left his son there to clear up one of the fires, but on returning to the engine-house heard the sound of an exploding boiler. At the boiler-house door he was met by a cloud of steam and smoke that obliged him to close the door again, leaving his son inside. It must have been an agonising decision to take. Later, with assistance, William's body was retrieved from the bottom of the steps; the lad was quite dead. From the evidence of Hugh Bray, 'engine-man' (? engineer) under Messrs. Sims and Son, who had had the superintendence of the Wheal Busy boilers ever since the present adventurers had taken over, it appears the boiler had burst through overheating of the tube, which was found crushed and torn asunder, and must have been almost red-hot. However, Mr. Sims was inclined to think the deficiency of water had arisen not from any negligence on Phillips' part, 'but from its sudden dispersion by some means.' Whether he meant that this boiler had been 'stealing' water from its neighbour – there were at least two in the house – or was making a veiled allusion to the 'exploding water' myth, is not clear. The boiler was a good one, and had been newly installed only twelve months before. James Phillips was said to have been employed as engineman at various mines for twenty-four years, and Mr. Sims gave him a very good character for attention and steadiness.

A boiler accident of a rather singular character was reported at Higher Menedue, Luxulyan, on January 17 1874. An iron mine had recently been opened there by Messrs. Chatwood, Oatey & Co., described as 'the well-known makers of burglar-proof safes'; and the engine, which was a very old one of ten horse-power, was in charge of Nathaniel Dyer. About six in the morning a terrible explosion took place in the engine-house, the bolts connecting the tube and boiler giving way. The tube was hurled a hundred yards in one direction and the boiler in the other. The tube carried Dyer before it and killed him, while the boiler was thrown a distance of sixty feet, being brought up by a pile of 'stuff' from the mine shaft. Two miners – William Borlase and Michael Borlase – were injured, but only slightly. The dead man was aged 51, and resided at Hallew, in the parish of Roche; he had formerly been the master of St. Columb workhouse, being obviously a man of parts! The accident was variously attributed to an excessive weight being places on the safety valves, and to the general weakness of the engine and boiler.

Another unusual accident took place at Cook's Kitchen on May 19 1892. The boiler, one of three supplying steam for the large pumping engine, was of the Cornish type measuring 30 feet long by six feet wide. It was the centre one of the trio, and known to be weaker than the others, but was not considered unsafe. Arrangements had been made for it to be cleaned and repaired, and this work would have been completed a week or two before the accident but for lack of skilled labour. The explosion occurred about nine in the morning, so severely scalding the engineman on duty that he died the following night. It was a most tremendous blast, as might be expected with a boiler of this size, and caused a great deal of damage; but accounts vary as to the effects on the boiler itself.

Underground in Cook's Kitchen (Courtesy Royal Institution of Cornwall)

According to the *Cornishman*, it blew out at both ends; but the *Cornish Telegraph* asserted that its front was blown away and the brick facing dislodged. The boiler-house was completely wrecked, a wall at the rear of the boiler being hurled through the main walls, and some of the stones carried to a considerable distance. When the steam had dispersed, the cause of the explosion was seen to be the collapsing of the upper portion of the tube, which had been torn down for some distance, the damage arising, in the opinion of the officials, from the weakness of one of the plates. Captain Charles Thomas and the other agents were quickly on the scene and did all they could to help the poor engineman whilst the engineer acted quickly to secure the two remaining boilers; so that by the time the balance-bob pit had been cleared of debris the old engine was bobbing away again.

The consequences were equally spectacular when the boiler of the large engine at Binner Downs exploded in March 1828. Seven miners were in the boiler house at the time; two of them, Daniel Dunn and John Daniel, were instantly killed, whilst the remaining five were so badly injured that the recovery of some seemed unlikely. The noise was heard at a great distance, whilst the house itself was completely destroyed. During August of that same year a boiler at Wheal Vor burst, fatally injuring one man and severely wounding another. The accident was said to have 'been occasioned by the in-attention of those left in charge.'

Chance, and luck — good or bad — often decided who lived and who died when a boiler blew up. This was strikingly illustrated at North Wheal Crofty on April 10th 1867 when the whim boiler exploded at twelve o'clock in the morning. Lugg, an odd-job man employed about the mine, was asked by the engine-man to go to the boiler house and check the feed. The boiler had lately been repaired and was thought to be in a sound condition, but just as he entered the boiler house the explosion occurred, killing him instantly. About ten minutes earlier three or four masons had been working in the house and would probably have shared his fate had they not left for dinner.

When a boiler exploded, those in its vicinity who were not actually killed frequently suffered dreadful injuries from the scalding steam. About one in the afternoon of October 13 1860 one of the boilers of Wheal Charlotte, near Perran, Marazion, burst, and six men — William Craze, from Goldsithney; James Williams, Thomas Ivey (or Ivery), John Semmens, James Semmens, and another known by the name of 'Lizard Jim,' all of Marazion — were dreadfully scalded. James Williams, aged 18, died the following night, and William Craze, aged 20, a day later. John Semmens and 'Lizard Jim' were both very ill, the other two being less seriously hurt. The boiler had been in use on the mine about nine months; it was second hand, but had been fully repaired at the works of Mr. R. R. Mitchell, and was considered the strongest of the three boilers on Wheal Charlotte.

It did not always require an actual explosion for men to be scalded. In April 1865 Francis Peters, for fifteen years engineman at East Pool, Bennett George, a trammer to the landers, William Bone and two others, were engaged in cleaning the boiler of the steam whim. By opening a valve and unscrewing all but four 'burrs' of the manhole they allowed steam and water to escape. Peters then told his assistants to sit down and wait. This they did for about ten minutes, and should have waited longer, when Bone, who had never previously been employed on such an operation, unknown to the others unscrewed the remaining manhole 'burrs;' as a result the cover was lifted and steam escaped. Peters did not move and was uninjured. Two others saved themselves by springing from a window six feet from the ground, but George fell into some boiling water, seriously scalding his back, legs and arms. He was taken home in a cart, but, despite medical attention, died some days later.

Another scalding accident occurred at Wheal Baddern, Chacewater, in January 1867. A miner named Francis Visick was ordered by the captain to get into the cistern for some purpose, and whilst he was there another workman entered the engine-house and put the engine to work, being totally unaware of Visick's perilous situation. Boiling water and steam at once rushed into the cistern and dreadfully scalded the legs of the unfortunate man. He was taken to his father's house where he eventually recovered under the care of Dr. Hugo of Chacewater.

To return to boiler explosions. Fatal as so many of these inevitably were some marvellous escapes have been recorded. On August 31 1857 the surface workers at Levant were greatly alarmed by the bursting of one of the boilers of the steam stamps. Fortunately there was no one in the boiler-house at the time, and although debris was scattered in every direction, the only casualty was a slight contusion sustained by a boy struck by a falling brick.

An even more wonderful instance occurred at the Gwennap United Mines on September 30 1851. The boiler of one of the large engines burst with such tremendous violence that the tube, weighing about three tons, was thrown bodily through the wall of the boiler-house to a distance of over a hundred feet, and large portions of the boiler and fireplace to still greater distances. The roof was blown completely off and the chimney stack thrown down; but though the ruins fell all about a boy, the only person in the house, he escaped with a cut on the temple from a falling brick. When the middle boiler of the engine of Trewavas mine in the parish of Breage burst on November 26 1842, great fears were entertained for the safety of those in its vicinity. However, no one was hurt, the engine-man and several miners having left the boiler-house a few minutes before the accident.

Although the United Hills mine, in St. Agnes, witnessed the most tragic of all Cornish boiler explosions in 1830 (as already described) it was also the scene of one of the luckiest escapes when an earlier mishap occurred there in February 1827. In this instance, the boiler blew up at half-past five on a Saturday afternoon with an appalling sound. Had the accident happened a few seconds before, the smallest number of lives likely to have been lost would have been around thirty or forty; but as it fortunately happened to be a general setting day nearly all the miners were absent. Two engine-men, one of the captains and several sumpmen were in the vicinity of the boiler-house, but none received any serious injury. The boiler, made of the thickest plate-iron, was rent in pieces, the roof and walls of the boiler-house blown to an amazing distance, and the boiling water, bricks and other debris showered into the valley, darkening the atmosphere for a time. Over a hundred men were thrown out of work by the accident, but neighbouring mines offered prompt help to get the damage repaired. The large number of fatalities that might have occurred on this occasion had it not been a setting day would presumably have arisen among the men who would otherwise have been changing over the boiler when it blew up.

No less than two boiler explosions took place at West Seton, Camborne, on the night of February 7 1889. The first happened at one o'clock at the stamps engine whilst the engine-man was at the back of the stamps attending to the flushets. The boiler-house roof was wrecked and a portion of the stamps' side carried away. The engine was equipped with two boilers, and was thus able to continue working. The second explosion occurred about five o'clock at the large eastern engine, known as Harvey's. This boiler had been cleaned the previous day, and the engine-man was preparing to rework it. The steam had only reached a pressure of 28lb. when the accident took place. The most serious result was the breaking of the steam-pipe connecting the boilers, which put the engine completely out of action. Fortunately, operations were then confined chiefly to the western part of the mine, which was forked by a second pumping engine; and as the water would have to rise to the 140 at Harvey's before going back to the western engine, it was thought no flooding would occur there. Not only was it remarkable that two boilers should explode on the mine in a single night; but each of them was fitted with a patent fusible plug which, should the feed get low, was supposed to melt, and therby prevent an accident, but failed to do so in each case!

About seven in the evening of February 17 1860, one of the boilers of the pumping engine at Balleswidden exploded, scatterng portions of the tube and boiler in almost every direction; so great was the power of the steam that it levelled the boiler-house to the ground and rent the boiler — a good one — in a manner that gunpowder itself could hardly have done. One portion of the tube, weighing about half a ton, was hurled up on to the high road, but luckily no person or vehicle happened to be passing at the time. Had the explosion taken place half-an-hour earlier or later, many lives would have been lost. Large numbers of miners even then were in the ladders and had almost reached surface when the accident occurred. Had they been up, they would have been in the boiler-house changing their clothes. The *Royal Cornwall Gazette* attributed the explosion 'to the gas of the cold water coming in contact with the steam, as the steam was at a high pressure at the time.' This sounds like yet another of those hoary old myths with which the engineers and boilermakers so cleverly covered their failures!

The engineman at Great Wheal Busy, near Chacewater, must have accounted himself a very fortunate man when one of the five boilers on the large pumping engine burst during November 1865, doing great damage to the boiler-house. He was in the act of opening the engine-house door when it burst; a moment more, and he would have fallen a victim to the rushing steam. Earlier that year (February) an explosion of the boiler of the pumping engine at West Wheal Damsel, Redruth, also had an extremely fortunate outcome. The blast hurled small portions of the boiler a considerable distance, whilst its main part was thrown forward about twenty feet. Somewhat remarkably, that portion of the tube immediately over the fire remained uninjured. Despite the great force of the explosion, no one was hurt. Again, in March of that same year, a boiler exploded at South Wheal Basset without fatal result; it was being set to work for the first time when the accident took place.

Engines were used on mines for a variety of purposes besides pumping, and these also sustained their full quota of accidents. In January 1841 the boiler of the crushing engine at the Carn Brea Mines burst with a tremendous explosion, killing the aged engineman, Thomas Kitto, of St. Austell. The machinery had been examined only the previous day, and appeared in perfect order. A steam stamps explosion occurred at Dolcoath just before six in the morning of February 18 1879, and was said to be attended by 'extraordinary and mysterious circumstances.' The boiler was the southernmost of three at the stamps, which were new. Downing, the engineman, was at the back of this boiler, which was divided by a wall from the others, when the explosion took place. He had just checked to see that everything was safe and in good working order. Dolcoath at that time had twenty-two boilers constantly in use; and this explosion was the first of its kind there for thirteen years.

The shocking condition in which some boilers were worked, to which Captain Teague had drawn the Mining Institute's attention in 1879, is amply confirmed by facts elicited at enquiries held into a number of boiler explosions. On the morning of March 28 1873, whilst a fifteen year old assistant engineman called Alfred Williams was cleaning the ash-pit outside the engine-house at Great Work mine, two miles north of Breage, the boiler suddenly exploded. His superior, James Dobb, who happened to be in the engine-house, fearing the lad might be endangered, went to see for him, but could find nothing save a heap of debris, whilst the pit was full of steam. Believing Williams had been buried under the rubbish, he procured assistance, and after the steam had been turned off from the other two boilers, they began to pull out the fire from one of them. Dobb then explored the ash-pit, and after some time found the youth in a terribly scalded state. He was immediately washed and taken home where he soon after died. At the inquest, Dobb, who had been engineman for six months, stated that the boiler was leaky, but he did not consider it dangerous so long as the feed could be kept up. This was not always possible; and then, to prevent an accident, the fires were immediately raked out. The boiler had been leaking on the day of the explosion and for some time previously; and he informed the engineer, who told him to rake out the fire if he could not keep up the feed. However, Dobb had been able to maintain the feed, so this was not done. After the explosion, he had examined the boiler plates; "and had I known" (he stated) "that they were so thin, I would not have worked the engine." Richard Hampton, the engineer, said he had examined the boiler during the morning prior to the accident, and found it leaking a little, but did not think there was danger while the feed was up. The boiler had been repaired a fortnight since; before that time he had considered it in a dangerous state. After the repairs had been made, the boiler remained tight for nearly a week; and when an inspection was made, the only weak place proved to be that which had been repaired! The leakage then continued until the explosion. Returning a verdict on William of 'accidentally killed by the explosion of a boiler,' the jury, whilst blaming no one, considered that 'greater attention should be paid to the state of the boilers on the mine.'

With the decline of Cornish mining, and the advance in safety measures, boiler explosions became quite rare towards the close of the nineteeth century, but did not entirely cease with it. In November 1907 one of five boilers in a building at East Pool burst during the night, destroying walls and a part of the roof, but no one was injured. The beam engines which survive today are treasured museum pieces, carefully preserved and highly regarded by enthusiasts of the great Age of Steam. But these magnificent machines — or, to be more precise, their powerful, high pressure boilers — were, let it not be forgotten, also killers, striking down their devoted attendants with sudden concussions of water and steam and wrecking the buildings which housed them.

FIRE — Above and Below

In the public mind, fires in mines are particularly, if not exclusively, associated with collieries. Coal mines are, of course, especially susceptible to this kind of disaster, as, apart from the coal seams themselves, large quantities of explosive dust and gas often accumulate in their workings, sometimes giving rise to the most appalling conflagrations. Metalliferous mines, happily, are free from these dangers; yet, paradoxically, fires have occurred in them, some of quite a serious nature. These have resulted from the timber work igniting from some cause or other; and when it is remembered that levels and shafts are often protected for considerable distances by a continuous framework of wood, this will not seem surprising. The only inhibiting factors are the generally damp conditions and restricted air supply; these apart, fire represents as great a potential hazard underground as in wooden buildings at surface.

Until comparatively recently miners depended on naked candles for their illumination, which were often stuck for convenience to a piece of timber, these proving the origin of most subterranean conflagrations. One of the most disastrous fires caused in this way took place in St. Ives Consols at the head of the Stennack Valley, St. Ives, on April 12 1844, which, after burning for six weeks, left an extremely rich section of the workings in a state of irretrievable ruin. St. Ives Consols was noted for the extraordinary deposits of tin to the south of the Standard lode to which the name *carbonas* was given. The most famous of these, the Great Carbona, proved to be one of the most remarkable deposits of tin ever known in Cornwall, the workings being excavated in enormous caverns ten or twelve fathoms high and equally wide. But the great mineral wealth which it contained was never fully extracted. A workman left a lighted candle stuck to the roof timbers in the entrance passage; this burned down, igniting the woodwork, and the flames were communicated to the vast stull (made of the largest timber procurable) which supported the sides and roof of the Great Carbona itself. The fire destroyed the entire section; but the mine as a whole was so rich that its output was not adversely affected.

On the night of January 8 1890 a fire broke out in some old stulls over the 235 fathom level near the man-engine shaft in Dolcoath, caused, it was believed, by a miner carelessly throwing a lighted candle-end among them. The men working on night shift in the 30 fathom level were driven from their pitches by huge volumes of smoke, and being unable to ascend by the man-engine shaft were obliged to escape through the new Eastern shaft, which was ventilated by a downward current. On the following day the quantity of smoke reaching surface had not lessened, and all underground work in the central part of the mine had to be suspended. Although there was no danger of the conflagration spreading to the main parts of the workings, the captains felt some anxiety for the security of the man-engine. Accordingly, two shaftmen called Trevarthen and Weekes descended to the 80 plot and there began to screw down the pole to prevent the 'plunger' from taking air. Trevarthen, however, succumbed to the smoke and fumes, and fell to the ground. Three times his comrade lifted him to his feet, but ultimately found his own strength failing, and, his legs giving way, they fell to the ground together, as they thought, to die. Eventually they became unconscious, and remained so for five hours. Two other shaftmen, called Sowden and Wake, who went below with them, managed to get away from the danger area and reached the Eastern shaft without being overcome.

Meanwhile, at surface, considerable anxiety was felt for the safety of these four men. Several rescuers went down by the new Eastern shaft to search for them, and the skip was lowered with a signal bell. On the skip being returned, it was found to contain two jackets, showing that two of them at least still lived. A timberman called Semmens with a companion went down in search of them, and walked down in the direction of the man-engine shaft until both fell to the ground, overpowered by smoke. With their remaining strength, and supporting each other, they crawled backwards, reflecting with bitterness on their inability to resuce their comrades. They eventually heard the sound of water falling from one of the upper levels, and making their way to it, were revived by the current of fresh air brought down by the stream. They continued their retreat to the new Eastern shaft, and on reaching the gig found to their great joy that Wake and Sowden had already arrived there from another level, and all four were drawn to the surface together.

The skip was lowered and raised again and again without further success whilst the anxious watchers at surface waited in a downpour of rain for a sign of the other missing shaftmen. Eventually a man named Eva expressed the opinion that they were in the 80 plot, and volunteered to go down in the skip if anyone would accompany him. John Rule, Trevarthen's brother-in-law, offered to go, and he and Eva were at once lowered into the shaft. Eva's surmise proved correct, for they found Weekes and Trevarthen lying on their faces in the 80 plot, still locked in each other's arms. When brought up, they were still insensible, and few thought they would recover. Although Trevarthen's mind was temporarily deranged by the experience he had undergone, both survived their fearful ordeal. Whilst they were lying unconscious in the plot, an exploring party passed and repassed within a few feet of them, shouting their names, but could not discern them in the darkness. In its feature *Mining Notes,* the *Cornish Telegraph* commented:

"A charge of cowardice, which seems to be not entirely unfounded, has been brought against some of the men who were at the surface when long absence of the four, who had gone down to examine the engine, created not unnatural anxiety. But Eva and Rule deserve every praise; indeed, they merit a substantial pecuniary reward for the ready manner in which they undertook a dangerous duty."

For some days afterwards smoke continued to pour out of Dolcoath's shafts, and Captain Josiah Thomas, the manager, forbade the men attempting to go underground until it cleared. Three days after the fire began two miners descended the new Eastern shaft by the gig, and went through the 314 level to New Sump shaft, where they opened the taps of the air compressor to help ventilate the workings. The smell of the fumes was noticed at West Seton mine, about a mile from Dolcoath, the gas having apparently found its way there through the adit level.[1]

Another stull took fire at Dolcoath in January 1903. On this occasion the conflagration was in the 290 level of New East shaft, and about eight hundred day men and boys were unable to proceed to their work. The outbreak was again ascribed to a carelessly discarded candle end. The fire obtained a firm hold among the large timber balks, and had to be allowed to burn itself out. As a result, underground operations were suspended for nearly a week — a serious matter both for the men and the adventurers. Two hundered miners at South Tincroft or Carn Brea mine were similarly thrown out of work for several days in January 1908 by an underground fire which filled the levels with thick smoke. Both the cause and location of this outbreak were said to be a mystery.

Many Cornish engine shafts underlay for part or whole of their depth; and the tremendous friction created where the heavy rods ran on rollers sometimes caused a fire. As shafts were ventilation outlets, and contained a plentiful supply of timber, the results were apt to prove spectacular. D.B. Barton gives two good examples in *The Cornish Beam Engine.* One occurred at South Frances, belonging to the Basset Mines, about a mile and a half south west of Redruth, when the flaming engine rods sent clouds of smoke issuing from the shaft mouth. Still more alarming was the conflagration at Wheal Basset in November 1870, the entire timbering of the upper part of Carnkie shaft and at surface being entirely consumed, flames rising fifty feet above the poppet head.

An interesting example of a shaft fire during recent times was reported from Wheal Jane, Baldhu, near Truro, on November 22 1973. When flames roared up three shafts on an abandoned section of the mine, men engaged in other parts of the underground workings were brought to surface for fear the smoke might penetrate into those areas. The mine's own rescue team went down to check on the smoke, whilst the Cornwall County Fire Brigade sent five appliances to the scene — two fire fighting machines from Truro, a water carrier and one fire fighting machine from

Camborne, and an emergency tender from Bodmin. After playing water down the shafts with little effect, two fire officers were lowered on ropes to take the hoses to the seat of the conflagration, which proved to be in an underground cavern about 60ft. long filled with blazing rubbish, including oily rags. The officers had an extremely difficult descent, being blinded by smoke, and had to be lowered very carefully, two feet at a time. They went down about 100ft., and a second team, which replaced them, descended about 130ft. The fire was extinguished without any danger to the mine or the underground workers.

By their nature, engine-houses were frequently the scene of sensational blazes. However, whilst the timberwork of the house was often totally destroyed, the walls and engine usually survived, enabling pumping operations to be resumed after a relatively short interruption. To describe even a tithe of these fires would involve giving many tedious variations on a common theme, so only a few representative examples will be mentioned here.

The first of these did not involve a mine engine at all, but took place in the house of the stationary engine used for hauling up carriages on the steep Angarrack incline of the old Hayle Railway. However, as this line was originally built for mineral traffic, it may legitimately be included here. About three o'clock in the morning of March 5 1847, the fire was seen by a man called Murley who lived at Gwinear Church Town, more than a mile distant, and he immediately hastened to the spot. The fire being visible for a great distance around, others emulated his example, but arrived too late to stop its progress. They succeeded, however, in saving the rope by which the carriages were raised and lowered on the incline. About five o'clock the roof fell in, leaving nothing standing but the walls. The engine was not much injured, owing to its being fixed upon iron props or stanchions. According to the *Penzance Gazette*, the fire was supposed to have originated in the sawdust placed round the cylinder, which then caught the first floor alight. No one was employed about the engine by night, and the men employed there by day had packed the piston the previous evening, leaving everything in good order.

On January 20 1874 someone carelessly placed a lighted candle against the wall of the engine-house of Wheal Kitty, Lelant. During the temporary absence of the man in charge this fell to the floor and ignited a quantity of hemp and grease. The flames quickly spread and damaged the roof, flooring, and wood connected with the engine before it could be brought under control with buckets of water, the damage being extimated at £150.

Towards the end of that same year (November 20) the engine-man on duty at Penhall's steam-stamps engine, St. Agnes, discovered flames rising from the boiler-house at about two in the morning, and before assistance could be obtained the fire had reached the engine-house. Very little could be done to arrest its progress, and most of the doors, windows and lintels were consumed, whilst the roof soon after fell in. The machinery was also damaged, and a great part of the engine-house walls so weakened that they had to be rebuilt. It was supposed that the fire originated from some old cylinder packing which had been deposited on the steam-pipes in the boiler-house. The mishap threw most of those engaged on the tin floors out of work for several weeks.

The most spectacular of all Cornish engine-house fires was that which took place at Tregurtha Downs mine, near Goldsithney, on January 4 1889. The engine involved — St. Aubyn's 80 inch — was one of the best and most powerful in the county, and when the fire broke out was working over eight strokes a minute and pumping five hundred gallons. At about a quarter to four that morning, whilst George Fox, the engine-man, was below attending to the boilers, a young man named Drewett, employed on the mine, entered the engine-house and ascended to the storey about the engine floor with a lighted candle. On that floor was stored a quantity of hemp tow, and a spark from the candle set it ablaze. The flames set oil and woodwork on fire, and in almost a moment the conflagration was out of control. The lad rushed down and called Fox, but by that time the whole place was on fire.

In order to summon help as quickly as possible, the engine-man had recourse to the steam hooter normally used to announce a change of shift at the mine. Sounding continuously at this unaccustomed hour, it soon roused many people in the vicinity. Captain Prisk, the chief resident agent, was quickly on the scene with a number of surface workers. Drewett was at once despatched to Marazion for the fire brigade and engine. He reached Marazion at ten minutes to five; but the arrangements for summoning and collecting firemen proved very unsatisfactory; and so it was not till 5.25 — more than half-an-hour after the first alarm — before they set off on their mission. However, the journey was completed quickly, considering the state of the roads, and the engine was immediately put to work. But it was already too late to save the building. In less than thirty minutes after the outbreak the roof had fallen in, and the place was now a mass of flames from top to bottom. The tinder-dry wood burnt furiously, and a column of fire one hundred feet high illuminated the hills of the entire district. By strenuous efforts the Marazion brigade succeeded in preventing the fire spreading to the adjoining boiler-house; but then they began to have trouble with their equipment. A hose burst, and was replaced; then the suction pipe failed; whilst the engine itself, which was a very old one and practically useless for such heavy work, broke its bed it two!

Captain Hosking thereupon despatched his horses and waggon to Penzance to borrow the engine belonging to the Corporation there, telegraphing in advance to have the machine ready on their arrival. Fresh horses were engaged at Penzance; and at nine o'clock, after a round journey of fourteen miles, the brigade had this engine playing water on the flames. They were not a moment too soon, as in another few minutes the fire, which had by now extended over the whole of the boiler-house, shears, bob plat and pitwork, would have been altogether unmanageable. With assistance of the mine captains, water was conducted from the mine reservoirs to provide a supply for the engine. This engine was said to be the *younger* of the two belonging to Penzance Corporation, and had already passed the mature age of ninety years! (In fact, it appears that as the Penzance mains were capable of sending up jets of water to a height of eighty feet, the engines were really not needed there, being only retained to help the neighbouring districts.)

The engine-house at Tregurtha Downs, shortly after its rebuilding
(Courtesy Royal Institution of Cornwall)

By now the engine-house had been practically burnt out, but several large masses of flaming woodwork remained in close proximity to adjoining buildings and the outside machinery. Through the firemen's efforts, the bob, plat, shears and other valuable items were saved. They also managed to prevent the total collapse of the engine-house, but it was not until after four in the afternoon that the flames were finally extinguished. In addition to the fire engines, fifty volunteers helped in the fire-fighting operations. Many of these were inhabitants of Marazion who had been awakened early in the morning by the cries of the boy who was sent for the brigade. Soon after the fire broke out, the men working underground on the night 'core' became alarmed by the sounding of the hooter and made their way to surface. On being assured there was no danger, they returned below for their tools, and then suspended work for the day.

The damage at first was thought to be considerable, being placed as high as £10,000, but later examination showed this to have been an over-estimate. A few of the brasses had been partially melted and some of the rods warped out of position by the heat, but the larger and heavier parts of the engine were not materially injured. As a result, the chief engineer, Michael Loam, who examined the wreckage a few days after the fire, believed it could be got ready to pump again in two weeks. Tregurtha Downs was not a very deep mine (eighty fathoms) but the workings were very wet, the average influx being 1,200 gallons per minute. With the engine out of action, the water rose rapidly, and within three days had reached the 40 fathom level. Work on rebuilding the engine-house and restoring the engine continued night and day, but in the meantime between three and four hundred people were thrown out of employment. Harvey & Co. of Hayle effected very rapid repairs, cutting Loam's estimate of the time required by half. The engine remained at Tregurtha Downs till 1902, and the following year started a fresh career on the new vertical Robinson's shaft at South Crofty. Here she gave faithful service till 1955, when replaced by electric pumps, being the last Cornish engine to work on a Cornish mine. She had been built in 1854 at Copperhouse Foundry for Alfred Consols, and later saw duty at Crenver and Wheal Abraham United before being transferred to Tregurtha Downs in 1881. Now owned by the National Trust, she is today one of the finest surviving relics of Cornwall's great mining history.

Another disastrous fire occurred in the engine hose at Poldory mine, part of the Mount Wellington complex in Carnon Valley, on January 8 1847. Strenuous efforts by agents and men failed to check the spread of the flames, and eventually all the woodwork was destroyed. The intense heat broke the cast iron bob of the engine, and it was estimated that ten days or a fortnight would be required to get it working again. The miners would be laid off for at least twice as long owing to the time required to fork the water – 'a calamity that will be seriously felt by the families of the workmen, especially at this season of the year, and with the present high price of provision.' 1847, it will be remembered, was the year when much unrest manifested itself in the Cornish mining districts, owing to the great scarcity and dearness of bread and foodstuffs, so that the authorities had good reason to feel apprehensive of the consequences that might follow a prolonged suspension of this mine.

A rare view of Poldory (Courtesy Royal Institution of Cornwall)

Besides engine-houses, other types of surface buildings were subject to outbreaks of fire. The blacksmiths' shops, where the men's tools were kept in good repair, provide a good example of this. An interesting case occurred at Dolcoath during March 1887. The smithy involved stood in an outlying sector of the mine, and was used as a 'dry' by several miners working in that part. As a result, it contained twenty suits of clothing when the fire broke out, all of which were burnt, whilst the roof of the building itself was destroyed. It was in this Dolcoath Valley smithy that Trevithick was said to have carried out much of the work required for the construction of his first locomotive. After the fire, a new roof was placed on the original walls, and the building continued to serve as a smithy for the mine.[2]

Although properly constructed 'drys' or changing houses for the men were much to be preferred to the primitive expedient of 'changing on the boiler' in engine houses or beside a blacksmiths' forge, on grounds not only of safety but of comfort and convenience as well, drys were themselves sometimes destroyed by fire, and with occasional loss of life. Such an event took place at Carn Brea Mines on December 7 1842. At six that morning, a large number of men were in the changing house preparing to go underground. Some were putting on their underground clothes, others getting their tools and materials ready. A young man called Waters began pouring powder from a cask into a canister to take down to his workplace in the mine when a candle which he was believed to have placed overhead dropped on the powder and caused a most frightful explosion. The building was in the form of a long, narrow shed, measuring about 150′ x 8′, with only one exit, and that near the end; and as the first explosion occurred by the door the lives of all inside were endangered. Waters was literally blown to pieces, whilst his father and nine other men were seriously injured and several other slightly hurt. Along each side of the house stood a range of cupboards in which the miners kept their clothes and materials. These were instantly in flames, and as several contained large quantities of gunpowder the fire spread with great rapidity, accompanied by frequent explosions. Escape through the door was thus impossible; but the men eventually managed to get out by breaking through the inner end of the building. The destruction of property was very considerable, much of it belonging to the miners themselves. Four hundred men were employed on the mine, each of whom, on average, sustained a loss of £1. But the worst aspect of the affair was the tragic number of deaths involved. For of the injured men, no less than seven subsequently died, their names being Waters (the father of the young miner with whom the accident originated), Harvey, Cock, Hocking, Martin, Nicholas, and Rogers. The jury which sat at Redruth on one of the victims appended to their verdict of 'Accidental Death,' a recommendation that the agents should make arrangements to obviate the necessity of keeping powder in the changing house.

About a hundred suits of clothes and shoes belonging to the underground miners were destroyed when the dry at Wheal Kitty caught fire in February 1873. The man who usually had charge by night of drying the clothes had been taken ill, and the shaftmen, before leaving to attend to their work, put in fresh coal and damped up the fireplace. The men were unable to go underground again until new clothes had been provided for them. The dry itself was very badly damaged in the blaze.

Early in the morning of November 8 1859, the dry of Levant was discovered to be on fire, and before any assistance could be procured, the whole building was destroyed, together with all the men's underground clothes, candles, powder and safety fuses. The total damage was estimated at not less than £400. In late March or early April 1865, the workmen at East Carn Brea mine also lost the greater part of their working clothes when the dry there burnt down. The origin of the fire was unknown. Fortunately, the smith's shop, account house and other nearby buildings were not involved. A somewhat remarkable fire occurred in the dry at St. Ives Consols on December 21 1881. About two in the morning, while a terrible storm was raging, people living in the higher part of the town, and particularly in the Stennack, heard a series of detonations, like minute guns. At first it was believed that these were signals of distress from a vessel on the coast, but then it was noticed that the sound did not come from the direction of the sea. They subsequently

A COPY OF
VERSES,

Composed on the tragical catastrophe that occured at Carn Brea Mine, on Wednesday, 7th December, 1842, by the burning of the barracks; one young man was blown to pieces by the explosion of a barrel of gun-powder, ten others were dreadfully scorched, the following of whom have since died.

WATERS AND SON.	**HOCKING,**
COCK,	**MARTIN.**
MITCHELL.	**HARVEY.**
NICHOLAS.	

Why am I with grief oppressed,
Dark forebodings fill my breast,
Plaintive accents flitting by.
Seem to whisper man must die.

Hark! methinks I hear a knell,
Pensive on the zephyr swell;
Ah! it tells some direful tale,
O! I listen till I'm pale.

Now the truth is brought to light,
See the flames are blazing bright,
Hark! the shrieking victim cries:
Ah! the burning Miner dies.

Lo! explosions quick and strong,
From gun-powder power along:
Awful accents rise between.
O! the horrors of the scene.

Mark th? clouds of smoke aspire,
Look! the barracks is on fire
Compass'd round with flames and death,
Ten poor Miners gasp for breath.

Mid the din of fire and air,
Hark! I hear the voice of prayer;
Burning, dying, death I see,
God be merciful to me.

Ten were rescued, scorched, and dried,
There was one dear youth who died,
Blown in pieces by the blast,
His remains were found at last.

Scorch'd by the consuming fire
Lay his poor afflicted Sire;
Crying, when the flames were o'er
Tell me is my son no more.

Now the roof begins to fall,
Blazing from the tottering wall,
Smoke in volumes soar away,
Death amid the ruins play.

By and by the flames expire,
And the rage of ruthless fire
Calmly dies, and now they strive
To save their comrades half-alive.

Some toward their homes were borne,
But they died before the morn,
Others with their sufferings wept
A few short days, and then they slept,

Seven, beside the youth are dead,
His dear Father too is fled,
Crying with his latest breath,
Jesus is my strength in death.

O what solace thus to see
Christ had set his spirit free,
Born on angels wings away
To the realms of endless day.

Now the Son and Father sleep
In yon gloomy grave so deep,
Where affection sits to mourn
Ever on their quiet urn.

Some have shouting cross'd the flood,
They were washed in Jesus blood,
Now before the throne they shine,
Clothed with victory divine.

Widow, dry the falling tear.
God will be thy husband here,
Orphan cease thy accents wild
God will be thy Father, child,

Now on him your griefs repose,
He will listen to your woes.
Feed you, guide you with his hand,
To that holy, happy land.

Fathers, do no longer cry:
Mothers, look beyond the sky:
Sisters, see your brother there,
Smiling in yon world so fair.

Deaths black shafts at random fly,
Reason tell us we must die,
Bids us seek to be forgiven,
Sends us at the gate of heaven.

Let us now for mercy cry,
Let us to the Saviour fly,
And procure a home at last,
Heavenly, when life's dream is past.

Edwards Printer &c, Camborne.

A broadsheet commemorating the Carn Brea disaster of 7 December 1842
(Courtesy Royal Institution of Cornwall)

learned that St. Ives Consols dry had taken fire by some unknown means, and there being no help at hand, it was burnt to the ground. Seven dynamite caps were in the building or close to it, and it was their exploding which caused the strange noises in the night. A similar nocturnal blaze destroyed the wooden dry at Trewey Downs mine, Zennor, in November 1907. About one o'clock in the morning, when a boy visited it, there was nothing wrong, but an hour later the engineman noticed it burning. The structure could not be saved. It was surmised that clothes left drying by the fire had ignited, and caused the blaze.

Fires in mine account houses appear to have been much rarer, which was fortunate, as the loss of records stored in these buildings could have the most serious consequences. The most dramatic fire of this description was probably that which destroyed the central part of Dolcoath account house on January 30 1895. No caretaker resided on the premises, and so the flames had obtained a good hold before the out-break was discovered. Camborne fire brigade was soon on the scene and began pumping water on the building from a large tank nearby, and when this was exhausted a long length of hose was run out to connect with the Camborne water mains. The firemen worked lustily at the pumps for five and a half hours, assisted by scores of willing helpers. At one time the blaze threatened to assume disastrous consequences, but by strenuous efforts the firefighters managed to confine it to the central portion of the building, the two wings being saved. Much of the history of this famous old mine perished in the flames. Perhaps the most serious loss was Herr Frankel's portrait of Captain Charles Thomas, father of Captain Josiah Thomas, the manager, which had been presented by a subscription of the adventurers, and for many years hung on the wall side by side with the plans of the mine. Other paintings destroyed were those of Mr. J. Francis Basset (uncle to the then Lord of Dolcoath, Mr. A. F. Basset) and of Sir William Williams, for many years chairman of Dolcoath committee. The loss of the plans was a great tragedy, but fortunately tracings or duplicates of these brought up to a recent date were preserved at the Tehidy office. Luckily, also, the most important books and documents had been stored in a fireproof room, whilst others were rescued from the burning building. 'Both the brigade and miners at the mine worked well and willingly,' states the *Cornishman*,

> ...and showed conspicuous bravery in attempting to subdue the ravages of the fire — indeed, at times their lives were in jeopardy amidst the columes of smoke and the falling of the burning timbers. By means of their plucky efforts, a mass of valuable books, papers and correspondence were saved, to say nothing of furniture and articles of lesser value.

However, Captain Josiah Thomas and his sons, Captain R. A. Thomas and F. W. Thomas, lost a large number of private papers, surveying and dialling instruments, and books and papers of the various companies with which they were associated. The cause of the outbreak remained unknown, but it was believed that it began at the rear of the premises and made its way right through the offices. The destroyed section comprised the general office of the mine, the large room used for meetings of shareholders, and the manager's private office.

On a few rare occasions fires swept through almost all the surface buildings on a mine, leaving behind a whole train of problems both for management and men. Such an event took place at Wheal Providence, Carbis Bay, on the night of November 7 1907. This mine had only recently been restarted after lying idle for about thirty years, and a considerable amount of new equipment had been put in and new buildings erected. The St. Ives fire brigade were summoned to the scene by telephone, and on arrival found the blaze had already assumed alarming proportions. Most of the buildings were of wood, with corrugated iron roofs, and these were blazing fiercely. There was a good supply of water, but it was very thick and muddy. This made hard work of the pumping, carried out by the old manual engine 'St. Eia,' but there were many willing helpers, and a good stream of water was soon playing on the flames. A quantity of valuable tools and materials in the fitting and blacksmiths' shops, and the brigade's main efforts were directed to saving these buildings, and in this they proved successful; but all the other places (including the offices, carpenters' shop, changing house, sample house, etc., with their contents) were entirely destroyed. The miners fared very badly, all the clothes of the afternoon and night men being consumed. The fire was first observed in the carpenters' shop, but how it originated was not known.

References

1. The names of other rescuers mentioned were Captain James; Captain Davies; and two youths, Pascoe and McCanister; but it is not made clear exactly what they did. All were affected in various degrees by the smoke.
2. Burrow, J.C., and Thomas, W., *'Mongst Mines and Miners, 1893.*

A Miscellany of Mishaps

So far this survey has covered the broader classification of accidents affecting Cornish mines. Besides these, however, there were many other types of mishap involving almost every aspect of the industry, and which for convenience have been grouped together in this final chapter.

A number of casualties occurred through the presence of 'foul air' in the workings. This term was used by miners to describe various types of vitiated or polluted atmosphere encountered underground. Prior to the introduction of compressed air for working drills in the 1870's and 1880's the ventilation of mines left much to be desired, and there were many 'ends' in which candles would not burn and where a man could easily be rendered unconscious or even die through lack of oxygen. On March 6 1843 Thomas Nicholls accidentally holed into a part of Levant mine, St. Just, that had for some time been abandoned, and fell apparently dead from breathing the foul air that escaped from it. His comrade immediately ran for assistance, and fetched seven more men, but as soon as they entered the place all fell in the same manner, and lay inert on the ground for some minutes. Purer air, however, soon followed, which revived them, and within a few days all were able to resume work.

Less fortunate were two young men called John Thomas Keast and James Beer, both eighteen years of age, who died from this cause at East Wheal Rose, near Newlyn East, in June 1845. The *Penzance Gazette* of July 9 stated that the lads were employed at the mine on surface work, dressing ores, and had no business underground. However, they went below one Saturday for some unknown purpose, and, it was supposed, having missed their way, endeavoured to get up through an old footway between the 20 and 30 fathom levels where there had been no working for several months past. When night came, and they had not returned home, an alarm was raised, and the following day some miners were sent down the mine to see if they were there. The two lads were both found in the footway, quite dead, apparently from having inhaled the impure air which had accumulated there.

The *Mining Journal* of September 4 1875 contained the account of a dramatic rescue carried out at Great Wheal Lovell, in the Wendron district, when some men were overcome by foul air. For several days the atmosphere had been bad in the 44 fathom level, which extended from the main shaft for about 50 fathoms. A new shaft was sinking, and all the customary means to ventilate the end, by burning furze and exploding powder (to induce a draught) had been taken. Captain Priske, the manager, had felt most anxious about the men working in that part. About two o'clock one morning three shaftmen — William Jones, John

Jenkin and Edward Rogers — descended the mine, being the last-core-by-night men; and Captain Priske was waiting at the landing for them at an early hour. When they failed to appear, the succeeding pare were sent underground with all speed, after being strictly cautioned about the foul air, which it seemed certain had overpowered the shaftmen. This group consisted of Daniel Treloar, his son, and six others. When they reached the shaft bottom the bad air began to affect their candles. Entering the level, they shouted as loudly as they could, but received no answer, nor was there any glimpse of light. So, carefully in the dimness the rescuers groped their way through the level. About two hundred feet from the main shaft and ninety feet from the new shaft, on which the missing men were employed, Jones was found, his head against the side of the level with a stream of water trickling on his temple. Treloar's party were already beginning to feel overpowered, but they took off their jackets and swung them about in the limited space to disperse the gas by which they and the senseless man at their feet were surrounded. Two of them then lifted Jones and carried him to the junction of the level with the shaft.

A fascinating view of Glebe Stamps, Wendron, illustrating the juxta position and close proximity of home and workplace in the Cornish mining districts
(Courtesy Royal Institution of Cornwall)

Not far from the spot where he had been found Jenkin and Rogers were also discovered, both lying with their heads towards the main shaft. It was not clear whether they had worked after arriving below, or had been at once stricken to the ground. Further men were now sent below to render assistance, as it was realised the rescuers themselves might be in danger. William Tonkin, who had been one of the first to go in after the missing shaftmen, was indeed by this time so far overcome that he gasped out "I am going," and soon became insensible. Daniel Treloar and his son, who had actively exerted themselves, were also exhausted, and while the unfortunate shaftmen were being attended to, they had to be sent up. As the kibble was required for the suffocated men, they had to ascend by the ladders, but this proved laborious work, and so weak had the rescue party become that they had to stop by the way. Young Treloar, whose father had been up and down the shaft three times, was lashed to the ladder about fourteen fathoms up, or he would have fallen and been dashed to pieces in the depths below. After hours of toiling, the shaftmen and those who had gone to their relief were all brought up and taken to the account house. They appeared like dead men, but intermittent breathing showed that life was not quite extinct. 'Pallid, almost pulseless, water dripping from their coarse mine clothes, and smeared with dirt, there they lay until the time arrived when it was prudent to remove them to their homes.' The men seem to have partly brought the trouble on themselves; for, having a good contract, they were anxious to prosecute their work with all speed, despite the repeated warnings about foul air which Captain Priske had given them. The task of bringing them to surface proved one of no small magnitude, as they had to be held up in the kibble by other men. Large numbers of rescuers from adjoining mines, with their captains, rendered most efficient help to Great Wheal Lovell in this dire emergency.

These miners indeed had a narrow escape, being only saved from asphyxiation by the courage and determination of their comrades. Foul air sometimes acted so quickly, however, that fatal results ensued even when ready help was at hand. John Stevens, a single young miner aged 21, living at Lelant Downs, and employed at Wheal Mary mine, had prepared and fired a hole in the 115 level on the morning of June 17 1873. When it failed to explode, he descended to discover the reason, but had scarcely reached the level when he signalled to his comrades to draw him up. This was done as quickly as possible, but he was found to have already been rendered insensible by the bad atmosphere, and soon afterwards expired.

Many accidents were caused by pumping engines and their associated machinery — a fact hardly to be wondered at considering the long lengths of unprotected rods working in the narrow shafts adjacent to ladder ways, and the great swinging balance-bob and other moving parts at surface. On August 19 1834 a sump-man called Richard Jenkin was killed whilst descending in a bucket to adjust one of the pumps at Lanescot mine, (a section of Fowey Consols, lying a mile N.E. of St. Blazey) apparently by the bucket-rod striking him on the head. At Duffield mine, in the parish of Gwinear, Edmund Angove, aged 21, received a similar injury by the engine striking him on the head whilst he was at work and he lived only an hour after being brought to surface. A very sad case involving a fatality caused by an engine-rod took place at Trumpet Consols, Wendron, on November 2 1874. Repairs were being carried out at the time in Wheal Dream shaft, and a section of the ladder-way had to be left open — *i.e.,* unprotected by a partition from the rod — for this purpose. A group of miners consisting of Amos Treloar Winn (19), his father, and two others called Josiah Pryor and Pearce were ascending this shaft when, on reaching the 40 fathom level, Pryor, who was behind Winn, saw the latter's legs hanging down and his body under a part of the pump rod. Pryor pulled the bell wire, and called to those above to stop the engine, but Winn was dead when taken up. At the inquest, Captain Quentrall, the manager, said he considered the ladder-way safe, despite the opening; but Dr. C. Le Neve Foster, Government Inspector of Mines, stated that in his view the place where the accident occurred was dangerous, and that something portable should have been placed there to protect the men. The jury returned of 'accidentally killed at Trumpet Consols by a blow from the pumping machinery,' and whilst exonerating the mining authorities from blame, recommended that the place should be secured to prevent the recurrence of such an accident.

Quite a number of engine-men met their deaths from being struck by the ponderous balance-bobs of their machines. An interesting early example occurred at Rosewall Hill mine, near St. Ives, on the morning of August 8 1801. Something having gone wrong with the engine, the engine-man passed beneath the bob to rectify the fault whilst the engine was still in motion. The bob came down upon him, causing such severe bruising that the poor fellow died within a few hours, leaving a wife and seven children to deplore his loss. The man had been a Private in the local Volunteer Artillery Company, and was interred with full military honours on the Sunday evening following in the parish of Towednack, the funeral being attended by many hundreds of sympathisers.

Between eight and nine o'clock on November 18 1873, William Grenfell, William Rowe (engine-man) and Mark Rowe were in the Crowns shaft of Botallack engaged in sending down a collar-launder. Mark Rowe was holding the lashing and Grenfell guiding it down, when the launder, by some means, became hitched in a man-hole. Grenfell was sent on before, and the lashing made fast to the staves of the ladder. Mark Rowe then came down to clear the launder, handing the lashing to Grenfell. Rowe said, "It is going," and Grenfell replied "Yes." Rowe then told Grenfell to let it go, which was done, until the former called out to him to "hold." Rowe tried to push the launder down, but did not succeed. He was then about three feet above Grenfell, who saw nothing further of his comrade until his hat dropped down at his side. On going up to see what was the matter, blood came down all over Grenfell's head and shoulders, but he could not get to his companion as the launder blocked the way. An alarm was made, when the engine-man at once stopped the engine and went for help. The kibble was sent down and Grenfell drawn to surface, after which Captain Oats went below by the ladder-way, accompanied by another man. They found the launder in the man-hole with Rowe in a sitting posture on it. His head was bowed, and they could not get him to speak. The unfortunate young man had received a violent blow on the side of the head; his jaw had fallen, and life was extinct. His body was brought to surface, and Captain Oats later went below again to look for the cause of the accident. He could find no marks of blood about the rod, but searching further, found some human hair at the bottom of the connection of the balance-bob. It was therefore concluded that Rowe, finding the launder would not come down easily, put his head out too far in the shaft over the protecting fence, and was struck by the bottom of the connecting-rod, which jammed his head against the fence-piece. At the inquest, Grenfell stated that the usual way of sending down a launder was by the capstan rope, but that the present method had been used instead by Rowe's express wish. The engine-man had previously asked him whether he should stop the engine whilst this work was going on, but he replied, "We shall not be in contact with the engine-rods, so you have no need to stop the engine."

A variety of other types of accidents with engines are recorded in the files of old Cornish newspapers. The *Penzance Gazette* of Wednesday February 16 1842 stated that on the previous Monday a lad called Edmund Moorshead was caught by the trousers by the crank of the fly wheel at St. Ives Consols mine, and his thigh smashed. Following amputation, his chances of recovery were thought to be good, but death occurred soon after. On August 20 1869 the fly wheel of the fire whim at Wheal Dream (a part of Trumpet Consols, in Wendron) broke in pieces, fortunately without injuring anyone. When a fly wheel disintegrates, it possesses something of the power of an exploding bomb; and in this case a large fragment struck the Coverack Wesleyan Chapel, tearing the roof and doing considerable damage.

An unfortunate tragedy took place at South Great Work, near St. Hilary, on the afternoon of May 17 1873 whilst maintenance work was being carried out on the engine. The packing of the cylinder had been completed, and a portion of the machinery lifted by a winch and chain, the chain remaining taut. As the engine made her first stroke, Ralph Courtice, of St. Hilary Downs, who happened to be near the winch, which was dragged violently round, received such a violent blow from its handle that his skull was fractured, death occurring within two hours.

Benjamin Snell, of St. Blazey, engine-man at Par Consols, was caught and killed by the wheel of his own engine at midnight on May 31 1853. The engine had been stopped whilst the men took their supper; having finished, a miner called Hancock put on the steam when by some unexplained means the accident occurred.

Engine maintenance, which sometimes involved the replacement of heavy pieces of equipment, could lead to mishaps. Whilst a new bob was being fixed at West Ding Dong in Madron during September 1852, it slipped and struck a man called Nicholas injuring his hand and leg and shattering his foot. Medical assistance was procured and every effort made to save the injured limb, but 'the painful process of amputation' — without anaesthetics in those days — 'was rendered necessary, this being the last recourse which held forth any chance of recovery.' He was later said to be doing well under the care of Dr. Quick of St. Just.

A sad feature of the Industrial Revolution was the large number of accidents, many fatal, involving young children, who were permitted to work near, and even operate, quite dangerous machines. Cornwall had its full quota of these, many of the miners' children being compelled, by sheer economic necessity, to be sent to work on the dressing floors and in other places about the mines where their puny strength and busy fingers could be of service. Many of the tasks to which they were set were, in themselves, not dangerous; but the whole area of a mine is filled with moving machinery, which, because of its fascination for children, could be all the more fatal to them. The fact that many of these accidents resulted from disobedience or playfulness makes them all the more horrifying, for it meant that they were the direct outcome of attempts to thwart and suppress these young people's natural instincts by putting them to work too early. A very grim example of this occurred at Dolcoath on April 21 1869. During the previous summer, the boys employed on the dressing floors adopted the practice of betaking themselves to the wooden roofs of the sheds, under which they worked, to eat their dinner. They preferred this elevated and airy perch to the room provided for them, but as this open-air dining injured the roofs and placed the lads in danger, they were scolded and fined for the offence. On the day in question, James Eva, a little boy of eight, living at Ponsferris, Gwinear, after working all morning packing kieves, was released at twelve for his dinner. Half-an-hour later, when Charles King and Charles Chapple returned from their dinner, they saw some of the machinery stop. King looked up at the rod, which had been revolving, and saw the poor little fellow twisted round it. He ran up to the roof and extricated him, but the child was quite dead. It was presumed that, while on the roof, his loose shirt became entangled with the rod, for his clothes were twisted round it, his right foot (including the ankle) was severed; the left arm was round the rod and nearly torn off; while the left ear had been cut off and blood came from the head. Comment on such a case as this would be utterly superfluous.

Another sad instance of a boy losing his life through acting in a foolish yet child-like way occurred on November 17 1874 at Wheal Basset. Mathew Bennett, aged 13, was employed as a clerk at this mine, a part of his duty being to hand out the powder to the miners. On this occasion, he took some powder to a distance from the mine and put a lighted match to it. The powder exploded, caught his clothes on fire, and burnt him so badly that he died three days later.

An even more dreadful powder accident, which resulted in the deaths of four little boys aged respectively 9, 7, 7 and 5 years, occurred at Dolcoath on June 20 1868. The miners there received their week's supply of powder and gun-cotton, amounting to 10 to 50 lbs. each, every Monday morning and stored it in lockers arranged in an open shed which had a roof but no walls. Each locker had a key which was kept by the 'pare' of men whose powder was stored there in cans and barrels. When transferring the powder from these containers small amounts were sometimes spilled on the floor, a fact well known to local children who were in the habit of collecting it to make 'fireworks.'

On that bright midsummer morning three brothers - James Oliver Walter, Augustus Walter and Alfred Lewis Walter, set out with their 13 year old sister, Fanny Ann Walter, from their home at Roskear Field, Camborne, to Pengegon Well where the girl was going to fetch water. They left her at the mine to go into the powder house, where they were joined by three other boys called Thomas Cahill, Benjamin Dorrington and Richard Wills. On returning from the well Fanny saw the boys picking up grains of powder and putting them into piles. She begged them to come away in case they burned themselves, but her words had no effect. She saw Dorrington take a match from his pocket and give it to James Walter, telling him to put it to the powder. The boy struck the match against a locker door and applied it to the powder grains on the floor. Fanny and Dorrington then ran off and had just got outside when a series of tremendous explosions occurred as all the lockers blew up one after another. The girl ran back, seized her little brother Walter and dragged him part way out of the house, but his clothes were on fire, and being nearly as heavy as herself she could not carry him any further.

John Harris, a miner, was going from the shaft to the smith's shop when he heard an explosion, and looking up saw the powder house on fire and two boys running away from the yard. Approaching the yard he saw a little boy, Alfred Lewis Walter, on the ground in flames, whilst three others, James Oliver Walter, Augustus Walter and Thomas Cahill, were being carried out from the powder house by rescuers, also with their clothes on fire.

The four children, severely burned and injured by the explosions, were taken to their homes and given medical attention, but three died that evening and the fourth the following morning. The Walter brothers were the sons of William Walter, a labourer earning 15s a week, with which he had to support a wife and eight children, including a little crippled girl.

At the inquest, the jury returned a verdict of 'accidental death' with a recommendation that 'for the future prevention of such accidents the walls on three sides of the court should be raised and the front protected by iron or wooden gates.' It is surprising they did not also recommend that the floor of the magazine should be regularly swept to remove all spilt gunpowder grains.

The children killed in this accident were, of course, trespassers on the mine. It is not clear from the recorded facts whether the same could be said of two others who died in an unusual mishap at Wheal Friendship, near Relubbas, in November 1857. The engine man had, as he supposed, let off all the steam from the boiler for the purpose of cleaning it, and soon after returned to descend through the manhole. A boy of 12 and a girl of 15 were standing near the cover. When he opened it a dense cloud of steam poured forth which enveloped all three. The man was badly scalded, but recovered; the two youngsters, however, died of the effects of the steam within a few hours.

The playful instincts of children working amidst potentially lethal mining machinery were responsible for a number of deaths. On September 14 1852 when James Thomas, an eleven year old ore-dresser at Great Wheal Baddern, near Bissoe Bridge, arrived at the mine he asked to be set a task, saying he wanted to leave work early to collect a new pair of shoes ordered some weeks previously. A task was given him, which he finished soon after three o'clock, but instead of going for his shoes he began riding in the cage of the horse-whim. His head reached above the cage, and every time he passed under the stay of the span beam he was obliged to duck. His employer pointed out the danger of his riding there, and ordered him to come down, which he did, but ten minutes later he got into the cage again, unknown to the whim driver and lander at the shaft, who had been ordered to allow no one to ride in that way. Whilst looking out over the cage his head got crushed between the span beam and the top bar, injuring him so severely that he died soon after.

Early on the morning of August 24 1867 John Dunn of Madron, described as a 'very steady' engine man at Ding Dong, was talking to Hannibal Eddy of Towednack, a boy employed on the mine, who lay across the rod which connected the flywheel of the engine with the tozing machine, resting on both hands. In this position the revolving rod suddenly caught his loose frock, flinging him round and round with such violence that it tore off one of his arms near the shoulder, and then threw him away, still carrying round the arm and some of his clothes. The engine was immediately stopped, and two doctors summoned, who amputated the fragments of the arm, but Eddy died three hours later.

Many children found employment at water stamps, and some of them were killed or injured by those dangerous appliances. On February 28 1853 nine year old Henry Floyd was assisting John Rowe, a tin dresser, in repairing some launders at Pins Stamps, North Country, Redruth. In reaching for a short launder which was being handed up to him by the little boy in the wheel pit, the wheel, which had been trigged, gave a sudden jerk and caught Floyd between the arm of the wheel and the pit, and it was found impossible to extricate him until part of the arm had been cut off. He was taken to his parents at Harmony account house, but died of his injuries six days later.

Although very young children were employed only at surface on the mines, at the age of twelve or thirteen they began to work underground, usually accompanied by their fathers who kept a watchful eye on them whilst they were learning the miner's trade. But, however careful the parental supervision accidents inevitably occurred from time to time. On July 24 1867 James Henry Gendall, of Trewellard, a lad of 13, was working with his father Richard Gendall at the 30 fathom level E. under adit in the Carnyorth part of Botallack. Gendall, senior, was in a winze, and the boy had to wheel stuff from him to another winze 30 fathoms further E. and there empty his barrow. This latter winze went from the 30 to 40, and was protected on top by three planks whose security had been checked by the boy's father only that morning. A miner named Clemens working at the bottom of the winze in the 40 was suddenly startled by a boy's desperate scream, and running quickly to the winze found the poor lad at the bottom lying against a large stone and bleeding from a head wound. It appeared that in emptying his first barrowful of stuff that day he must have slipped and fallen 60 ft. with it. The barrow and leather slings were at the top of the pile of stuff at the base of the winze, but he had rolled to the bottom. James Henry Gendall was got to surface as quickly as possible and attended to by Drs. Quick and Harvey, but died of concussion within a few hours.

Benjamin Thomas, of West Place, St. Just, began his underground working career at the very early age of nine years, attending on a pare of men in Balleswidden mine. On November 19 1866, when aged eleven, he was working with his brother Martin Thomas and John Hocking in the 160 fathom level. A day or two previously the two men had examined the ground there which appeared to be weak, but thought the timber in the back of the level adequate to support the weight. About an hour after they commenced work Benjamin was coming back in the level with water in a box — presumably drinking water — when a 'queer' of ground about a ton in weight suddenly came away, completely burying the child except for his head. The men extricated him from the rubble as quickly as possible, but he was quite unsensible. They got him to surface and tried to obtain the services of one or other of the three surgeons living at St. Just. One was not at home; another insisted on attending one of his own patients first but would come to the mine afterwards; whilst the third, who was not a surgeon of the mine, refused to attend unless paid in advance! After this, Dr. Davy, a Balleswidden mine surgeon who lived at Penzance, six miles distant, was sent for, and arrived within ninety minutes, but the boy died at midnight from his injuries. At the inquest, the Coroner recommended to Captain Veale, one of the Balleswidden agents, that an immediate understanding should be come to with the St. Just doctors who were not appointed surgeons of the mine, to attend any future case of this kind, when called on to do so by the mine's agents, and to guarantee the payment of their fees. Captain Veale promised to call the purser's attention to the matter.

Conduct that would have merited censure in an adult, yet is excusable in a child, cost thirteen year old Peter Toy his life at the Basset and Grylls mine, Wendron, on February 21 1881. Half-an-hour before the accident occurred his master cautioned him against going up a ladder, by the water wheel, but he ignored the warning. When half-way up the ladder, his comrade called him back, but he went on, and was caught by the driver or crank and killed on the spot. Machinery of this type was particularly lethal to children. In November 1863 a twelve year old lad named Phillips working at the stamping mill belonging to the Lanivet Steam Works, had his smock caught by the stamps; he was dragged among them and his head instantly crushed.

The most shocking of all accidents involving children were surely those which caused the deaths of young bal-maidens. For a typical example, a case occurring at Ding Dong — that strange old mine situated in the heart of the West Penwith moorland — on July 8 1873 will serve as well as any. Alice Ann Stevens and Eliza Jane Hall worked together at the stamps; during the dinner hour they met in the stamps' boiler house and from there went to the whim house. Stevens then walked across to a nearby stream, whilst Hall climbed on to the crown wheel of the whim, the appliance at that time not being in motion. She remained there about two minutes; and Stevens, whilst washing her hands, looked up and said to the foolish girl, "Eliza, don't you know better than to get up there?" Hall made no answer to this, but got down from the wheel. Just at that moment the bell rang, indicating that the whim was about to commence work, which it immediately did. Ignoring a second warning from Stevens, Hall got on the wheel again whilst it was in motion, exclaiming "I will go round!" The wheel, of course, had the motion of a roundabout, but a very dangerous one it proved to ride, for in an instant the girl's clothes were caught in it, and she was dragged to the ground. Stevens screamed, and James Berriman, the whim-driver, stopped his machine. He found Hall lying partly on the ground and partly in the cog of the wheel. She was freed, and it was then found that her right leg had passed through the wheel, and was crushed and broken, whilst the left foot had been caught in the cogs and was much fractured. Blood was also dropping from her on the ground. Despite prompt medical aid the poor girl died seven hours afterwards. During the subsequent inquest held at Towednack, Berriman states that the crown wheel had been in use at the mine for over thirty years, but this was the first accident that had ever happened with it. No boy or girl had any business on or near the wheel.

Equally tragic was the case of a young woman called Buzza, of Gwennap, aged about seventeen. During the 'crowst' break on May 15 1823 she retired to a stamps' shed on Poldice mine, but going too near the axle by which the stamps were set in motion her clothes were caught by one of the caps. The poor girl was drawn in between the stamps and the wall and crushed to death.

Bal maids and children were however by no means the only victims of mishaps involving tin stamps and water wheels. Many a stamps-man met his death between the cogs of his cumbrous machine. On February 10 1843 Sampson Chynoweth, who worked the stamps at Royal Polberow Consols, St. Agnes, was about to apply some oil to the cog wheels when his clothing became entangled with them, and he was drawn in and crushed to death by their teeth. No one saw the accident and the pieces of cloth caught between them, showed plainly enough how it must have happened. The body, when found, had fallen from the machinery into the pass behind the stamps heads; and had it remained undiscovered an hour longer it would have been pounded to atoms and washed off along with the tinstuff. At Wheal Budnick, Perranzabuloe, Nicholas Scobell, the stamps-man, had his right hand caught between the cog wheels on December 14 1839, his arm being crushed nearly to the shoulder-joint. He was taken almost lifeless to the Royal Cornwall Infirmary on a litter, but after an operation hopes were entertained for his recovery. A very grim fate overtook James Lukes, a carpenter, when repairing the stamps at Lanescot mine on April 26 1834. He had propped up one of the iron lifters and placed his head under it in order to adjust the machinery, when the support gave way, the lifter fell, and he was crushed to death.

On May 28 1866 John Rodda, aged 19, of St. Just engine driver of St. Just United steam stamps, noticed something amiss with the stamps and ran outside to put it right. This was not part of his duties, but that of the stamps-man, but he kindly volunteered his services. The stamps axle had some time previouly cracked, and a band, with screws, was put round it, to make it safe. Forgetful of this band, he stooped, and the revolving and projected band struck him on the head, knocked his brains out, and he died in a minute on the spot.

Men were killed not only in operating stamps but also when erecting them. John Budge, of the parish of North Hill, was excavating a wheel pit at North Phoenix mine, near Darley, in Linkinhorne, on August 28 1857 and had just sent up a kibble of stuff which men above were wheeling off in barrows, when one large stone fell into the pit, striking him on the back of the head and neck. He died within two hours of a fractured skull.

Water wheels continued in use until quite recent times; and as a consequence accidents with them were not unknown in the early part of this century. One such occurred at Tregurtha Downs mine in April 1913. Three water wheels were connected to the tin-dressing plant by a slowly revolving shafting; and as a workman who had just finished his night's work was leaving for home his foot slipped and he was caught by the shafting. He was twisted around it several times before his plight was seen and the machinery stopped. He was in a pitiable condition when extricated, his injuries including two broken legs, a fractured arm and cut head. He died soon after at Penzance Hospital.

Some mine accidents were attended by the most extraordinary circumstances. While Captain Robert Williams, of Redruth, was setting a pitch to a workman in Poldice mine during August 1812, the scaffolding gave way with a great quantity of earth, and they both fell into sixty fathoms of water. It was estimated that a year's work would be required to get out their bodies. Some miners, again, seemed pursued by a strangely malignant fate, so that no matter what job they undertook, a mishap was bound to befall them. In 1837 a miner called Collins, of Camborne, while working in North Roskear mine, lost an arm and an eye by a premature explosion of gunpowder, and being thereby rendered unfit for underground labour, obtained a situation at one of the whim engines on the same mine. However, whilst cleaning a part of the engine in March 1840 his remaining arm became entangled in the machinery and was so dreadfully shattered that amputation became necessary, the operation being performed by the same surgeon who had taken off the other arm. 'The unfortunate man,' stated the *Royal Cornwall Gazette,* 'although in a most deplorable condition, is in pretty good spirits, and is doing as good as might be expected.'

Tramming accidents were a frequent source of death and injury to miners. Nicholas Rowe, engine-man at Wheal Owles, St. Just, wished to speak to Richard Lavis one day in April 1873, but could not find him on the tramroad at surface where he was accustomed to work. Half-a-minute after Lavis was missed, Alfred Goninan, a tin-dresser at

Botallack, ran up and said that from a distance of three hundred yards he had seen Lavis push a truck from the mouth of the skip shaft to the end of the embankment — mine-burrow is apparently meant by this term — which was about 30 feet high. Lavis went round to the tail of the truck and took the pin out, then came back, stooped down and put the chain on the end of the vehicle. One end of this chain was fastened to a staple driven into the runner which formed part of the road, whilst the other was intended to be attached to the wagon to prevent it going over the incline when the load was tipped. He raised the truck by its handles, but very little of the stuff came out, as it was wet. He was leaning forward on the truck, when Goninan saw it suddenly topple over the bank and carry poor Lavis with it. When Goninan and Rowe reached the place they found him lying on his right side, the wagon across his legs, his skull fractured with blood flowing from the wound, and moaning pitifully. He died as he was being carried home. When Captain Tregear later examined the wagon, he found that a new staple, put into the runner that same afternoon, had parted owing to a flaw in the iron. This liberated the chain and allowed the truck to fall.

Another tramming accident took place in the submarine part of Levant on February 15 1881. William Davey and Richard Rowe carelessly let their wagon run too fast, so that it went six feet beyond its intended stopping place. Davey was walking by its side, and his foot accidentally went over the edge of the board, causing him to fall into the plat. They had placed a stone at the end to stop the wheel of the wagon, but because of the wagon's speed it was driven along and the stone slipped to one side. There ought to have been a board alongside the tramway where the wagon stopped. Boards had, in fact, previously been placed there, but when the tramroad was temporarily taken away two months before, these were removed and had not been replaced. Samuel Harvey, who was working in the 260 fathom level when Davey fell into the plat, went to his aid, and found him lying on his face bleeding from a bad head wound. Although all speed was used, it took them three hours to bring him to surface, but he died on the way up. At the inquest, Henry Harvey, timber-man, states that three weeks earlier Captain Trezise ordered him to repair all dangerous places in the 260 fathom level. This he did, but carried out no repairs to the place where the accident took place, as he saw no hole open there. The hole was covered by loose boards, and he asserted that no one could have fallen through unless these had been removed. The jury found 'that deceased was killed by falling through a hole in the 260 fathom level of Levant mine, and that Henry Harvey should be severely censured by the Coroner for not securing certain boards which had covered the hole through which deceased fell, but which boards had previous to the accident been removed by some person unknown.' It may thus be said that Davey's life was lost for the want of a few nails.

The tall headgear and buildings on mines were not infrequently struck by lightning and sometimes set on fire by it, whilst the effects of the shock were sometimes felt a considerable distance underground. During a severe thunderstorm at Wheal Sisters, Lelant, in August 1886, a large stack was thrown down, many large stones from it being found more than a hundred yards away. The current then travelled down the shaft to the 200 fathom level, and entered the level itself. Here two men were at work, one of whom received a shock as though struck on the back by a hilt.

West Kitty mine was affected in much the same way during a blinding hailstorm in March 1905. Lightning played up and down steel cable at the shaft, and several miners working a hundred fathoms in the stope at the 110 fathom level were knocked down by the shock. Its effects were also felt at Wheal Friendly during this storm.

During a severe storm on October 20 1862 the stack of the engine house at Ding Dong, built four years previously, was struck by lightning and toppled to the ground. The boiler house was also completely demolished and part of the engine house, through the falling of the heavy masonry. Fortunately there was no one present but the engine man, and he providentally escaped.

The ores in some Cornish mines contained a high proportion of arsenic which had to be removed, prior to smelting, by a process of roasting or calcination. The arsenic thus expelled was discharged into the atmosphere as a vapour; but when it came to be realised that this highly poisonous substance possessed considerable commerical value for medical, agricultural, chemical and other applications, efforts were made to reclaim it by condensing the fumes in long horizontal flues. The manufacture of arsenic, indeed, provided some mines with an appreciable part of their income; but the men engaged in this dangerous work often suffered severely in health. The following extract from the *West Briton* of March 2 1899 illustrates this point only too well:

> 'The recent development in the manufacture of arsenic in Cornwall and Devonshire has, it appears, been affected at a terrible cost to the health and lives of the workers. From a report presented to the Tavistock Board of Guardians by thier medical officers of health last week it seems that in the parish of Calstock, Cornwall, a large number of former arsenic workers, now in receipt of poor relief, were all suffering from diseases of the respiratory organs, the effects of arsenical fumes. The average age at which they were disabled from following their employment was forty; while a few at thirty-two were practically wrecks. On visiting the works the doctors found that furnacemen wore no protection against the deadly fumes of the poison; and that the other employees were protected only by a covering of lint over the nostrils, tied by a handkerchief extending over the mouth — this being, in the doctors' opinion, altogether inadequate.'

The engine house damaged by lightning at Wheal Sisters in April 1886
(Courtesy Royal Institution of Cornwall)

Wheal Sisters, with repairs to the lightning-struck engine-house (on the right) effected
(Noall collection)

It was not only the workers who suffered from the effects of this deadly substance. It was impossible to trap all the arsenic in the flues; and the remainder, emitted from chimneys, fell like a poison rain on the adjacent countryside, killing crops, injuring livestock, and endangering the health of everyone living near. Those affected by these evil exhalations sometimes sought redress in the courts, with varying success. During the spring of 1865 in the action of Matthews *v.* King, tried at Bodmin assizes, a farmer complained of a nuisance alleged to be caused by the roasting of ore and manufacturing of arsenic at Chacewater, the defendant being a shareholder in the offending tin and copper mine. The jury returned a verdict for the plaintiff but such an outcome could not always be looked for, as the mining interest, which formerly had great influence in some parts of the county, was sometimes able to tip the scales of justice in its own favour.

A notable case of this kind — and one with an amusing side, also — was heard at the county assizes in March 1878. The plaintiff was himself a man of some standing — Mr. C. W. Reynolds, J.P., the owner of Trevenson, Pool — whilst the adversary he had chosen to engage was the formidable East Pool mine, represented in the person of Mr. Martyn, its purser. Reynolds sought to recover £50 damages, the value of a horse alleged to have been poisoned by arsenical fumes emanating from a chimney belonging to the mine. He stated that smoke from the stacks drifted over his property. The smoke was suffocating and of a most pungent taste. A plantation had been destroyed and the ground left bare. The animal he claimed for was a brood mare, for which he would not have taken a hundred guineas. He had lost four colts in the same field within the last four years. The mare had been running in the field (known as Stamps' Field) for the past four years, but she became such a wretched object that he ordered her throat to be cut.

Mr. Sampson Taylor Rowe, analyst to the Truro Agricultural Exchange, gave evidence on Reynolds' behalf. This chemist had appeared in so many cases of this kind that he had earned himself the soubriquet of 'Arsenic Rowe' — because he could 'find arsenic in everything'! He certainly lived up to his reputation on this occasion, testifying that he had discovered arsenic in all parts of the unfortunate mare's body, and in samples of grass and leaves collected from the field.

Richard Martyn, the defendant, said he had received no complaint about damage by arsenic fumes until this horse died. They condensed fifty tons of arsenic and produced forty tons of tin a month. The prevailing wind was S.W., and that would blow everything away from Trevenson. Mr. Maynard, the mine manager, asserted they had gone to a great deal of expense to condense the arsenic. The flue was over 3,000 feet long, and beyond a point in it some distance from the chimney they never found arsenic in any appreciable amount. He had seen bullocks and sheep recently grazing in the field where the horse died, and added that this animal 'was buried in a lot of rubbish which had been gathered from different places.' Dr. Oxland, of Plymouth, believed the flues were effective, and claimed that no arsenic could ever reach Reynolds' house, but conceded that 'a few pounds of arsenic' might escape from the chimney in the course of a year. He had found no arsenic in grass taken from the field, but there was some in the ground. Mr. Collins, the Cornwall County Analyst, brought a part of the horse to him; they examined it together, and found an exceedingly small trace of arsenic — 'no more, in fact, than I would expect to find in any Cornishman living in a mining district'!

The judge said the questions to be answered by the jury were — did plaintiff's horse die of arsenic? and if so, did the fumes from the mine poison the animal? If the jury did not believe that the mare died of arsenic, then there was an end of the case. Those 'twelve good men and true' almost immediately returned a verdict for the defendant. A few weeks later it was announced that Reynolds was about to sell Trevenson and leave Cornwall. 'It is believed,' said the *Western Morning News,* 'that the adverse decision of the jury in the late action at the Assizes with regard to arsenical fumes from an adjoining mine has had some influence in this decision.'

An equally entertaining case occurred in 1865, when William Kitto, a Breage farmer, sought to recover £80 10s. damages from the adventurers of Wheal Grylls mine, on Kenneggy Downs, for injury and death caused to his stock by arsenic fumes emitted by a burning house. The plaintiff had a pure Jersey cow, which he had imported, and which took the prize at one of the cattle shows, but having eaten poisoned herbage in a field near the arsenic stack she became ill and died. Remonstrances were made to the Captain of Wheal Grylls, after which some flues were made to prevent the escape of the arsenic, but from faulty construction or design they did not answer and the arsenic continued to escape as before. Kitto now had three other cows and several growing animals, all of whom were sick. 'They lose all their flesh, and their ribs are bare and their backbones stick up like a saw.'

Following further representations, the mine put a 'freeth' - a triangle stuffed with furze - over the top of the chimney to catch the arsenic, and also placed a donkey in Kitto's field to ensure there was no arsenic present before he put in his cattle again. 'The arsenic kills donkeys; it killed a pretty many about there.' James Pope, agent at Wheal Grylls, testified that the burning house was erected in 1862. There were four chambers in the flue for precipitating the arsenic. This arsenic was not sold, as they recovered so little of it, but was put down an old shaft. Edward Rogers, Captain of Wheal Grylls, declared that the flues were

417 feet long. They were cleared out once every two months. The long flue was used when the wind was strong enough to create sufficient draught. He had the long flue built 'to keep Kitto quiet.' Cracks sometimes appeared in the flue, and he sent a man to mend them. Other witnesses hinted that Kitto's stock was in 'low condition' as a result of bad management on his part; in particular, it was alleged that the farm lay high and exposed to the wind, and that the Jersey cow ought to have had shelter. However, William Vellanoweth, a wheelwright, who had some fields south of the stack, said his animals had suffered from eating arsenic. 'I have seen the arsenic lying on the ground – it fell like snow as the wind blew over.' The jury found a verdict for plaintiff, but awarded him only 40s. damages.

When an arsenic works was sited on the outskirts of a town the consequences could be highly injurious to the health of the inhabitants. During the 1850's an arsenic calciner was erected at Pednandrea mine, adjacent to Redruth, and its effects were considered so deleterious that the local Board of Health issued a notice to stop further production. The calciner accordingly closed for a short period, but in November 1856 work there was resumed, and the Board announced their determination to prosecute the mine adventurers unless their orders were strictly obeyed. A public meeting was convened in Redruth Town Hall to discuss the matter, during which Mr. Cardozo, chief secretary of the mine, from London, promised that no expense should be spared to prevent the escape of arsenic and to render the works harmless to the inhabitants. On receiving this assurance, the meeting passed unanimously a resolution requesting the Board to suspend further proceedings against Pednandrea Calcining Works for three months to give the adventurers time to place it in a satisfactory condition.[1]

The adventurers of Wheal Prosper, Marazion, were mulcted of heavy damages in February 1865 in respect of cattle and horses poisoned by their calciner. On Otober 5 1864 Mr. Benjamin Thomas of New Dairy Farm, Marazion, placed a large number of cattle to feed by the side of the stream which passed through Prosper United on its way to the sea. That evening he found several showing symptoms of poisoning; six died and six were injured, causing him a total loss of £45. He had samples of water from the leat, and the contents of the animals' stomachs analysed; all yielded arsenic. On enquiry, he found that a few days before Prosper had stamped ten tons of stuff from the burning house flue, and that stuff the nearest to the fires which was consequently the most impregnated with arsenic. He accordingly brought a claim against the mine which both sides agreed to submit to arbitration at Penzance. During the hearing it was proved that ten tons of similar stuff had been frequently stamped during the past two years, but the 1864 summer was unusually dry and the water became a strong solution of arsenic. The arbitrator awarded £30 and costs.

At the same time a claim was heard by Mr. John Laity, of Trevarthian, for £180, the value of horses lost while grazing near the mine. Mr. Laity's case was that Wheal Prosper tin had recently burnt very foully owing to the fact that a boiler which had been attached, under Captain Thomas Richards' management, to the long flue of the buring house to damp the fumes and arrest its exit from the flue, had been removed by his successors, so that arsenic poured from the stack and poisoned about 40 acres of ground. Horses worth about £180 had been so poisoned, whilst two others were killed by drinking arsenic water and two more by falling into shafts. For the mine, it was contended that the animals had drunk from a pool to which they had no right. The arbitrator awarded the complainant £108.

The famous photograph of Pednandrea in the mid-1860s
(Courtesy Royal Institution of Cornwall)

Improved production methods have happily done away with the brooding menace of the tall chimney wafting its insidious poison over the countryside to the detriment of all living things in its vicinity.In the same way, new mining techniques have abolished many hazards for the miner, both above and below grass, as well as greatly lightening his toil and enabling much higher outputs to be achieved. Nevertheless, innovations bring their problems and sometimes dangers. So as mining was transformed from its traditional picturesque pattern into one of streamlined efficiency, a few new types of accident began to appear, arising directly from the use of more sophisticated methods and machines.

The first great revolution in mining technique was the introduction of boring machines in the early 1870's. These proved something of a mixed blessing. On the positive side, they eliminated the arduous toil of hand drilling and also ensured far better ventilation through the plentiful supply of compressed air required to operate them. Against this, far more dust was produced - deadly rock dust, which led to a marked increase in silicosis among the men who worked with these machines. Conditions were particularly bad in places where overhead drilling was carried out, the dust falling down upon the men standing below, and also where 'wet' drilling was not employed making use of a jet of water to lay the dust. As a rule, the onset of silicosis was slow and gradual, not showing its full effects till some years later; but sometimes it ran its fatal course far more rapidly. In September 1909 a fifty-one year old miner at East Pool complained of feeling unwell when leaving work. After taking a rest, he felt rather better, and walked from the 310 fathom level to the shaft to ascend to surface. Here, he complained of being worse, fell forward, and expired. He had been operating a boring machine; and at the inquest a doctor stated that both his lungs were completely destroyed by miner's phthisis, which had produced syncope.

Accidents with compressors, which provided the air supply for boring machines, were not unknown. An attendant was fatally injured whilst adjusting machinery in the compressor and crushing house on Williams' shaft, Dolcoath, in July 1912; he appears to have been the victim of his own carelessness.

Electric power came into fairly widespread use in mines from about 1905 onwards. As a public supply grid was not then available, the mining companies were obliged to erect their own power plants; and here, too, mishaps sometimes occurred. An unusual one was recorded at St. Ives Consols power house in 1911. A workman, whilst trying to replace a missing guard between a flywheel and the generator, fell into the flywheel pit and was immediately killed. In this instance, the man's keenness on his work led to the tragic result.

Reference

1. Pednandrea is one of the oldest and most interesting mines in Cornwall. The following is taken from the *Cornish Telegraph* of February 3 1869:

   One of the most prominent objects presented to the eye of the visitor upon his entrance to the town of Redruth, from any point of the compass, is the fine old massive chimney stack of the above mine, standing in the centre of the extensive surface works and rising to an altitude of 132 ft. (from base to top), the highest of the kind in the county. The stack was built in 1824, and upon its completion a barrel of ale was drunk on the top, and it has served as a landmark and engine stack to the present time. Curiously enough, in 1832, upon its summit were burnt several tar barrels by way of rejoicing upon passage of the Reform Bill, and a ladder-way was afterwards constructed within for purposes of observation.

Pednandrea Mine itself has existed as a mine for nearly two centuries, but until about fifty years ago bore the name of 'Suit and Cloak,' being thus named by an early adventurer, who upon being successful in his speculation, bought his lady a red cloak and himself a suit of broadcloth, both of which were then obtainable only at a considerable cost.

A curious incident in connection with Pednandrea mine occurred in 1749. An adventurer named Zacharias Johns, who was also an innkeeper keeping the Old Inn at the corner of Cross Street, bearing the sign of a Mackeral on a Cross, having had, in a lawsuit respecting his mining property, to visit London, which he did on horseback, and having returned the victor, had a kibble of punch suspended to his sign, and every miner who chose to drink did so until the kibble was dry.

Up to 1824 no great amount of profit was got out of Pednandrea, but for seven years after that she was worked for copper with varying success. Again she was knocked, and in 1852 the present adventurers commenced in earnest to develop the mine, and to erect suitable machinery for the return of the tin stone which was being broken in large quantities, but of low quality. For the last fourteen years the number of hands employed has varied very little up or down of 400, while the returns of tin for the same period have averaged about 20 tons per month; the amount expended from the year 1852 to the present time giving a monthly average of about £1,500.

The Botallack Mine Tragedy

ST. JUST, APRIL 18th, 1863.

How swift the moments pass away,
  How soon a day is gone,
And weeks and months they disappear,
  And years as quick roll on.

In health and strength some heedless pass
  The time that God has given;
Not thinking that it soon may close, -
  The thread of life be riven.

Thousands in life are passing on,
  Their journey soon will end,
Who scarcely ever seem to think
  To where their footsteps tend.

What dangers do our path surround,
  Unseen by mortal eye, -
A moment's space and we are gone,
  Into eternity.

Prepar'd or not prepar'd to die,
Whate'er the life had been, -
The saint or sinner - each must go
  Into a world unseen.

List, reader, to a tale of woe,
  Which I shall now relate,
How by a dreadful accident,
  Nine met an awful fate.

In Cornwall, on the western coast,
  St. Just, near the Land's-end,
Botallack mine, a wondrous place,
  Upon the cliffs is seen.

Near half-a-mile beneath the sea,
  Men labour day and night,
Searching for tin and copper ore
  By candles' glimmering light.

Their path-way down the gloomy shaft,
  Four hundred fathoms deep,
Is cut through adamantine rocks -
  And rugged, dark, and steep.

A 'skip' or gig, goes up and down,
  Bearing its living freight,
Of miners to their work below,
  Or back when 'tis complete,

By engine power it is drawn up,
  And by the same let down,
On iron rails made sure and firm,
  As on the solid ground.

On Saturday, at three o'clock,
  April - eighteenth day,
Nine miners were being drawn up,
  That dark and lonesome way.

On, on they came, and near'd the top,
  Nor dream'd of danger nigh,
When suddenly the chain was broke,
  And back the skip did fly.

No power could stay its rapid course,
  Down, down the dark abyss;
One hundred miles an hour it ran -
  A fearful speed was this.

And those within that fatal 'skip',
  The fatal car of death,
Were in the twinkling of an eye
  Deprived of mortal breath.

Down, down it went with fearful crash
  Its living freight was lost!
Filling the shaft with sparks of fire,
  And sickening clouds of dust.

But then within the engine-house,
  Sad tokens too were seen,
That something serious had occur'd, -
  What could that rumbling mean?

Soon the alarm was spread around;
  And to the rescue came
Brave-hearted men; but, ah! too late;
  Extinguish'd was life's flame.

Down in the gloomy depths below,
  They hasted for to see,
If any living could be found,
  Or what the injury.

But there a fearful scene they view'd;
  Nine human bodies lay,
Wrap'd in the cold embrace of death,
  Which fill'd them with dismay.

Richard Nankervis first they found -
  A lad - and he was dead;
A blow had kill'd him on the spot,
  That struck him on the head.

John Eddy next, a ghastly corpse
  Upon the road was found,
His arms and ribs all frightfully crush'd
  His head smash'd on the ground.

Beneath the skip John Chappel lay,
  A steady, quiet man,
And by his side, his eldest son,
  Shocking to look upon.

Young Peter Eddy's head was gone,
  Upon the skip he lay,
The sollar struck him as they pass'd,
  And took his head away.

Yet further down were others found,
  Thomas and Richard Wall,
Father and son - an awful sight -
  Lay in that dreadful hole.

Thomas Nankervis lay to death
  An awful sight to view,
And Michael Nicholas by his side,
  Both bruis'd and mangled too.

Each one was injur'd fearfully,
  Bruis'd, broken, smashed and dead;
A sickening spectacle! for some
  Had lost part of the head.

The horrid news soon spread around,
  And thousands gather'd there -
Friends and relations, in the crowd,
  With cries did rend the air.

At length the bodies were brought up,
  And borne unto their homes,
Where loving wives and children dear,
  Mingled their cries and groans,

Near twenty children now are left
  Without a father's care;
Three widows for their husbands mourn,
  In sorrow and despair.

The widow'd mother too is left,
  Her only son is gone;
His earnings did her wants provide,
  Nought else to live upon.

On Sunday in each house of God,
  Dry eyes could scarce be seen, -
The preachers spoke of the event,
  While sobs did intervene.

They spoke of humble pious men
  Whose fate they did deplore,
Who lately join'd with them in praise,
  To Him they did adore.

That although suddenly cut off
  They long had been prepar'd —
Their lives were lives of holiness,
  Their God they always fear'd.

How blessed are the dead, who die
  In Jesus sanctified;
Whose only hope was in the Lord,
  Who for them bled and died.

And they while living here below,
  Prepar'd for that sad hour,
By seeking pardon for their sins -
  The Holy Spirit power.

They trusted in the living God,
  They feared not to die;
Living or dying all was well,
  With Jesus ever nigh.

Then borne unto the silent tomb,
  What thousands gather'd there,
To mingle with the relatives,
  Sorrow's lingering tear.

Since life with all uncertain is,
  And death is sure to come,
How should we live - Heaven to gain!
  And 'scape eternal doom.

An accident, or sudden death,
  Above or underground,
May call thee, reader! but how blest
  If waiting thou art found.

The mourn not, weeping friends, for those
  That suddenly are gone;
In Heaven they from their labours rest,
  Before the great white throne.

Prepare! prepare! to follow them,
  While yet it's called to day!
Lest unprepar'd, grim Death should come,
  And summon you away.

Index

MINES

MINING FAMILIES

Editor's note: The *General* index includes the vast majority of ordinary proper names appearing in the text. That for *Mines* is more specialist and includes all mine workings referred to by Cyril Noall. Inevitably, there are some difficulties, ambiguities and perhaps inconsistencies, for several mines had more than one name, or changed their names over time, or at some point absorbed their hitherto independent neighbours. Still others consisted of distinct setts or operationally semi-independent components, known by their individual names. Wherever possible, Cyril Noall's usage in the text has been taken as the guide but occasionally editorial judgement has been resorted to. The *Mining Families* index is similarly specialist. Names are identified by family surname only, avoiding the alternative of impossibly long lists of similarly or identically - named individuals with the common Cornish patronymics such as Richards, Williams and Thomas. The inclusion here of separate, specialist indexes is designed to assist particularly those readers concentrating specifically on mining or family history research *P.J.P.*